# Low Carb Keto Chaffle Cookbookr

*Kickstart Your Day With These Keto Chaffles And Feel Energetic And Glowing*

**By**

**Dora Gray**

# Table of Contents

## The Complete Ketogenic Guidebook for Women Over 50



## Gourmet Keto Diet Cookbook For Women After 50

## Intermittent Fasting for Women Over 60

## Keto Dessert & Chaffle Cookbook 2021 with Pictures

## Intermittent Fasting for Women

## Keto diet Cookbook

# The Complete Ketogenic Guidebook for Women Over 50

*Easy Anti-inflammatory Recipes to Lose Belly Fat, Boost your Metabolism, and increase your energy above the age of 50*

**By**

**Dora Gray**

# Table of Contents

# Introduction

A Keto diet is one that is very low in carbohydrates but rich in fats and is normal on protein. Through the years, the Keto diet has been used to treat a variety of diseases that people have learned to face. This includes: rectifying weight gain as well as managing or treating diseases of human beings like treating epilepsy in youngsters. The Keto diet enables the human body to use its fats instead of consuming its carbohydrates. Typically, the body's carbohydrates, which are present in the foods you eat, are transformed into glucose. Glucose is a consequence of the body burning off its carbohydrates which are typically distributed throughout the body. A dietary strategy and a balanced lifestyle are, thus, an important necessity for all the citizens who choose to prevent early mortality. Health problems are widely prevalent in women over the age of 50 since they suffer from normal bodily adjustments related to menopause.

Osteoporosis, hypertension, high blood pressure, overweight, and inflammation are popular among women of this category. An effective metabolism is a secret to good health! The level of metabolism does not stay the same, though! As an individual age, the body naturally moves through a slow metabolic phase. This phase of aging speeds up as we eat unhealthy food and live an unhealthy lifestyle, resulting in a variety of metabolic disorders and other associated diseases. It's a popular myth that you'll be consuming bland and fatty food while you're on a ketogenic diet. Although basic foods are a necessity, there are so many ways to bring the spice back into your diet.

Doing keto doesn't just include consuming any type of fat or having ice cream on the mouth. Instead, it's about choosing products that are high in healthy fats and poor in carbohydrates cautiously. If you aren't sure where to go, don't be afraid. Some really good, fantastic keto meals are out there promising to be eaten.

# Chapter 1: Introduction to Ketogenic Diet

A ketogenic diet is widely known as a diet which is low in carbs and in which the human body generates ketones to be processed as energy in the liver. Several different names are related to a keto diet, lower-carb diet, lower-carb high fat (LCHF), etc. Patterns of diet come and go, and it seems like the formula mostly includes a low-carb plan. At the top of the chart right now is the ketogenic diet. The keto diet, also referred to as the ketogenic diet, relies on having more of the calories from protein and a few from fat while eliminating carbohydrates dramatically.

## 1.1 How Does The Ketogenic Diet Work?

A high fat, medium protein, low carbohydrate diet plan, which varies from standard, balanced eating recommendations, is the ketogenic diet. Many foods abundant in nutrients, including vegetables, fruits, whole grains, milk products, are sources of carbohydrates. Carbs from both types are highly constrained on a keto diet. Keto dieters, therefore, do not eat bread, grains, or cereals with the intention of holding carbs below 50 g a day. And since them, too, contain carbohydrates, even fruits and vegetables are restricted. The keto diet involves making drastic changes about how they normally consume for most individuals.

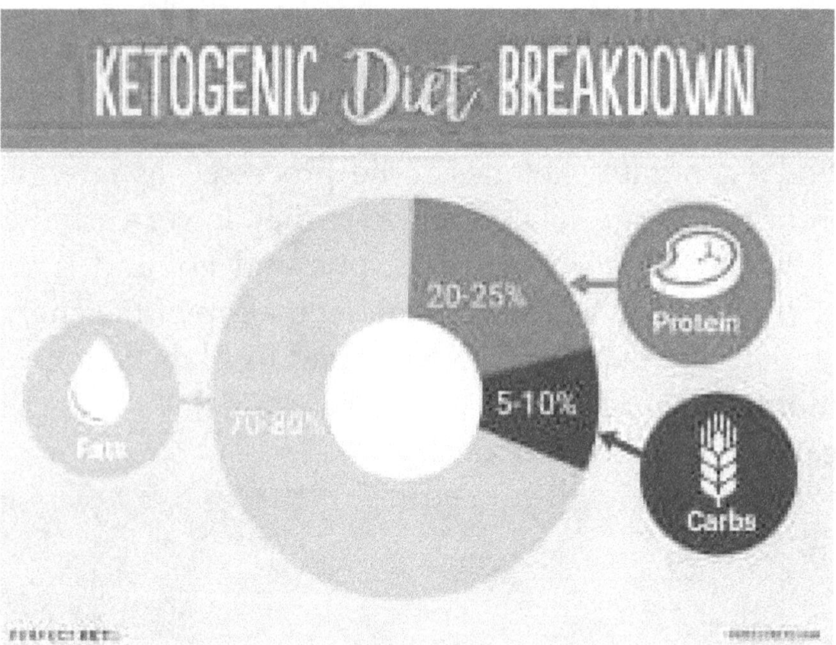


**What is Ketosis?**

Ketosis is a metabolic condition where the body utilizes fat and ketones as the main source of fuel instead of glucose (sugar).

A critical part of beginning a keto diet is knowing how Ketosis works. Ketosis, irrespective of the number of carbohydrates you consume, is a phase that the body goes through on a daily basis. This is because if sugar is not readily accessible, this method provides humans energy from ketones.

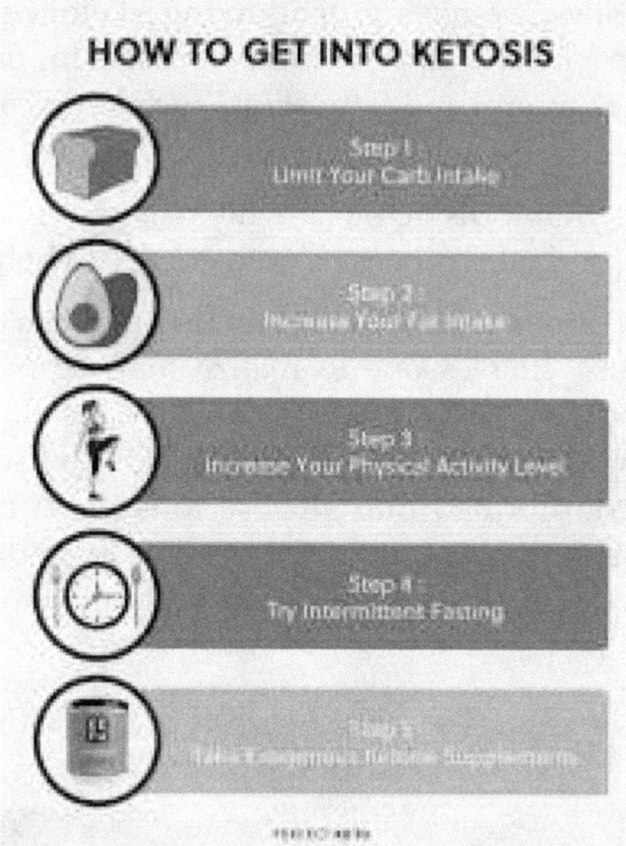


The body tends to raise its ketone levels if the requirement for energy grows, and carbohydrates are not sufficient to satisfy the need. If a more extended period of time (i.e., more than three days) is limited to carbohydrates, the body can raise ketone levels much more. These deeper ketosis rates produce several favorable benefits in the body, results that are achieved when adopting the ketogenic diet is the best and healthiest manner practicable.

Most individuals, however, seldom get Ketosis and never feel its advantages because the body tends to use sugar as its main source of power, even if the diet provides plenty of carbohydrates and protein.

### How does Ketosis happen?

The body would turn any of its accumulated fat into extremely effective energy molecules called ketones while the body has no access to healthy food, like while you are resting, exercising, or adopting a ketogenic diet. (We should credit our body's capacity to alter metabolic processes for that.) After the body breaks down fat into glycerol and fatty acids, such ketones are synthesized.

While in certain cells in the body, fatty acids and glycerol may be directly converted into food, brain cells do not use them as energy at all. This really is because they are so gradually processed into energy to help the brain work.

That's why sugar appears to be the brain's primary source of fuel. Interestingly, this also enables one to realize that we make ketones. Thus providing an alternate source of energy, because we do not eat sufficient calories, our brain will be incredibly susceptible. Our muscles will be quickly broken down and transformed into glucose to support our brains that are sugar-hungry before we have enough power left to find food. The human species would most definitely be endangered without ketones.

## 1.2 Types of Ketogenic Diet

There are a variety of aspects in which ketosis can be induced, and so there are a number of diverse ketogenic diet variations.

**Keto Diet Standard (SKD)**

This is a really low carb diet, a medium protein diet yet high fat. Usually, it comprises 70 to 75% fat, 20% protein, and only 5 to 10% carbohydrates.

A traditional standard ketogenic diet, in terms of grams per day, will be:

- Carbohydrate between 20-50g
- Around 40-60g of protein
- No limit specified for fat

The bulk of calories should be given by fat in the diet for this to be a keto diet. As energy needs might differ greatly among individuals, no limit is set. A large number of vegetables, especially non-starchy veggies, should be included in ketogenic diets, as they are very low in carbs.

In order to help people reduce weight, increase blood glucose regulation and improve cardiac health, standardized ketogenic diets have repeatedly demonstrated success.

**Very-low-carb diet ketogenic (VLCKD)**

Very-low-carb is a traditional ketogenic diet, and so a VLCKD would normally correspond to a traditional ketogenic diet.

**Ketogenic Diet Well Formulated (WFKD)**

The word 'Well Formulated Keto Diet' derives from one of the main ketogenic diet experts, Steve Phinney.

As a traditional ketogenic diet, the WFKD maintains a similar blueprint. Well-developed ensures that weight, protein & carbohydrate macronutrients align with the ratios of the traditional ketogenic diet and thus have the greatest likelihood of ketosis happening.

**Ketogenic Diet MCT**

This fits the description of the traditional ketogenic diet but insists on providing more of the diet's fat content through the use of medium-chain triglycerides (MCTs). MCTs are present in coconut oil and are accessible in the liquid state of MCT oil and MCT dispersant.

To treat epilepsy, MCT ketogenic diets are being used since the idea is that MCTs enable individuals to absorb more carbohydrates and protein, thus sustaining ketosis. That's because multiple ketones per gram of fat are produced by MCTs than the long-chain triglycerides found in natural dietary fat. There is a dearth of research, though, exploring whether MCTs have greater advantages on weight loss and blood sugar.

**Ketogenic diet Calorie-restricted**

Unless calories are reduced to a fixed number, a calorie-restricted ketogenic diet is identical to a normal ketogenic diet.

Research indicates that, whether calorie consumption is reduced or not, ketogenic diets seem to be effective. This is because it helps to avoid over-eating of itself from the nutritious impact of eating fat and staying in ketosis.

**The Ketogenic Cyclical Diet (CKD)**

There are days on which more carbohydrates are ingested, like five ketogenic days accompanied by two high carbohydrate days, in the CKD diet, frequently recognized as carb back loading.

The diet is meant for athletes who can regenerate glycogen drained from muscles during exercises using the high carbohydrate days.

**Ketogenic Diet Targeted (TKD)**

Even though carbs are eaten around exercise hours, the TKD is equivalent to a typical ketogenic diet. It is a combination between a regular ketogenic diet as well as a cyclical ketogenic diet that requires every day you work out to eat carbohydrates.

It is focused on the assumption that carbohydrates eaten before or during a physical effort can be absorbed even more effectively, while the need for energy from the muscles rises while we are engaged.

**Ketogenic Diet of High Protein**

With a proportion of 35 percent protein, 60 percent fat, and 5 percent carbohydrates, this diet contains more protein than a regular keto diet.

For people who need to lose weight, a study shows that a high-protein keto is beneficial for weight loss. Like in other types of the ketogenic diet, if practiced for several years, there is an absence of research on which there are any health risks.

## 1.3 Benefits of Ketogenic Diet

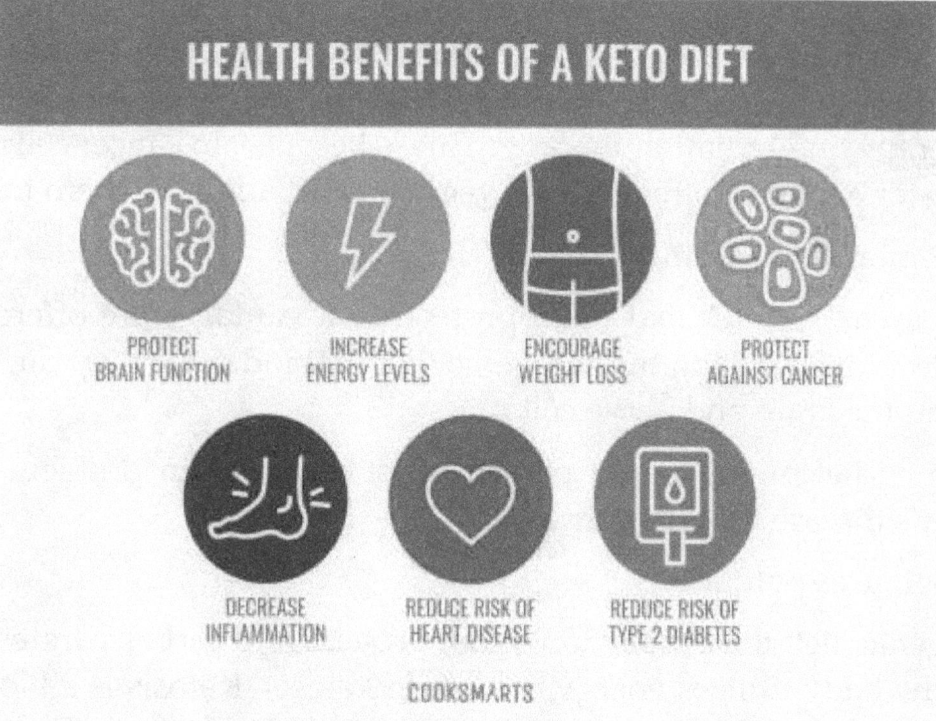


A keto diet has many advantages, including:

**Weight Reduction**

A person's keto diet will help them lose weight. The keto diet help encourages weight loss in many aspects, particularly metabolism boosting and appetite reduction. Ketogenic diets comprise foods that load up an individual and can minimize hormones that trigger appetite. For these factors, it may suppress appetite and encourage weight loss by adopting a keto diet.

**Helps improve acne**

In certain persons, acne has many common reasons and can have associations with diet and blood sugar. Consuming a diet rich in highly processed carbs can change the equivalence of intestinal bacteria and cause major rises and declines in blood sugar, both of which would negatively impact the health of the skin.

**It can decrease the risk of certain cancers**.

The implications of the ketogenic diet have been studied by experts to potentially avoid or even cure some cancers. One research showed that in patients with some cancers, a ketogenic diet could be a healthy and appropriate complementary medication to be used in addition to chemotherapy and radiation therapy. This is because, in cancer cells, it might cause greater oxidative stress than in regular cells, allowing them to die.

**It can safeguard brain function.**

Some research indicates that neuroprotective advantages are offered by the ketones developed during the ketogenic diet that indicates they can reinforce and defend the brain and nerve cells.

A ketogenic diet might help a person resist or maintain problems such as Alzheimer's disease for this purpose.

**Lessens seizures potentially**

In a ketogenic diet, the proportion of fat, protein, and carbohydrates changes the way the body utilizes energy, results in ketosis. Ketosis is a biochemical mechanism in which ketone bodies are being used by the body for energy.

The Epilepsy Foundation indicates that ketosis in people with epilepsy, particularly those who have not adapted to other types of treatment, might decrease seizures. More study is required on how efficient this is, as it seems to have the greatest influence on children who have generalized seizures.

**Improves the effects of PCOS**

Polycystic ovary syndrome (PCOS) may contribute to surplus male hormones, ovulatory instability, and polycystic ovaries as a hormonal syndrome. In individuals with PCOS, a high-carbohydrate diet can trigger negative impacts, like skin problems as well as excess weight.

The researchers observed that many markers of PCOS are strengthened by a ketogenic diet, including:

- Loss in weight
- Balance of hormones
- Ratios of follicle-stimulating hormone (LH) and luteinizing hormone (LH) (FSH)

- Insulin fasting levels

A different research analysis showed that for people with hormonal conditions, like PCOS and type 2 diabetes, a keto diet has positive benefits. They also cautioned, though, that the findings were too diverse to prescribe a keto diet as a specific PCOS treatment.

# Chapter 2: Easy ketogenic Low Carb Recipes

It may be challenging to adopt different diets: all the foods to quit, to consume more, to purchase new products. It's enough to make bonkers for everyone. But the ketogenic, or "keto," diet, as well as its keto meals, are one type of eating that has been gathering traction lately.

Doing keto doesn't only involve eating some sort of fat or putting ice cream on your mouth. Rather, it's about picking items that are rich in good fats and low in carbohydrates carefully. If you aren't sure where to start, don't be scared. Some very healthy, excellent keto meals are out there appealing to be consumed.

## 2.1 Keto Breakfast Recipes

### 1. HIGH PROTEIN COTTAGE CHEESE OMELET

**Serving: 1**

**Preparation time: 5 minutes**

**Nutritional Values: 250kcal Calories | 18g Fat | 4 g Carbs | 18.7g Proteins**

**Ingredients**

- 2 eggs - large
- 1 tbsp. of whole milk or 2% milk
- Kosher salt about 1/8 tsp.
- Pinch of black pepper, freshly ground,
- 1/2 tbsp. of butter - unsalted
- 1 cup spinach (about 1 ounce)
- Cottage cheese 3 tbsp.

**Directions**

1. In a moderate pan, put the eggs, milk, salt, & pepper and stir until the whites & yolks are thoroughly combined, and the eggs are a little viscous.
2. In an 8-inch non - stick roasting pan over medium heat, add the butter. Flip the pan until the butter covers the bottom equally. Include the spinach and simmer for around 30 seconds before it is ripened. Put the eggs in and turn the pan directly so that the eggs cover the whole bottom.
3. To softly pull and move the cooked eggs from the sides into the middle of the pan, use either a silicone or rubber spatula, leaving room for the raw eggs and creating waves in the omelet. Rig a spatula underneath the edges to enable raw eggs to run beneath the cooked part, holding and swiveling the pan. Cook for around 2 minutes until the sides are settled, and the middle is moist but no longer soft or gooey.
4. Let the pan away from the heat. Whisk over half the eggs with the cottage cheese. Cover the egg carefully over the filling using a spatula. On a plate, transfer the omelet.

## 2. DEVILED EGGS

**Serving: 4-6**

**Preparation time: 15-20 minutes**

**Nutritional values: 280kcal Calories | 23g Fat | 3.4g Carbs | 15g Proteins**

**Ingredients**

- 12 eggs - large
- 8 oz. of full-fat cream cheese, warmed for 1 hour or more at room temperature,
- Kosher salt about 1/2 teaspoon
- 1 shred of black pepper
- 2 tablespoons of all the bagel seasoning

## Directions

1. A dozen eggs become hardboiled according to your chosen method. (The most critical part is to layer with ice water, raise to a boil, then lift from the heat and leave for 8 to 10 minutes to remain.) In an ice bucket, soak and chill the eggs. And peel them.
2. Cut the eggs laterally in half and use a tiny spoon to pick the yolks out and put them in a dish.
3. Take the cream cheese and transfer it to the yolks into rough parts. Use a hand beater or stick mixer to mix until smooth and blended, starting at lower speeds and then at high speed. Bang in the pepper and salt. Uh, taste. If needed, tweak the seasonings.
4. Load the egg whites with the yolk mixture using a spoon or piping bag. (It would be stiff; to soften it any further if possible, microwave it in very fast bursts of 2 to 3 seconds.)
5. With the all-bagel seasoning, dust the tops of the loaded eggs appropriately. In two hours, serve.

## 3. 90 SECOND KETO BREAD

**Serving: 1**

**Preparation time: 90 seconds**

**Nutritional values: 99kcal Calories | 8.5g Fat | 2g Carbs | 3.9g Proteins**

**Instructions**

- 1 egg - large
- 1 spoonful of milk
- Olive oil about 1 tablespoon
- 1 tablespoon flour of coconut
- 1 tablespoon flour of almonds or hazelnuts
- 1/4 tsp. powder for baking
- Pinch of salt

**Add-ins optional:**

- 1/4 cup of grated cheese

- 1 tbsp. scallions or herbs chopped

**Directions**

1. In a small cup, mix together the egg, milk, oil, coconut flour, almond flour, baking powder, and salt. If using, incorporate cheese and scallions or herbs and mix to blend.
2. To induce any air bubbles to lift and burst, pour into a wide microwave-safe mug and strike the bottom tightly on the counter multiple times. Reheat for 1 minute, 30 seconds, on maximum.
3. On a chopping board, transpose the mug and enable the bread to drop out. Slice into 1/2-inch-thick strips crosswise. For the toast, heat a teaspoon of oil across moderate flame in a small pan until it glistens. Add the strips and toast, around 30 seconds on either side, before golden-brown.

## 4. KETO FRITTATA

**Serving: 4-6**

**Preparation time: 25 minutes**

**Nutritional values: 155kcal Calories | 8.9g Fat | 11.4g Carbs | 7.9g Proteins**

**Instructions**

- 6 large eggs, sufficient for the ingredients to fill
- Heavy cream 1/4 cup
- 1 tsp. of kosher salt, split-up
- 4 thick-cut bacon (8 oz.) pieces, diced (optional)
- 2 tiny, stripped, and finely diced Yukon gold potatoes
- 1/4 tsp. of black pepper, freshly ground

- 2 cups of spinach (2 ounces)
- Garlic 2 cloves, chopped.
- 2 tsp. of fresh leaves of thyme
- 1 cup of Gruyere, Fontina, or Cheddar crushed cheese

**Directions**

1. Preheat oven. In the center of the oven, position a brace and warm it to 400 °F.
2. Stir together the cream and eggs. In a medium bowl, stir together the eggs, whipping cream, and 1/2 teaspoon salt; hold.
3. Just prepare the bacon. Put the bacon in a non - stick 10-12-inch cold cooking pan or cast-iron skillet, and keep the heat to moderate. Cook the bacon until translucent, stirring regularly, for 8 to 10 minutes. Move the bacon to a paper towel-lined dish with a slotted spoon and skim off all but 2 tbsp. of the fat. (If the bacon is excluded, heat the pan with 2 tablespoons of oil, then finish incorporating the potatoes).
4. Simmer the potatoes in the fat of the bacon. Mix the potatoes and spray with the pepper and the remaining 1/2 teaspoon salt. Switch the pan to a moderate flame. Heat, stirring regularly, for 4 to 6 minutes, until soft and golden brown.
5. Crumble the spinach with thyme & garlic. Put the spinach, garlic, and thyme in the pan and cook, mixing, for 30 seconds to 1 minute, or until the spinach is wilted. Transfer the bacon again to the skillet and swirl to spread uniformly.
6. Add some cheese. Scattered the vegetables, compressed with a spatula, into an even layer. Over the top, spread the cheese and let it only begin to melt.
7. In the pan, add the egg mixture. Place over the vegetables and cheese with the egg mixture. To be sure that the eggs settle equally over all the vegetables, rotate the skillet. Wait for a minute or two before you observe the eggs starting to set at the ends of the pan.

8. Around 8 to 10 minutes, oven the frittata. Bake for 8 to 10 minutes unless the eggs are ready. Cut a tiny slit in the middle of the frittata to test. Bake for a few more minutes if uncooked eggs run into the cut; if the eggs are fixed, take the frittata out of the oven. At the end of cooking, hold the frittata underneath the broiler for a couple of minutes for a crisped, charred layer.
9. For 5 minutes, chill in the skillet, then cut into slices and serve.

## 5. CHEESE, HAM, AND EGG WRAPS

**Serving: 4**

**Preparation time: 15-20 minutes**

**Nutritional values: 371kcal calories | 27g Fat | %g Carbs | 27g Proteins**

**Ingredients**

- 8 eggs - large
- 4 tsp. of Water
- 2 tsp. of all-purpose or cornstarch flour
- Half a teaspoon of fine salt
- 4 tsp. of coconut or vegetable oil
- 1 1/3 cups of Swiss grated cheese
- 4 ounces of ham extremely thinly sliced
- 1 1/3 cups of watercress loosely wrapped

**Directions**

1. In a wide bowl, put the eggs, water, flour or cornflour, and salt, and stir until the starch or cornflour is fully dissolved.
2. In a 12-inch non - stick saucepan, heat 1 tsp. Of oil unless glinting, over moderate flame. To cover the surface with the oil, move the pan. To brush the bottom part in a thin coating, incorporate 1/2 cup of the egg mixture and stir. Cook for 3 to 6 minutes before the wrapping is fully set on the sides and on the surface (the top may be a little damp but should be apparently set).
3. Soften the sides of the wrap using a wide spatula and move it under the wrap, ensuring that it will slide across the pan quickly. With the spatula, turn the wrap. Slather 1/3 cup of cheese instantly over the wrap and simmer for around 1 minute before the second side is ready. Drop it onto a chopping board or work surface (the cheese may not be completely melted yet). Put a single coat of ham over the egg when it is still hot. Put 1/3 of a cup of watercress in the middle of the wrap. Firmly roll it up.
4. Repeat the leftover wraps by cooking and filling them. Slice each wrap crosswise into 6 (1-inch) bits using a steak knife.

## 6. BACON GRUYERE EGG BITES

**Serving: 9**

**Preparation time: 10-20 minutes**

**Nutritional values: 208kcal Calories | 18g Fat | 1g Carbs | 11g Proteins**

**Ingredients**

- Fat or butter of bacon, to coat the pan
- 9 large eggs
- 3/4 cup Gruyere cheese grated (2 1/4 oz.)

- 1/3 cup (about 2 1/2 oz.) cream cheese
- Kosher salt about 1/2 teaspoon
- 6 pieces of thick-cut, cooked, and imploded bacon

**Directions**

1. In the center of the oven, place a rack and warm it to 350°F. Graciously cover an 8x8-inch (broiler-safe if you like a crisped top) cooking dish with bacon fat or butter.
2. Put the eggs, Gruyere, cream cheese, and salt in a mixer and combine for around 1 minute, at moderate speed, until quite smooth. Drop it into the pan for baking. Slather bacon with it. With aluminum foil, cover firmly.
3. Take the oven rack out from the oven midway. Upon on the oven rack, put a roasting tray. Put in 6 extremely hot tap water pots. Place the baking dish in the hot skillet with the eggs. Bake until the center is just ready, 55 minutes to 1 hour.
4. Pull the roasting pan from the oven cautiously. Remove the roasting pan from the baking dish and unfold it. (For a browned surface: Heat the oven to sauté. Sauté 4 to 5 minutes before the top is golden-brown.) Slice and serve into 9 squares.

# 7. RADISH TURNIP AND FRIED EGGS HASH WITH GREEN GARLIC

**Serving: 2**

**Preparation time: 10-12 minutes**

**Nutritional values: 392kcal calories | 34g Fat | 10g Carbs | 13g Proteins**

**Ingredients**

- 2 to 3 tiny turnips (approximately 1 1/2 cups cubed) clipped, peeled, and sliced into 3/4-inch cubes
- 4 to 5 tiny, rinsed and clipped radishes, and sliced into 3/4-inch cubes (approximately 1 1/2 cubed cups)
- Crushed Salt of the Sea
- Pepper freshly crushed
- 2 tbsp. of grapeseed oil, or other heat-tolerant, neutral oil
- 1 green garlic stalk, clipped and diced (just white and light green parts)
- 2 spoonful's of unsalted butter

- Four eggs
- 1 tablespoon parsley chopped

**Directions**

1. Place the water in a wide skillet and raise it to a boil. Stir in 2 teaspoons of sea salt. Transfer to a bowl with a slotted spoon, skim off any extra water and set it aside. Simmer turnip cubes only until moist, 3 to 4 minutes. Next, quickly boil the radishes for 30 to 60 seconds; scrape with a slotted spoon in a pan, skim off any extra water, and set it aside.
2. Place a sauté pan of cast iron over moderate flame. Include the grapeseed oil and add the turnips & radishes when warm, and pinch the sea salt and pepper with each one. Cook for 8 minutes or until golden-brown, flipping vegetables just once or twice. Switch the heat to medium, bring in the green garlic and simmer for a minute or so. Place the vegetables to the edges, melt the butter in the center of the pan, and add the eggs. Cook unearthed for 4 to 6 minutes for over-easy eggs; close pan for 3 minutes for over-medium eggs, then unfold and continue to cook only until whites are ready, 2 to 3 minutes further. To taste, finish with chopped parsley and sea salt and pepper. Instantly serve.

## 8. CAULIFLOWER RICE BURRITO BOWLS

**Serving: 4**

**Preparation time: 20-25 minutes**

**Nutritional values: 374kcal Calories | 15g Fat | 46g Carbs | 21g Protein**

**Ingredients**

- 1 (15-ounce) canned washed and cleaned black beans.
- 1 cup of corn kernels - frozen
- 2 spoonful's of water
- Chili powder about 1/2 teaspoon
- 1/2 teaspoon of cumin powder
- 3/4 teaspoon of kosher salt, distributed
- 1 tablespoon of olive oil
- One cauliflower of a medium head (just around 1 1/2 lbs.), riced (or one 16oz sack riced cauliflower)
- 1/3 cup of fresh cilantro minced, distributed

- 1/4 cup of lime juice, freshly extracted (from 2 to 3 lemons)
- 1 cup roasted chicken chopped or shredded (optional), warmed if necessary
- 1 cup of gallo pico de or salsa
- One large, drained, pitted, and diced avocado

**Directions**

1. In a small pan, put the beans, corn, water, chili powder, cumin, and 1/4 tsp. over moderate flame. Cook for 3 to 5 minutes, mixing periodically until hot. Distance yourself from the steam.
2. In the meantime, over a moderate flame, heat the oil in a wide, large skillet until it shimmers. Transfer the cauliflower and the residual 1/2 teaspoon salt to the mixture. Process until the cauliflower is cooked through though soft, 3 to 5 minutes, mixing periodically. Remove from the heat. Transfer the cilantro and lime juice to 1/4 cup and mix to blend.
3. Divide into four bowls the riced cauliflower. Cover with the mixture of bean and corn, chicken if used, pico de gallo or salsa, and pieces of avocado. Slather with the cilantro that persists and serve hot.

## 9. KETO LOAF

**Serving: 1**

**Preparation time: 10-12 minutes**

**Nutritional values: 239kcal Calories | 22g Fat | 4g carbs | 8g Proteins**

**Ingredients**

- Two cups of fine powdered almond flour, especially brands like King Arthur
- 1 tsp. powder for baking
- 1/2 tsp. of gum xanthan
- Kosher salt about 1\2 tsp.
- 7 eggs - large

- 8 tbsp. (1 stick) of melted and chilled unsalted butter
- 2 tbsp. of concentrated, processed, and chilled coconut oil

**Directions**

1. In the center of the oven, place a rack and warm it to 351°F. Cover the bottom part of a parchment paper 9x5-inch metallic loaf pan, having the surplus spill around the long sides to create a loop. Just set aside.
2. In a wide dish, mix together the flour of almond, powder for baking, xanthan gum, as well as salt. Just placed back.
3. Put the eggs in a bowl equipped with the whisk extension of a stand blender. Beat at moderate pressure until soft and drippy. Lower the level to moderate, incorporate the butter and oil of coconut gradually, and whisk unless well mixed. Lessen the intensity to medium, incorporate the mixture of almond flour gradually, and mix unless mixed. Rise the pace to moderate and beat for around 1 minute before the mixture thickens.
4. Pour and scrape the top into the primed pan. Bake for 45 to 55 minutes unless a knife placed in the middle comes out clean. Let it cool for around ten minutes in the pan. Take the loaf over the skillet, grab the parchment paper, and shift it to a cutting board. Cool it down completely until slicing.

## 10. BREAKFAST SALAD

**Serving: 4**

**Preparation time: 10 minutes**

**Nutritional values: 425kcal Calories | 34g Fat | 16g Carbs | 17g Proteins**

**Ingredients**

- Spinach 8 Oz (about 6 packed cups)
- 1/2 a cup of blueberries
- 1 medium-sized avocado, chopped
- 1/3 cup red roasted quinoa
- 1/4 cup of pumpkin seeds - toasted

- Bacon - 6 strips
- 4 eggs of large size
- 1/4 cup of apple cider vinegar
- 2 tsp. of honey
- Kosher salt about 1\2 tsp.

**Directions**

1. In a large bowl, add the spinach, avocado, berries, pumpkin seeds, and quinoa and toss them to mix. Distribute the salad into deep plates or pots.
2. Put the bacon over moderate heat in a large cast-iron pan. Cook until the fat has dried out and the bacon is crunchy, tossing halfway around for a total of around 10 minutes. Shift the bacon to a tray that is lined with paper towels. Cut the bacon into little crumbles until it is cold.
3. Lower the heat and fry the eggs to the perfect braising in the dried bacon fat. Keep the pan away from the heat. Place the toppled bacon and an egg on top of each salad.
4. Upon emulsification, mix the vinegar, honey, and salt into the residual bacon fat in the dish. Sprinkle over the salad with the warm dressing and serve promptly.

## 2.2 Keto Lunch & Dinner Recipes

# 1. CAULIFLOWER FRIED RICE

**Serving: 4**

**Preparation time: 20- 25 minutes**

**Nutritional values: 108kcal Calories | 1g Fat | 21g Carbs | 7g Proteins**

**Ingredients**

**For Fried Rice**

- 1 cauliflower head, sliced into cloves
- Balanced Oil 2 tbsp. (such as vegetable, coconut, or peanut)

- 1 bunch of finely sliced scallions
- 3 cloves of garlic, chopped
- 1 tbsp. natural ginger diced
- 2 peeled and finely chopped carrots
- 2 stalks of celery, chopped
- 1 bell pepper, red, chopped
- 1 cup of peas - frozen
- 2 tbsp. vinegar for rice
- 3 spoonful's of soy sauce
- Sriracha 2 tsp., or enough to taste

**For Garnishing**

- Balanced oil about 1tbsp. (such as vegetable, coconut, or peanut)
- Four eggs
- Salt and black pepper finely processed
- 4 tbsp. of fresh cilantro, diced
- 4 tbsp. of scallions thinly diced
- 4 tsp. of seeds of sesame

**Directions**

1. **For Fried Rice:** Pump the cauliflower in the mixing bowl for 2 or 3 minutes before the mishmash resembles rice. Just set aside.
2. Heat oil over a moderate flame in a wide skillet. Include the scallions, garlic, and ginger and mix for around 1 minute, unless aromatic.
3. Incorporate the carrots, celery & red bell pepper, and braise for 9 to 11 minutes until the veggies are soft.
4. Add the cauliflower rice, then stir-fry for another 3 to 5 minutes, once it starts to turn golden. To blend, mix in the frozen peas and toss properly.

5. To combine, incorporate rice vinegar, Sriracha, and soy sauce & swirl. Just set aside.
6. **For Garnishing:** Add the oil in a large skillet over moderate to high flame. Crack the eggs straight into the skillet and stir for 3 to 4 minutes before the whites are assertive, but the yolks are still watery. With pepper and salt, sprinkle each one.
7. Distribute the cauliflower rice into four dishes to serving and serve each one with a fried egg. Sprinkle with 1 tablespoon of cilantro, 1 tablespoon of scallions, and 1 teaspoon of sesame seeds on each dish. Instantly serve then.

## 2. LOW CARB THAI CURRY SOUP

**Serving: 6**

**Preparation time: 22 minutes**

**Nutritional values: 324kcal Calories | 27g Fat | 7g Carbs | 15g Proteins**

**Ingredients**

- 4 Leg pieces of boneless skinless chicken,
- 14.5 ounces (411.07 g) full-fat coconut milk
- 2 tsp. of Thai paste of yellow curry
- 2 tsp. of fish sauce
- Three tsp. of Soy Sauce
- 1 tsp. of Agave or honey nectar
- 2 green Scallions minced
- Garlic 4 cloves, minced
- 2 inch (2 inches) coarsely chopped diced ginger

**Veggies to add in soup**

- One Can of Straw Mushrooms (optional)
- 74.5 g (1/2 cup) of Cherry Tomatoes, half-sliced
- Cilantro, 1/4 cup (4 g), diced
- 3 green Scallions diced
- 1 lime, juiced

**Directions**

**For the Instant Pot**

1. Put the essential soup components and lock in an Instant Pot.
2. Process it under heat for 12 minutes by using the SOUP key. The soup button avoids it from boiling and extracting the coconut milk.
3. Discharge the pressure immediately and detach and cut the chicken. Place it in the broth again.

4. Transfer the warm broth to the vegetables. In the hot broth, you want to bring them a little scorching but not to mold them though you can actually taste the flavor of the vegetables and herbs.

**For the Slow Cooker**

1. In a slow cooker, put the essential soup ingredients and steam for 8 hours on lower or 4 hours on average.
2. Over the last half-hour, place in vegetables and herbs. In the hot broth, you want to bring them a little scorching but not to mold them though you can actually taste the flavor of the vegetables and herbs.
3. Remove the chicken and cut it. Place it in the broth again.

- It's actually cheaper to purchase Thai Yellow Curry Paste than to prepare it. At your nearest Asian food store, you will find it.
- With the provided directions, prepare this in your Instant Pot or slow cooker. If required, you may use heavy whipping cream for coconut milk.

## 3. JALAPENO POPPER SOUP

**Serving: 3**

**Preparation time: 25 minutes**

**Nutritional values: 446kcal Calories | 35g Fat | 4g Carbs | 28g Proteins**

**Ingredients**

- 4 bacon strips
- 2 spoonful's of butter
- Medium-sized 1/2 onion, chopped
- 1/4 cup of pickled, diced jalapenos
- 2 cups broth of chicken
- 2 cups of shredded chicken, cooked
- Cream cheese 4 ounces
- Heavy cream 1/3 cup

- 1 cup of Fresh Cheddar Shredded
- 1/4 tsp. powdered garlic
- Pepper and salt, to taste
- If needed, 1/2 tsp. xanthan gum for thick soup [Optional]

**Directions**

1. Fry the bacon in a pan. Crumble when cooked and put aside. Place a large pot over the moderate flame while the bacon cooks. Include the onion and butter and simmer until the onion becomes porous.
2. Transfer the jalapenos and half the crumbled bacon to the pot.
3. Pour in the broth of the chicken and the shredded chicken. Take to a boil, then cook for 20 minutes, and reduce.
4. Put the cream cheese in a medium bowl and microwave for around 20 seconds; once soft until smooth, mix. Stir the cream cheese and the heavy cream into the soup. It may take a few minutes for the cream cheese to be completely integrated. Turn the heat off.
5. Include the shredded cheese, and whisk until it is completely melted. Add xanthan gum at this stage if the thick soup is preferred.
6. Serve with the leftover bacon on top.

## 4. PEPPERS & SAUSAGES

**Serving: 6**

**Preparation time: 2 hrs.5 minutes**

**Nutritional values: 313kcal Calories | 22g Fat | 11g Carbs | 16g Proteins**

**Ingredients**

- 1 tablespoon olive oil
- Six medium links of Pork sausage
- 3 of the large Bell peppers (cut into strips)
- 1 onion of large size (cut into half, the same size as the pepper shreds)
- Garlic 6 Cloves (minced)
- 1 tbsp. seasoning Italian
- Sea salt about 1/2 tsp.
- Black pepper 1/4 teaspoon

- 1 and a half cups of Marinara sauce

**Directions**

1. To activate a kitchen timer whilst you cook, toggle on the times in the directions below.
2. Heat the oil over moderate heat in a large pan. Include the sausage links until its warm. Cook on either side for around 2 minutes, only until golden brown on the outer side. (Inside, they will not be prepared.)
3. In the meantime, in a slow cooker, add the bell peppers, onions, garlic, Italian spices, salt, & pepper. Toss it to coat it. Softly spill the marinara sauce over the veggies.
4. Once the sausage links are golden brown, put them on top of the veggies in the slow cooker.
5. Cook on low flame or 2-3 hours on high flame for 4-5 hours, unless the sausages are cooked completely.

## 5. SHRIMPS WITH CAULIFLOWER GRITS AND ARUGULA

**Serving: 4**

**Preparation time: 25-30 minutes**

**Nutritional values: 123kcal Calories | 5g Fat | 3g Carbs | 16g proteins**

**Ingredients**

**For Spicy Shrimp**

- 1 pound of cleaned and roasted shrimp
- 1 tablespoon of paprika
- 2 teaspoons of powdered garlic
- 1/2 tsp. of pepper cayenne

- 1 tablespoon of olive oil extra virgin
- Salt and black pepper freshly processed
- GRITS of CAULIFLOWER
- Unsalted butter about 1 tablespoon
- Riced cauliflower about four cups
- 1cup of milk
- 1/2 cup of goat's crushed cheese
- Salt & black pepper freshly processed

**For Garlic Arugula**

- 1 tablespoon of olive oil extra virgin
- 3 cloves of garlic, finely minced
- 4 cups of baby arugula
- Salt & black pepper freshly processed

**Directions**

1. **Prepare the Spicy Shrimp:** Put the shrimp in a big plastic zip-top pack. Mix the paprika in a tiny bowl with the garlic powder as well as the cayenne to blend. Place the mixture with the shrimp into the packet and shake well before the spices have covered them. Refrigerate the grits while preparing them.
2. **Prepare the Cauliflower "Grits"**: Melt the butter over a moderate flame in a wide bowl. Integrate the cauliflower rice and simmer for 2 to 3 minutes once it sheds some of its steam.
3. Whisk in half the milk and raise it to a boil. Continue to boil, stirring regularly, for 6 to 8 minutes, before some milk is consumed by the cauliflower.
4. Add the leftover milk and boil for another 10 minutes before the mixture is smooth and fluffy. Mix in the cheese from the goat and add salt and pepper. Just hold warm.

5. **Prepare Garlic Arugula:** Warm olive oil over moderate heat in a large pan. Add the garlic and simmer for 1 minute unless tangy. Include the arugula and simmer for 3 to 4 minutes, unless softened. Use salt and pepper to season, take from the pan, and put aside.
6. Heat the olive oil over low heat in the same pan. Include shrimp and simmer for 4 to 5 minutes until completely cooked. Use salt and pepper to season.
7. Divide the grits into four dishes to serve, then top each one with a fourth of the arugula & a quarter of the shrimp. Immediately serve.

## 6. CHICKEN CHILI WHITE

**Serving: 4**

**Preparation time: 35-45 minutes**

**Nutritional values: 481kcal Calories | 30g Fat | 5g Carbs | 39g Proteins**

**Ingredients**

- 1 lb. breast of chicken
- Chicken broth about 1.5 cups

- 2 cloves of garlic, thinly chopped
- 1 can of sliced green chills
- 1 jalapeno sliced
- 1 green pepper chopped
- 1/4 cup onion finely chopped
- Four tablespoons of butter
- 1/4 cup of heavy whipped cream
- Four-ounce cream cheese
- 2 teaspoons of cumin
- 1 teaspoon of oregano
- Cayenne 1/4 teaspoon (additional)
- To taste: salt & black pepper

**Directions**

1. Season the chicken with cumin, cayenne, oregano, salt, and black pepper in a wide pan.
2. Braise both sides unless golden, under medium-high heat,
3. Transfer the broth to the pan, cover, and cook for 15-20 minutes or until the chicken is completely cooked.
4. Melt the butter in a moderate pan while the chicken is frying.
5. In the pan, incorporate the chills, chopped jalapeno, green pepper, and onion, and simmer until the vegetables soften.
6. Add the chopped garlic and simmer for an extra 30 seconds, switching off the heat and put aside.
7. When the chicken is fully done, slice it with a fork and transfer it to the broth.
8. In a chicken & broth pan, incorporate the sautéed veggies and cook for 10 minutes.

9. Soften the cream cheese in the microwave in a mixing bowl so you can blend it (~20 sec)
10. Mix the cream cheese and heavy whipped cream
11. Add the mixture of chicken and vegetables into the pot and whisk rapidly.
12. Simmer for an extra 15 minutes.
13. Serve with preferred toppings such as cheese from the pepper jack, slices of avocado, coriander, sour cream.

## 7. BOWL OF CHICKEN ENCHILADA

**Serving: 4**

**Preparation time: 40-50 minutes**

**Nutritional values: 570kcal Calories | 40g Fat | 6g Carbs | 38g Proteins**

**Ingredients**

- 2 spoonful's of coconut oil (for searing chicken)
- 1 pound of chicken thighs that are boneless, skinless
- 3/4 cup sauce of red enchilada
- 1/4 of a cup of water
- 1/4 cup onion, minced
- 1-4 oz. green chills Can - sliced

**Toppings**

- 1 Avocado, sliced
- 1 cup of cheese, crushed
- 1/4 cup of pickled jalapenos, diced
- 1/2 of a cup of sour cream
- 1 tomato Roma, diced

**Directions**

1. Heat up the coconut oil on a moderate flame in a pan or a Dutch oven. Braise the chicken thighs unless finely brown when hot.
2. Place in the enchilada sauce as well as the water. After this, add the onion and also the green chilies. Lower the heat to a boil and cover it. Cook the chicken for 17-25 minutes or until the chicken is juicy and heated to an inner temperature of approximately 165 degrees.
3. Remove the chicken cautiously and put it on a chopping board. Then put it back into the pot. Cut or shred chicken (your preference). To retain flavor, let the chicken boil uncovered for an extra 10 minutes and enable the sauce to minimize some more.
4. For serving, cover with avocado, cheese, jalapeno, tomato, sour cream, or any other toppings you want. Feel free to adjust them to your taste.

If preferred, serve individually or over cauliflower rice; just refresh your personal nutrition details as required.

## 8. CHIPOTLE HEALTHY KETO PULLED PORK

**Serving: 10**

**Preparation time: 8 hrs.15 minutes**

**Nutritional values: 430kcal Calories | 34g Fat | 3g Carbs | 27g Proteins**

**Ingredients**

- 1 Mid-yellow onion chopped

- 1 cup of water
- 2 tablespoons of fresh garlic diced
- 1 tablespoon of Coconut Sugar
- 1 tablespoon of salt
- 1 teaspoon of chili powder
- 1/2 teaspoon of cumin powder
- 1/2 Tablespoon Adobo sauce
- Smoked paprika 1/4 teaspoons
- 3 1/2-4 lbs. pork shoulder, Extra fat should be removed
- Whole wheat or hamburger buns without gluten OR salad wraps for serving
- Paleo ranch, to be garnished
- Coleslaw blend for optional garnish
- Lime Juice, to be garnished
- Green Tabasco for garnishing

**Directions**

1. Cut the onion and chop the garlic, and put it in the base of the slow cooker—a spill in a cup of water.
2. In a small bowl, mix all the ingredients for the seasoning and set it aside.
3. Slice off the pork shoulder some large, noticeable parts of fat and spread it all over with the seasoning until it is uniformly covered.
4. Over the top of the garlic, onions & water, add the pork and simmer until soft and juicy, 6-8 hours on maximum or 8-10 hours on reduced.
5. If the pork is cooked, extract much of the liquid from the crockpot and put the solids directly into the crockpot (which comprises the garlic and onions).
6. On a chopping board, move the pork and slice it with two forks.

7. In the slow cooker, shift the sliced pork back and combine with the onions and garlic. Cover unless ready to be served, and keep it warm.
8. On a bun or lettuce, place the pulled pork, served with a ranch coleslaw blend and a pinch of lime juice as well as green tabasco.
9. Enjoy.

## 9. STIR FRY ZOODLE

**Serving: 4**

**Preparation time: 15-22 minutes**

**Nutritional values: 113kcal Calories | 3g Fat | 20g Carbs | 6g Proteins**

**Ingredients**

- Sesame oil 11/2 tsp. (or 1 tbsp. of olive oil)
- 1 bunch of thinly chopped scallions
- 2 cloves of garlic, chopped
- 1 tablespoon of fresh ginger, diced

- Two carrots, chopped into thin strands
- One red pepper bell, cut into small strands,
- Two cups of snap peas
- Four zucchini, sliced into noodles (using a utensil like this)
- 1⁄4 cup of soy sauce
- 3 tbsp. vinegar for rice
- 1⁄4 cup of fresh cilantro, diced

**Directions**

1. Add the oil in a wide sauté pan over medium heat. Integrate the scallions, garlic, and ginger and simmer for 1 to 2 minutes, unless aromatic.

2. Include the bell pepper, carrots, snap peas & zucchini noodles. Sauté for 5 to 6 minutes until the vegetables just start to become soft.

3. Integrate the soy sauce & rice vinegar and proceed to cook unless the vegetables are quite soft and juicy, frequently tossing, for another 3 to 4 minutes.

4. Seasoned with cilantro, serve hot.

## 10. TEX MEX CHICKEN SALAD

**Serving: 4**

**Preparation time: 25 minutes**

**Nutritional values: 546kcal Calories | 41g Fat | 12g Carbs | 30g Proteins**

**Ingredients**

- For the seasoning of the fajita:
- 2 tsp. of powdered chili
- 1 tsp. of cumin
- 1 tsp. of powdered garlic
- 1 teaspoon powdered onion
- 1 tsp. of paprika. smoked
- 1/2 tsp. of or to taste salt

**For the fajitas**

- Two spoonful's of olive oil
- 1/2 tsp. ground mustard OR 1 tbsp. of Dijon mustard as required
- 1 lemon juice
- 2 medium breasts of chicken hammered to even density
- 2 tablespoons divided butter
- 4 finely diced medium bell peppers into slices
- 1 medium red onion finely sliced into slices
- 2-3 leaves of buttered lettuce
- 2-3 leaves of romaine lettuce

**To serve**

- Slices of lime
- Avocado sliced

**Directions**

1. Mix all the ingredients for the condiments in a tiny compostable jar. Enclose well and squish. For bell peppers, save 1 1/2 tsp.
2. Integrate two tbsp. of olive oil, lemon juice, and 5 tsp. of fajita condiments in a wide, zip lock bag. In the bag, add the chicken and secure it. Push the marinade into the chicken and enable the vegetables to marinate while preparing them (or freeze in the fridge unless ready to use).
3. Cut the bell peppers as well as onions.
4. Heat 1 tbsp. of butter over moderate heat in a large skillet. Add the onions and cook for approximately 4-5 minutes, or until tender and succulent. Transfer the bell peppers and squirt 1 1/2 tsp. of fajita condiments with the restrained ones. Cook for almost 3-5 minutes if you like the peppers with a lovely crunch. And if you like it softer, end up leaving it on for about two to three minutes long. Set aside and move to a plate.

5. Melt 1 residual tablespoon of butter and brown the chicken in the same pan. Cook for 5-6 minutes, or until properly cooked.
6. In a wide salad bowl or tray, organize the lettuce and top it with chicken as well as bell peppers. Add your chosen sliced avocados, lime slices, and any other seasonings.

## 11. KETO BROCCOLI CHEDDAR SOUP

**Serving: 4**

**Preparation time: 20 minutes**

**Nutritional values: 285kcal Calories | 25g Fat | 3g Carbs | 12g Proteins**

**Ingredients**

- 2 spoonful's of butter
- 1/8 cup of onion, white
- 1/2 tsp. of finely chopped garlic
- 2 cups of broth of chicken
- Pepper and salt, to taste
- 1 cup of broccoli, cut into bite-sized pieces
- 1 spoon of cream cheese
- Heavy whipping cream 1/4 cup
- 1 cup of cheddar cheese, crushed
- Bacon 2 loaves, cooked and Imploded (Optional)
- 1/2 tsp. of gum xanthan (Optional)

**Directions**

1. Simmer the onion and garlic with butter in a wide pot over medium heat until the onions are seamless and textured.
2. Add broth as well as broccoli to the pot. Until soft, cook broccoli. Add the salt, pepper, and seasoning you want.
3. Put the cream cheese in a medium bowl and heat for ~30 seconds in the microwave until smooth and easy to mix.
4. Mix in the soup with heavy whipping cream and cream cheese; bring to the boil.
5. Turn off the heat and mix the cheddar cheese swiftly.
6. If required, stir in the xanthan gum. Allow for stiffening.
7. Serve hot with implodes of bacon (if desired)

## 12. SPICY THAI BUTTERNUT SQUASH SOUP

**Serving: 4**

**Preparation time: 30 minutes**

**Nutritional values: 450kcal Calories | 35g Fat | 35g Carbs | 8g proteins**

**Ingredients**

- 11/2 tbsp. coconut oil, refined
- 1 large onion, yellow, sliced
- 1/4 cup of a paste of red curry
- One 2-inch slice of grated or finely chopped garlic
- Four teaspoons of cloves of garlic, diced

- 4 cups vegetable stock with low sodium or water
- 1 peeled and finely diced medium butternut squash (about 41/2 cups)
- One 13.5-ounce coconut milk full-fat can
- 1/4 cup cashew butter or almond butter in natural form
- Lower tamari 1 tbsp.
- 1 tablespoon maple syrup or nectar of Agave
- Kosher salt about 1 tsp., plus more to flavor
- Three teaspoons of freshly pressed lemon juice
- 1/2 cup of fresh, chopped cilantro, plus more for garnishing
- Serve with coconut yogurt, roasted peanuts, scallions & sesame seeds

**Directions**

1. Choose the Instant Pot Sauté mode, then add the coconut oil after several minutes. When the oil is warm, add a bit of salt to the onion, and then cook for 6 to 7 minutes before it starts to brown. Transfer the curry paste, ginger, and garlic; simmer for about 1 minute, constantly stirring, until quite tangy.
2. Spill the stock in and use a wooden spoon on the bottom of the pot to pick off some browned pieces. Stir in butternut squash, coconut milk, tamari, salt, cashew butter, and maple syrup. To blend properly, mix.
3. Shield the cover and seal the pressure release. Choose the high-pressure setting for the soup and specify the cooking time to 12 minutes.
4. Enable an organic pressure release for 5 minutes when the timer goes off, and then undergo a speedy pressure release.
5. Open the pot, add the lime juice and mix. Mix, so you have a nice and creamy broth using an electric mixer. Conversely, using a dish towel to shield the mixer cap to keep steam from spreading, you should pass the broth in batches to a mixer.
6. Stir in the minced cilantro until the broth is pureed—seasoning with coconut yogurt, peanuts, sesame seeds, and scallions as needed.

## 13. KETO PHO RECIPE

**Serving: 4**

**Preparation time: 35 minutes**

**Nutritional values: 220kcal Calories | 5g Fat | 8g Carbs | 33g Proteins**

**Ingredients**

- 4 Entire Star Anise
- 2 entire pods of Cardamom
- 2 entire sticks of Cinnamon
- 2 Whole Cloves
- 1 tbsp. seeds of Coriander
- 1 tsp. of ginger
- 8 cups of bone broth of beef

- 1 tablespoon of Fish sauce
- 1 tbsp. Allulose Mix of Besti Monk Fruit (optional, to taste)
- Salt (optional, to taste)

**Soup Pho**:

- Flank steak 12 oz. (trimmed, or sirloin)
- 2 large Zucchinis (spiraled into zoodles)

**Pho toppings optional:**

- Thai basil
- Cilantro
- Wedges of lime
- Slices of red chili pepper (or jalapeno peppers)
- Scallions
- Sriracha

**Directions**

1. For 30 minutes, put the steak in the refrigerator to make it easy to slice finely.
2. In the meantime, over moderate heat, warm a Dutch oven, minus oil. Bring the star anise, pods of cardamom, sticks of cinnamon, garlic, seeds of coriander, and fresh ginger. Toast, until aromatic, for 2-3 minutes.
3. Combine the fish sauce as well as bone broth. Mix together—Cook the pho broth and stew for 30 minutes.
4. In the meantime, to make zoodles out from the zucchini, use a spiralizer. Split the noodles from the zucchini into 4 bowls.
5. Pull it out and slice rather thinly against the grain until the steak in the refrigerator is stable. Put the steak inside each bowl on top of the zoodles.

6. Mix in the sweetener to disintegrate (if used) and modify the salt to taste whenever the broth is finished simmering. In a different pot or bowl, extract the soup. Discard all the spices that are trapped in the strainer.
7. Although the broth is already simmering, spill it over the preparing bowls instantly, making sure that the steak is immersed, so it cooks completely. (Conversely, the steak should first be stirred into the boiling broth.)
8. Thai basil, coriander, lemon slices, jalapeno or chili pepper strips, scallions, and Sriracha, and garnish with condiments of you're choosing.

## 14. PORK CARNITAS

**Serving: 8**

**Preparation time: 7 hrs.15 min**

**Nutritional values: 442kcal Calories | 31g Fat | 9g Carbs30g Proteins**

## Ingredients

- 1 white, halved, and finely chopped onion
- Five cloves of garlic, chopped
- 1 jalapeño, chopped,
- 3 lbs. of cubed shoulder pork
- Salt and black pepper finely ground
- 1 tablespoon of cumin
- 2 tbsp. of fresh oregano minced
- Two Oranges
- 1 lemon
- 1⁄3 cup of broth of chicken

## Directions

1. At the base of a slow cooker, put the onion, jalapeño garlic, pork together. Add the salt, pepper, oregano & cumin.
2. The oranges and lime are zested over the pork, then halved, and the juice is squeezed over the pork. Also, spill the broth over the pork.
3. Put the cover on and adjust the heat to medium on the slow cooker. Process for 7 hours or unless the meat is soft and quick to squash with a fork.
4. Shred the pork with two forks. The pork may be eaten instantly or frozen in an airtight jar for up to 5 days in the fridge or for up to one month in the freezer.

## 15. CHICKEN MEATBALLS AND CAULIFLOWER RICE WITH COCONUT HERB SAUCE

**Serving: 4**

**Preparation time: 45 minutes**

**Nutritional values: 205kcal calories | 13g Fat | 3g Carbs | 20g Proteins**

**Ingredients**

**For meatballs**

- Non-stick spray
- 1 tablespoon of extra virgin olive oil
- 1/2 of the red onion
- 2 cloves of garlic, chopped

- 1 lb. of ground chicken
- 1/4 cup of finely minced parsley
- 1 tablespoon of Dijon mustard
- 3/4 tsp. of kosher salt
- 1/2 tsp. of freshly ground black pepper

**For sauce**

- One 14-ounce of coconut milk can
- 11/4 cups of fresh, chopped parsley, distributed
- Four scallions, minced roughly
- 1 clove of garlic, peeled and crushed
- Juice and zest of one lime
- Kosher salt and black pepper, recently ground
- Red pepper flakes to serve.
- 1 Cauliflower Rice recipe

**Directions**

1. **Prepare the meatballs:** Set the oven to 375°F. Cover a baking sheet with aluminum foil and coat it with a non-stick spray.
2. Heat the oil in a wide skillet over medium heat. Integrate the onion and simmer until soft, about five minutes. Integrate the garlic and simmer until tangy for around 1 minute.
3. Shift the onion and garlic to a mixing saucepan and let it cool completely. Mix in chicken, parsley, and mustard, sprinkle with salt. Turn the paste into 2 tablespoon balls and shift to the parchment paper.
4. Cook the meatballs for 17 to 20 minutes until firm and fully cooked.
5. **Prepare the sauce:** In a food processor pan, blend coconut milk, scallions, parsley, garlic, lime juice & lemon zest and stir unless buttery; season with salt and pepper.

6. Cover with the red pepper flakes as well as the leftover parsley. With the sauce, end up serving over the cauliflower rice.

## 16. KETO RAINBOW VEGGIES AND SHEET PAN CHICKEN

**Serving: 4**

**Preparation time: 40 minutes**

**Nutritional values: 380kcal Calories | 14g Fat | 35g Carbs | 31g Proteins**

**Ingredients**

- Spray for Nonstick
- 1 lb. of boneless chicken breasts without skin
- Sesame Oil 1 tbsp.

- 2 spoonful's of soy sauce
- Honey about 2 tablespoons
- 2 bell peppers, red, chopped
- 2 bell peppers yellow, chopped
- Three carrots, diced
- 1/2 broccoli head, sliced into cloves
- 2 red, chopped onions
- Extra virgin olive oil about 2 tablespoons
- Kosher salt and black pepper, recently ground
- 1/4 cup of fresh parsley, minced, for serving

**Directions**

1. Heat up the oven to 400 degrees F. Slather a baking sheet lightly with non - stick spray.
2. Put the chicken on the baking tray. Stir the sesame oil and soy sauce together in a medium bowl. Dust the blend over the chicken equally.
3. On the baking dish, place the red and yellow bell peppers, broccoli, carrot & red onion. Sprinkle over the vegetables with olive oil and softly toss to coat; season with salt and pepper.
4. Roast it for 23 to 25 minutes until the veggies are soft and the chicken is thoroughly cooked. Take it out of the oven and seasoned it with parsley.

## 17. CAULIFLOWER POTATO SALAD

**Serving: 6**

**Preparation time: 30-40 minutes**

**Nutritional values: 90kcal Calories | 4g Fat | 9g Carbs | 5g Proteins**

**Ingredients**

- 1 head cauliflower, sliced into chunks that are bite-sized
- 3⁄4 cup of Greek yogurt
- 1⁄4 cup of sour cream
- 1 tbsp. Mustard from Dijon
- 2 tbsp. apple cider vinegar
- 1 tablespoon of fresh parsley minced

- 1 tbsp. fresh dill minced
- Celery 4 stalks, finely chopped
- 1 bunch of green, finely chopped onions
- 1⁄3 cup of cornichons diced
- Kosher salt and black pepper, freshly processed

**Directions**

1. Put the cauliflower, then coat it with water in a large container. Take the cauliflower to a simmer over moderate flame and boil until it is just fork soft, 8 to 10 minutes (do not overcook it, because, in the salad, it may not keep up).
2. Gently soak and cool the cauliflower to normal temperature. Meanwhile, mix the Greek yogurt, sour cream, mustard, vinegar, parsley, and dill together in a wide cup.
3. To incorporate, add the cauliflower, celery, green onions, and cornichons to the bowl and mix well. Sprinkle with salt & pepper.
4. When eating, chill the salad for a minimum of 1 hour. It is possible to prepare the salad 1 day in advance and keep it in the fridge until ready to eat.

## 18. PROSCIUTTO WRAPPED CAULIFLOWER BITES

**Serving: 8-10**

**Preparation time: 15 minutes**

**Nutritional values: 215kcal Calories | 15g Fat | 5g Carbs | 15g Proteins**

**Ingredients**

- 1 tiny cauliflower
- 1/2 cup of paste of tomatoes
- 2 spoonful's of white wine
- 1/2 tsp. of black pepper
- 1/2 cup of Parmesan cheese grated
- 20 Prosciutto slices
- 6 tbsp. of extra-virgin olive oil

**Directions**

1. Start preparing the cauliflower: Cut the base, and any green leaves, away from the cauliflower. Halve the cauliflower, and slice the halves into 1-inch-thick pieces. Based on the size of the slice, divide the slices into 2 or 3 bite-size bits.

2. Bring a big saucepan of salted water to a boil. In the water, parboil the cauliflower until almost soft, for 3 to 5 minutes. With paper towels, rinse the cauliflower well enough and pat off.
3. Add the tomato paste with the white wine & black pepper in a small dish to blend. On the edges of each slice of cauliflower, distribute 1 tsp., then dust with 1 tsp. of Parmesan. A prosciutto slice is carefully wrapped over each piece of cauliflower, pushing softly at the edge to seal it (it should twig well to the tomato-paste blend).
4. Continuing to work in chunks, heat two tablespoons of olive oil over moderate heat in a large pan. Add the cauliflower while the oil is hot and simmer unless the prosciutto is crispy and golden, 3 to 4 minutes on either side. Repeat till all the pieces are ready, with extra oil and cauliflower. Let it cool slowly, then serve right away.

## 19. CAULIFLOWER TORTILLAS

**Serving: 6**

**Preparation time: 45 minutes**

**Nutritional values: 45kcal Calories | 2g Fat | 5g Carbs | 4g Proteins**

**Ingredients**

- 1 head cauliflower
- 2 eggs, pounded lightly
- 1/2 tsp. cumin
- 1/4 tsp. of cayenne pepper
- Salt and black pepper, freshly processed, to taste

**Directions**

1. Heat up the oven to 375°F. Use parchment paper to cover a baking sheet.
2. Split the cauliflower into thin strips. Cut the delicate portion of the stems roughly (discard the tough and leafy parts).
3. Move the cauliflower to the mixing bowl, filling it just halfway, working in bundles. Compress the cauliflower until it looks like rice, around 45 seconds to 1 minute. Repeat for the cauliflower that remains.
4. Move the cauliflower to a dish that is microwave-safe. Microwave around 1 minute, mix well, and microwave for an extra 1 minute.
5. Move the cauliflower to a tidy kitchen towel in the center. In a twist, cover the cauliflower up. Keep the towel over the basin and curl the ends to suck the humidity out of the cauliflower.
6. Take the cauliflower back to the bowl. Add the eggs, cumin, cayenne, salt, and black pepper, and mix well.
7. Ridge the lined baking sheet with 1/4 cup of cauliflower scoops. Distribute the cauliflower into 1/8-inch-thick circles using a tiny spoon.
8. For around 8 to 9 minutes, cook the tortillas until the bottoms are crispy. Then use a spatula to turn the tortillas over cautiously and cook for another 8 to 9 minutes unless crispy on the other side.
9. The tortillas can be eaten hot, instantly, or frozen for up to five days in an airtight jar in the fridge (with parchment pieces among them).

## 20. KETO SALMON SUSHI BOWL

**Serving: 3-4**

**Preparation time: 15 minutes**

**Nutritional values: 45kcal Calories | 6g Fat | 8g Carbs | 9g Proteins**

**Ingredients**

- Cauliflower Rice 3/4 Cup
- Smoked salmon about 1/2 packet
- 1/2 cup of cucumber spiraled
- Avocado 1/2
- 2 sheets of seaweed-dried
- 1 teaspoon of low sodium soy sauce
- Pepper & salt, to taste

- Wasabi 1/2 teaspoon, optional

**Sauce**

- 3 tbsp. mayonnaise
- Sriracha 1-2 teaspoon (adjust to preference)

**Direction**

1. Steam the cauliflower rice and incorporate salt and black pepper ( I used premade bag)
2. Put the rice layer with soy sauce as well as seasoning in the bottom of the small dish.
3. Fill the bowl with salmon, cucumber, seaweed, and avocado
4. Integrate mayo and Sriracha for sauce, adapting to the preferred heat.
5. Spread the sauce over a dish.
6. If desired, add sesame seeds as well as pepper for garnishing.

## 2.3 Keto Snacks

# 1. BAKED GARLIC PARMESAN ZUCCHINI CHIPS

**Serving: 6**

**Preparation time: 20-30 minutes**

**Nutritional values: 155kcal Calories | 10g Fat | 10g Carbs | 5g Proteins**

**Ingredients**

- Chopped 3 to 4 zucchini into pieces of 1/4-inch and 1/2-inch
- 3 tbsp. of Omega-3 DHA Extra Virgin Olive Oil STAR
- Salt to taste and freshly ground pepper
- 1 cup bread crumbs of panko

- 1/2- cup of Parmesan grated cheese
- 1 tsp. of oregano that is dried
- 1 tsp. of powdered garlic
- Cooking spray
- Non-Fat simple yogurt, for serving,

**Directions**

1. Preheat the cooking oven to 450.
2. Line 3 foil-based baking sheets; brush lightly with cooking spray, then set it aside.
3. Incorporate the zucchini pieces, olive oil, salt, and pepper in a wide mixing bowl; whisk until well mixed.
4. Incorporate the crumbs, cheese, oregano, plus garlic powder in a different dish.
5. Dip the zucchini pieces in the cheese mixture and cover on both ends, press to remain with the coating.
6. On the prepared baking sheets, put the slices of zucchini in a thin layer.
7. Spray every slice lightly with cooking spray. This would help to achieve a texture that is crispier.
8. Flip the pan and finish frying for 8 - 10 mints, or until the chips are nicely browned—bake for ten min.
9. Remove it from the oven.
10. With Non-Fat Simple Yogurt, serve it.

## 2. KETO PIZZA ROLL-UPS

**Serving: 8-10**

**Preparation time: 15 minutes**

**Nutritional values: 138kcal Calories | 12g Fat | 8g Carbs | 6g Proteins**

**Ingredients**

- 12 mozzarella cheese slices
- Chunks of pepperoni, or you may use small pepperoni as well.
- Seasoning - Italian
- Marina Sauce - Keto

## Directions

1. Heat the oven to 400°F.
2. Using a baking mat and parchment paper, cover a cookie sheet.
3. Position the slices of cheese on the baking mat, then place them in the oven for 6 mints, or unless the slices of cheese tend to brown across the corners.
4. Take it out from the oven and leave to cool the cheese moderately. If you like, make the slices to chill and scatter with Italian seasoning, as well as include pepperoni.
5. With your chosen dipping sauce, wrap & serve! Enjoy

## 3. STUFFED MUSHROOMS WITH SAUSAGE

**Serving: 8**

**Preparation time: 30-40 minutes**

**Nutritional values: 280kcal Calories | 20g Fat | 6g Carbs | 15g Proteins**

**Ingredients**

- 1 pound of mild Italian sausage
- Cremini mushrooms about 1 pound
- 4 ounces of cream cheese
- 1/3 cup mozzarella - shredded
- Salt, as necessary
- ½ Teaspoon flakes of red pepper
- 1/4 cup of Parmesan grated cheese

**Directions**

1. To 350F, set the oven. Wash and cut the stems from the mushrooms.
2. Cook the sausage in a wide skillet over moderate heat. Transfer it to a wide mixing bowl until it has been cooked.
3. Add the mozzarella cheese, cream cheese, and mix to combine. Season to taste, then add salt & red pepper if required.
4. Spoon onto the mushroom caps with the sausage combination. Use Parmesan cheese for scattering. Put in a pan or casserole platter that is oven-safe.
5. Bake for 25 mints, unless the cheese is golden brown and the mushrooms are tender.

## 4. EASY KETO PIZZA BITES

**Serving: 30**

**Preparation time: 30-35 minutes**

**Nutritional values: 82kcal Calories | 7g Fat | 1g Carbs | 4g Proteins**

**Ingredients**

- 1 lb., cooked as well as drained Italian sausage
- Cream cheese, 4 ounces, softened.
- 1/3 of a cup of cocoa flour
- 1/2 tsp. powder for baking
- 1 tsp. of garlic diced

- 1 tsp. of seasoning - Italian
- 3 large, beaten eggs
- 1 1/4 cup mozzarella crushed

**Directions**

1. Preheat the oven to 350°F.
2. Mix the prepared sausage & cream cheese unless fully fused together.
3. To give the flour time to ponder the moisture, rest of the ingredients until well mixed and cool for 10 minutes.
4. If you forget to chill the dough, they will deflate while they cook and will not be pleasant round balls.
5. Use a tiny cookie scoop to transfer onto a greased baking sheet (I prefer using the silicone baking mats).
6. Bake until lightly browned for 18-20 minutes.
7. This made 30, so it depends on the scale of the scoop you're using and how closely you're packing it.

## 5. CUCUMBER SLICES WITH HERB AND GARLIC CHEESE

**Serving: 16**

**Preparation time: 5 minutes**

**Nutritional values: 42kcal Calories | 3g Fat | 1g Carbs | 1g Proteins**

**Ingredients**

- 1 Diced English cucumber into 16 slices
- The Chives
- 6.5 ounces of Boursin or Alouette Herb & Garlic Cheese

**Directions**

1. To include some novelty, cut short slices of the cucumber skin with the help of a vegetable peeler.

2. Cut the cucumber to a thickness of around 1 mm.
3. Put the cheese in a pastry bag equipped with the edge of a large star.
4. The cucumber tips could clear every moister with a paper towel pat.
5. Puff each cucumber with the cheese and cover with a piece of chives.

## 6. KETO POPCORN - PUFFED CHEESE

**Serving: 5**

**Preparation: 10 minutes**

**Nutritional values: 80kcal Calories | 7g Fat | 0.3g Carbs | 5g Proteins**

**Ingredients**

- cheddar 100g/3.5 ounces

Directions

1. Slice the cheese into 0.5 inches / 1 cm pieces if you use diced cheddar. If you are using a block of cheddar, crush it to the same size using your fingertips.
2. Use a cloth/kitchen towel to wrap the cheese to keep it from being gritty and let it stay for up to 3 days in a hot, dry spot. You would like the cheese to be solid and dried absolutely.
3. Preheat oven to 390 Fahrenheit / 200 Celsius. On a baking tray covered with parchment paper, spread the cheese and bake for 4-five minutes before the cheese bursts. Put a new baking tray securely over the tray to keep it from popping out over the oven.

## 7. BACON WRAPPED BRUSSELS SPROUTS

**Serving: 4**

**Preparation time: 40 minutes**

**Nutritional values: 170kcal Calories | 15g Fat | 3g Carbs | 2g Proteins**

**Ingredients**

12 bacon slices

12 Brussels sprouts, cut stems

Balsamic Dip:

Mayonnaise 5 tbsp.

Balsamic vinegar about 1 tbsp.

**Directions**

1. Preparation: Set aside baking sheets and 12 toothpicks, covered with parchment paper or a baking mat that would be non-stick—preheat the baking oven to 400 F.
2. Wrap Sprouts: Put 1 slice of bacon on each sprout of Brussels, seal it with a toothpick, and put on the baking sheet in a thin layer.
3. Bake: Bake discovered at 400 F until the bacon is translucent and the Brussels are quite juicy around 40 minutes.
4. Serve: In a medium bowl, blend the mayonnaise & balsamic vinegar altogether unless creamy. Serve Brussels sprouts covered with bacon on a plate, along with the dip.

## 8. KETO ASPARAGUS FRIES

**Serving: 6**

**Preparation time: 1hour**

**Nutritional values: 202kcal Calories | 14g Fat | 7g Carbs | 14g Proteins**

**Ingredients**

- 1 pound of asparagus chopped (thick if possible)
- Salt and pepper to taste
- 1 cup of Parmesan cheese
- 3/4 cup of almond flour

- 1/4 tsp. of cayenne pepper
- 1/4 tsp. of baking powder
- 4 pounded eggs
- avocado oil spray

**Directions**

1. Use a fork to cut the asparagus spikes with gaps—season well with a minimum of 1/2 teaspoon of salt. Put on paper towels and let it rest for 30 minutes.
2. In the meantime, mix 1 cup of Parmesan, cayenne pepper, almond flour & baking powder in a dish. Sprinkle with salt to taste.
3. Pound the egg in a different dish.
4. Soak the asparagus segments in the eggs, then cover with the blend of the cheese.
5. Your air fryer should be preheated to 400 degrees.
6. Organize the asparagus in one layer and, if required, cook in chunks. Spray the oil well—Cook for five minutes. Turn, and then respray.
7. Fry unless the asparagus is soft for the next 4 or 5 minutes.

## 9. EGG, BACON, AND CHEESE SLIDERS

**Serving: 6**

**Preparation time: 10 minutes**

**Nutritional values: 237kcal Calories | 18g Fat | 3g Carbs | 15g Proteins**

**Ingredients**

- 6 peeled, boiled eggs
- 6 Thin cheddar cheese strips

- 3 Slices of bacon that has been cooked
- 1/2 of Avocado
- 1/2 teaspoon Juice of a lime
- 1/2 Teaspoon cumin

**Directions**

1. In a mixing bowl, place 1/2 of an avocado.
2. Stir in the cumin as well as lime juice. Mix until completely smooth. To taste, incorporate the salt.
3. Cut each hardboiled egg lengthwise in half.
4. Put on the lower half of the egg one piece of thinly cut cheddar cheese.
5. Place 1/2 a slice of cooked bacon on edge.
6. On the edge of the bacon, put a spoonful of the avocado mixture on top.
7. To make a little sandwich, place the remaining half of the egg face right over the top. Protect the bite of the egg with a toothpick placed down the center.
8. For your remaining eggs, replicate steps 4-7.
9. Add salt and pepper to each bite of the egg to taste & serve.

## 10. TURKEY BACON WRAP RANCH PINWHEELS

**Serving: 6**

**Preparation time: 15 minutes**

**Nutritional values: 133kcal Calories | 12g Fat | 2g Carbs | 5g proteins**

**Ingredients**

- 6 ounces of cheese cream
- 12 strips of smoked turkey deli (about 3 oz.)
- 1/4 teaspoon powdered garlic
- 1/4 teaspoon of chopped dried onion
- Dried dill weed 1/4 teaspoon
- 1 tablespoon of crumbling bacon

- 2 tablespoons cheddar shredded cheese

**Directions**

1. Among 2 pieces of plastic wrap, place the cream cheese. Stretch it out until it's approximately 1/4 inch thick. Scrape the plastic wrap off the top piece. On top of the cream cheese, place the slices of turkey on the edge.
2. Cover and switch the whole item over with a fresh layer of plastic wrap. Chop off the plastic bit that is on the upper right now. Slather it on top of the cream cheese with the seasoning. Spray it with cheese and bacon.
3. Roll the pinwheels up such that the exterior is the turkey. Refrigerate for 2 minimum hours. On the edge of low-carb crackers or diced cucumber, cut into 12 bits and serve.

## 2.4 Keto Desserts

# 1. KETO BROWN BUTTER PRALINES

**Serving: 10**

**Preparation time: 16 minutes**

**Nutritional values: 338kcal Calories | 36g Fat | 3g Carbs | 2g Proteins**

**Ingredients**

- 2 Salted butter sticks

- Heavy cream 2/3 cup
- 2/3 Cup of Sweetener Granular 1/2 tsp. of xanthan gum
- 2 Cups Pecans diced
- Maldon Sea salt

**Directions**

1. Use parchment paper or a silicone baking mat to make a cookie sheet.
2. Cook the butter in a skillet over medium flame, stirring regularly. It's going to take less than five min. Whisk in the heavy cream, sweetener, and xanthan gum. Extract it from the heat.
3. Mix in the nuts and put in the fridge, stirring regularly, for 1 hour to tighten up. The mixture's going to get really dense. Scrape onto the prepared baking sheet into 10 cookie styles and spray, if necessary, with the Maldon salt. Let the baking sheet freeze until frozen.
4. Store and keep stored in the fridge until served in an airtight dish.

## 2. KETO CHOCOLATE MOUSSE

**Serving: 4**

**Preparation time: 10 minutes**

**Nutritional values: 220kcal Calories | 25g Fat | 5g Carbs | 2g Proteins**

**Ingredients**

- 1 Cup of Whipped Heavy Cream
- 1/4 cup Cocoa powder unsweetened, sifted
- 1/4 Cup Sweetener Powdered
- 1 tsp. extract of vanilla
- Kosher salt about 1/4 teaspoon

**Directions**

1. Use the cream to whip into stiff peaks. Include the cocoa powder, vanilla, sweetener, and salt, then mix until all the products are mixed.

## 3. KETO CHEESECAKE FLUFF

**Serving: 6**

**Preparation time: 10 minutes**

**Nutritional values: 260kcal Calories | 27g Fat | 4g Carbs | 4g Proteins**

**Ingredients**

- 1 Cup of Whipping Heavy Cream

- 1 Eight oz. Cream Cheese Brick, Softened
- 1 Lemon Zest
- 1/2 Cup of Sweetener Granular

**Directions**

1. In a stand mixer, combine the heavy cream as well as stir until stiff peaks are made. A hand blender or a whisk can also be used by hand using a whisk.
2. In a different bowl, scrape the whipped cream and put it aside.
3. In the stand blender bowl, add the textured cream cheese, zest, and sweetener, then beat until sturdy.
4. With the cream cheese, add the whipped cream into the stand blender dish. Mix carefully until it is halfway mixed with a spatula. To finish whipping until sturdy, use the stand mixer.
5. Serve with a favorite topping of you.

## 4. LOW CARB BLUEBERRY CRISP

**Serving: 2**

**Preparation time: 20-25 minutes**

**Nutritional values: 390kcal Calories | 35g Fat | 17g Carbs | 6g Proteins**

**Ingredients**

- 1 Cup of Fresh or Frozen Blueberries
- 1/4 Cup Halves of Pecan
- Almond Meal/Flour 1/8 cup
- Butter around 2 tbsp.
- Granular Sweetener 2 tablespoons - distributed

- 1 tablespoon of flax
- Cinnamon 1/2 Teaspoon
- ½ teaspoon Extract from vanilla
- Kosher salt about 1/4 teaspoon
- Heavy cream 2 tablespoons

**Directions**

1. Heat the oven to 400F.
2. Put 1/2 cup of blueberries and 1/2 tablespoons of swerve sweetener in 2, 1 cup ramekins. Blend and combine.
3. Incorporate the pecans, almond flour, butter, 1 tbsp. sweetener, cinnamon, ground flax, vanilla, and kosher salt into the food processor. Pulse while you mix the ingredients.
4. Place on top of the blueberries with the blend. Put the ramekins on a baking sheet and cook for 15-20 minutes in the middle of the oven or until the topping turn's toasty brown. Serve with 1 tablespoon of heavy cream slathered on top of each one.

## 5. 1 MINT LOW CARB BROWNIE

**Serving: 1**

**Preparation time: 3 minutes**

**Nutritional values: 196kcal Calories | 17g Fat | 2g Carbs | 8g Proteins**

**Ingredients**

- 2 tablespoons almond flour
- 1 tablespoon of preferred granulated sweetener
- 1 tablespoon powdered cocoa
- Baking Powder 1/8 teaspoon

- Almond butter 1 tablespoon. * See notes
- 3 tablespoons of milk, unsweetened almond milk,
- 1 tablespoon of chocolate chips of preference - optional

**Directions**

1. A tiny microwave-protected cereal bowl or ramkin is lightly greased with cooking spray and placed aside.
2. Integrate all of your dried ingredients in a medium mixing bowl and blend well.
3. Integrate the creamy almond butter and milk in a separate bowl and mix them together. Place the wet and dry ingredients together and blend properly. Roll them through if chocolate chips are used.
4. Microwave at intervals of 30 seconds until the optimal texture has been reached. Take from the microwave then, before eating, let settle for one min.

## 6. KETO PEANUT BUTTER BALLS

**Serving: 18**

**Preparation time: 20 minutes**

**Nutritional values: 195kcal Calories | 17g Fat | 7g Carbs | 7g Proteins**

**Ingredients**

- 1 cup of finely diced salted peanuts (not peanut flour)
- 1 cup of peanut butter
- 1 cup of sweetener powdered, like swerve
- 8-ounce chocolate chips free from sugar

**Directions**

1. Combine the diced peanuts, peanut butter, and the sweetener, respectively. Distribute the 18-piece crust and mold it into balls. Put

them on a baking sheet covered with wax paper. Put it in the fridge until they're cold.

2. In the oven or on top of a dual boiler, heat the chocolate chips. Mix chocolate chips in the microwave, swirling every 30 seconds till they are 75percent melted. Then stir before the remainder of it melts.
3. Soak the chocolate for each peanut butter ball and put it back on the wax paper. Until the chocolate settles, put it in the fridge.

# 7. WHITE CHOCOLATE PEANUT BUTTER BLONDIES

**Serving: 16**

**Preparation time: 35 minutes**

**Nutritional values: 105kcal Calories | 9g Fat | 2g Carbs | 3g Proteins**

**Ingredients**

- 1/2 cup of peanut butter
- Softened butter around 4 tablespoons
- Two Eggs

- Vanilla 1 teaspoon
- 3 tbsp. fresh cocoa butter melted
- 1⁄4 cup of almond flour
- 1 tablespoon of coconut flour
- 1⁄2 cup sweetener
- 1⁄4 cup of fresh cocoa butter diced

**Directions**

1. Preheat the baking oven to 350. Use cooking spray to cover the base of a 9 into 9 baking tray.
2. Beat the first 5 ingredients with an electric mixer until creamy. Bring the flour, sweetener, and sliced cocoa butter into the mixture. Scattered in a baking dish that has been prepared. Bake until the middle no longer jostles, and the corners are golden, for 25 minutes.
3. Cool thoroughly, and then, before slicing, chill in the freezer for 2-3 hours.

## 8. LOW CARB BAKED APPLES

**Serving: 4**

**Preparation time: 20 minutes**

**Nutritional values: 340kcal Calories | 88g Fat | 8g Carbs | 4g Proteins**

**Ingredients**

- 2 ounces. cheese,
- 1 oz. Walnuts or Pecans
- 4 tablespoon coconut flour
- Cinnamon 1/2 tsp.
- Vanilla extract around 1/4 teaspoon
- One tart/sour apple

**To serve**

- 3/4 cup of heavy whipped cream
- Vanilla extract about 1/2 teaspoon

**Directions**

1. Heat the oven to 175°C (350°F). In a crispy dough, mix the hot butter, diced almonds, coconut flour, cinnamon & vanilla together.
2. Wash the apple, but don't eliminate the seeds or chop it. Cut both edges off and cut 4 slices through the center portion.
3. In a greased baking dish, put the slices and place dough crumbs on top. Bake fifteen minutes or more or until light brown appears on the crumbs.
4. To a moderate bowl, incorporate heavy whipping cream as well as vanilla and whisk until soft peaks appear.
5. For a minute or two, let the apples chilled and serve with a spoonful of whipped cream.

## 9. FROZEN YOGURT POPSICLES

**Serving: 12**

**Preparation time: 10mins 2hours**

**Nutritional values: 73kcal Calories | 60g Fat | 28g Carbs | 13g Proteins**

**Ingredients**

- 8 oz. Mango chilled, chopped
- 8 oz. Strawberries chilled
- 1 cup of Greek full-fat yogurt
- 1/2 cup of heavy whipped cream
- 1 teaspoon extract of vanilla

**Directions**

1. Let the strawberries and mango defrost for 10 to 15 minutes.
2. In a mixer, place all the materials and combine until creamy.
3. End up serving as fluffy ice cream instantly or pipe into Popsicle shapes and chill for at least a few hours. If you do have an ice cream machine, it can be used, of course.

## 10. CHOCOLATE AVOCADO TRUFFLES

**Serving: 20**

**Preparation time: 35 minutes**

**Nutritional values: 65kcal Calories | 76g Fat | 19g Carbs | 5g Proteins**

**Ingredients**

- 1 (7 ounces.) ripe, diced avocado
- Vanilla extract about 1/2 teaspoon
- 1/2 lemon, zest
- About 1 pinch of salt
- Five ounces. Dark chocolate containing cocoa solids of at least 80 percent, finely diced
- 1 spoonful of coconut oil
- 1 tbsp. cocoa powder unsweetened

**Directions**

1. Use an electric mixer to mix the avocado and vanilla extract. The use of ripe avocado is necessary in order for the mixture to be fully creamy.

2. Add a tablespoon of salt and mix in the lemon zest.
3. In boiling water or oven, melt the chocolate & coconut oil.
4. Incorporate the chocolate & avocado and blend properly. Let it rest for 30 minutes in the fridge or until the batter is compact but not fully solid.
5. With your fingertips, shape little truffle balls. Likewise, use two teaspoons or a tiny scoop. Morph and roll in the cocoa powder with the hands.

## 11. CRUNCHY KETO BERRY MOUSSE

**Serving: 8**

**Preparation time: 10 minutes**

**Nutritional values: 256kcal Calories | 26g Fat | 3g Carbs | 2g Proteins**

**Ingredients**

- Two cups of heavy whipped cream
- Three ounces. Fresh strawberries or blueberries or raspberries
- 2 oz. Pecans diced
- 1/2 of a lime, zest
- Vanilla extract around 1/4 teaspoon

**Directions**

1. Drop the cream into a container and whip until soft peaks appear using a hand mixer. Towards the top, add the lime zest, then vanilla.
2. Cover the whipped cream with berries & nuts and stir thoroughly.
3. Wrap with plastic and allow for 3 or even more hours for a stable mousse to settle in the fridge. While you don't like a less firm consistency, you can also experience the dessert instantly.

# Conclusion

Ketogenic' is a name for a diet that is low-carb. The concept is for you to obtain more protein and fat calories and fewer carbs. You reduce much of the carbs, such as sugar, coffee, baked goods, and white bread that are easily digestible.

If you consume fewer than 50 g of carbs a day, the body can gradually run out of resources (blood sugar) that you can use instantly. Usually, this takes 3 or 4 days. Then you're going to start breaking down fat and protein for nutrition, which will help with weight loss. This is classified as ketosis.

A ketogenic diet plan intended to induce ketosis, disintegrate body fat into ketones and enable the body to perform on ketones instead of glucose to a great extent. Since samen is the ultimate aim of these diets, there are typically a lot of connections between the various forms of the ketogenic diet, especially in terms of being low in carbohydrates and high in dietary fat. A program that focuses on high-fat and low carbohydrates is the Ketogenic Diet, and it has many advantages.

It is necessary to remember that a short-term diet that emphasizes weight reduction rather than medical benefits is a ketogenic diet. To reduce weight, people use a keto diet more commonly, although it may help treat some medical problems, such as epilepsy, too. People with heart problems, some neurological disorders, and also acne can even be supported, although further research in those fields needs to be conducted.

# Gourmet Keto Diet Cookbook For Women After 50

**By**

**Dora Gray**

# Table of Contents

# Introduction

If you're just a woman over 50 years of age, you may be much more involved in weight loss than you would have been at 30. Most women face a slower metabolism at this age at a rate of around 50 calories a day. A slower metabolism will make it incredibly difficult to control weight gain, along with reduced exercise, muscle degradation, and the propensity for increased hunger pangs. There are several diet options available to help lose weight, but the keto diet is amongst the most famous lately. The keto diet (or ketogenic diet, for short) is indeed a low-carb, high-fat diet that promises numerous health benefits. We have obtained several questions about keto's feasibility and how to adapt the diet in such a healthier way. More than 20 studies have shown that sort of diet can lead to weight loss and health enhancement. Diabetes, cancer, epilepsy, and Alzheimer's can still benefit from ketogenic diets. To make the body burn its very own fat stores more effectively, Keto is a diet that involves reducing carbohydrates and growing fats. Analysis has also shown that a keto diet is suitable for general health and weight reduction. In particular, ketogenic diets have enabled certain individuals to lose excess body fat without the extreme hunger pangs characteristic of most diets. Any patients with type 2 diabetes have also been shown to be able to use keto to manage their signs. At the core of a ketogenic diet are ketones. As an alternative energy source, the body creates ketones, a fuel molecule, while getting short on blood sugar. When you decrease carb consumption and eat only the proper levels of nutrients, ketone production happens. Your liver will convert body ketones when you consume keto-friendly foods, which are then used by your body as an energy supply. You are in ketosis as the body uses fat for energy supply. This causes the body, in some situations, to dramatically increase its fat burning, which helps to minimize pockets of excess fat. This fat-burning approach not only lets you lose some weight, but it could also fend off cravings during the day and eliminate sugar crashes. While it's straightforward to assume that the keto diet is high in fat and low in carbohydrates, while you're in the supermarket aisle, it still feels a little more complicated. If Keto is right for you or not depends on several variables. A ketogenic diet can have many advantages, especially for weight loss, providing you don't suffer from health problems. Eating a perfect mix of greens, lean beef, and unrefined carbohydrates are the most significant thing to note. It is possible that keeping the whole foods is the most successful way to eat healthily, mainly because it is a sustainable strategy. It is important to remember that a lot of literature suggests that it is impossible to continue with ketogenic diets. For this cause, discovering a safe eating plan that appeals to you is the right advice. It's cool to try good experiences, but don't leap headfirst. If you are a female over 50 and want to change your lifestyle, this book will teach you what you need to learn about the keto diet. Breakfast, lunch, dinner recipes, and some tasty keto snacks and smoothie recipes are tasty, convenient, and straightforward to make for you. To sustain a balanced lifestyle after 50, let's just begin reading.

# Chapter 1: The Keto Diet: A Better Way Towards Improved Health for Women Over 50

## 1.1. Keto diet in a nutshell

The keto diet is a high-fat, low-carbohydrate diet similar to Atkins & low-carb diets. It involves substantially reducing the consumption of carbohydrates and replacing them with fat. "Ketogenic" is a low-carb food idea (like the Atkins diet). The idea is to get more calories from proteins, fats, and less from carbohydrates. One has to remove carbohydrates such as starch, soda, pastry, and white bread, which are simple to digest. This reduction in calories takes the body to a regular cycle of the body, which is called ketosis. When this happens, the liver is extremely energy efficient when processing fat. It also transforms fat into ketones in the liver that can supply energy to the brain. Ketogenic diets can contribute to substantial decreases in blood sugar and insulin levels. This, combined with the increased ketones, has a range of health effects. If you eat less than 50 grams of carbohydrate a day, your body will eventually run out of fuel (sugar in your blood) and eat it easily. It normally takes about 3 and 4 days. Then you start to break down protein and energy fat that can help you drop weight. It's referred to as ketosis. It is necessary to note that the ketogenic diet is not about dietary benefits, but rather about a short-term diet that focuses on weight loss. People use ketogenic diets to lose weight most frequently, although they may also help to address certain medical problems, including epilepsy. People with heart disease, brain diseases, and even acne can benefit, but more research in these fields is required. First, talk to your doctor about whether a ketogenic diet is healthy, particularly if you have type 1 diabetes.

## 1.2. Yes, keto is fine for women over 50

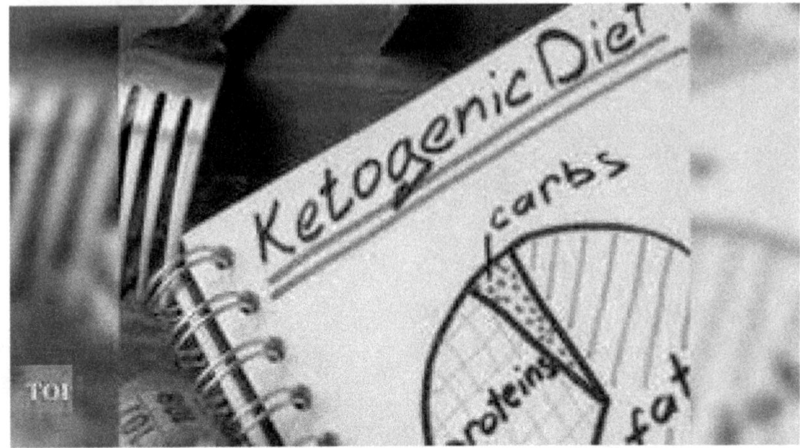


There are certain common dangers and issues that relate to anyone who consumes keto, such as the need to add electrolytes to prevent cramps. It's crucial for anyone to grasp the diet and do it appropriately. Especially for women above 50, it could mean paying particular attention to calcium or making sure they have enough food to remain well-nourished. There are still individuals - both men and women - who simply don't work on low-carb diets for a particular reason, and that's all right.

Some several unique concerns and subjects relate mainly or exclusively to women. Yet overall, there is very little proof that healthy women who are just not pregnant may be more worried about keto than some other diet. There is no proof that people necessarily cannot or cannot consume keto - in fact, there are many women who do keto and enjoy keto! And there is also some proof that keto diets can be beneficial to some female-specific problems, such as PCOS.'

## 1.3. Key takeaways for women above 50 on keto Diet

- Get the correct protein quantity
- Don't eat far too much fat.
- fast intermittently
- Look out for the creeping carb
- Cut the alcohol out
- Evite the sweeteners
- Do a weightlifting workout
- Get ample sleep right now
- Reducing tension
- Be rational about this

## 1.4. Problems to be aware of regarding keto diet in over 50 women

One issue that women can face with keto diets about the under-eating to the extent of a physically unsafe energy deficiency or a lack of body fat underneath a safe amount. It's quite likely to consume less on keto, deliberately or accidentally. Many people who pursue keto seem to be healthy-conscious individuals who want to exercise out a lot, which only increases the issue when they consume less, then drives themselves into intense exercises that need more protein and calories to recover.

This is much more harmful to women than for men since the female body is vulnerable to malnutrition. The reduction of bone mass, a higher likelihood of bone stress fractures, a higher risk of anemia, stomach issues, and psychiatric symptoms.

Dieting to the extent of missing your time can even happen without some workout at all, and it's almost as risky that way! Nutrition Disease

None of this is special to keto. It's all like the calorie deficit. But the appetizing benefits of keto diet increase the risks that women attempting to lose weight will not know how severe they are, mainly because they'll actually receive nothing but compliments about how "safe" they're eating and how "sweet" they're consuming absolutely nothing.

Although, of course, the repression of hunger often renders the diet appealing to women living with eating disorders. It's not exactly a "keto danger;" it's a danger of violating keto, but it does occur. It's outside the meaning of a single post to really consider coping with it, so it sounds like someone you meet, reach out to - you could be saving a life.

# Chapter 2: Keto Breakfast recipes for women over 50

Let's be realistic; one of life's biggest pleasures is a carbohydrate-rich breakfast. There are plenty of safe and tasty keto-friendly breakfast meals. And there is a lot you're probably going to save them from trying someday.

## 1. Keto Hot chocolate shake

Servings: 1 cup | Total time: 10 min

Calories: 193 | Proteins: 2g | Carbohydrates: 4 g | Fat: 18g

**Ingredients**

- Two tablespoons unsweetened cocoa powder
- Two and a half teaspoon sugar
- One-fourth cup of water
- One-fourth cup heavy cream

- One-fourth teaspoon pure vanilla extract
- Some whipped cream, for the purpose of serving

**Steps of preparation**

- In a medium bowl on medium-low heat, mix together chocolate, swerve, and around two tablespoons of water until everything is smooth and absorbed. Increase down to a simmer, introduce remaining water & cream, and periodically whisk until heated.
- Stir in the vanilla, and dump in the cup. Start serving with whipped cream or chocolate powder.

## 2. Keto delicious Cereal

Servings: 3 cups | Total time: 35 min

Calories: 188 | Proteins: 4g | Carbohydrates: 7 g | Fat: 17g

**Ingredients**

- Cooking spray
- One cup almond, chopped walnuts
- One fourth cup sesame seeds
- Coconut flakes
- Two tablespoon flax seeds
- Two tablespoon chia seeds
- Half teaspoon ground clove
- One and a half teaspoon ground cinnamon
- One teaspoon pure vanilla extract

- Half teaspoon kosher salt
- One large egg white
- One-fourth cup melted coconut oil

**Steps of preparation**

- Preheat the oven to 350 ° C then oil the baking tray with a cooking spray. In a wide cup, add coconut flakes, almonds, sesame seeds, walnuts, and chia seeds and linseeds Stir with garlic, vanilla, salt, and cinnamon,
- Now Beat the egg white into foamy and mix in the granola. Apply the coconut oil and mix until all is well covered. Pour over the baking tray and scatter over a consistent layer. Bake for 20 mins just until it gets crispy, stirring gently halfway through. Let it just to cool completely.

## 3. Keto Sausage Sandwich

Servings: 3 | Total time: 15 min

Calories: 411 | Proteins: 38g | Carbohydrates: 7.3 g | Fat: 27g

**Ingredients**

- Six large eggs
- Two tablespoons heavy cream
- Pinch of red pepper flakes
- Pinch of Kosher salt
- Three slices cheddar
- Six frozen sausage patties
- Freshly ground black pepper
- One teaspoon butter
- Avocado in sliced pieces

**Steps of preparation**

- Beat the eggs, red pepper flakes, and heavy cream in a shallow cup. Season to taste with salt carefully. Melt the butter in a non - stick pan over medium heat. In the bowl, pour approximately 1/3 of the whites. Place the cheese mostly in center and then let it rest for around

1 minute. Place the corners of the egg in the center, shielding the cheese. Remove from heat and perform the same on remaining eggs.

- Serve the eggs in two avocado sausage patties.

## 4. Ketogenic Cabbage Hash Browns

Servings: 2 | Total time: 10 min

Calories: 230 | Proteins: 8g | Carbohydrates: 6 g | Fat: 19g

**Ingredients**

- Two large eggs
- Half teaspoon garlic powder
- Half teaspoon kosher salt
- Grounded black pepper
- Two cups shredded cabbage
- One fourth small yellow onion
- One tablespoon vegetable oil

**Steps of preparation**

- In a big cup, mix together eggs, salt and garlic. Season with salt and pepper. Apply the cabbage and the onion to the beaten egg and mix to blend.
- Heat the oil skillet over medium-high flame. Roughly divide the prepared mixture into four patties in the skillet and pressure the spatula to compress. Cook until yellow golden and juicy.

## 5. Ketogenic Pancakes for breakfast

Servings: 6 | Total time: 15 min

Calories: 268 | Proteins: 9g | Carbohydrates: 6 g | Fat: 23g

**Ingredients**

- Half cup almond flour
- Four oz. cream cheese
- Four large eggs
- One teaspoon lemon zest
- Butter

**Steps of preparation**

- In a medium cup, blend together the rice, the eggs, the cream cheese, and the lemon zest until soft and smooth.
- Melt 1 tablespoon of butter on medium heat in a frying pan. Pour in approximately 3 teaspoons of the batter and simmer for 2 minutes until golden. Flip and cook for 2 more minutes. Move to the plate and continue for the remainder of the batter.
- Serve with some sugar and butter.

## 6. Keto breakfast quick Smoothie

Servings: 6 | Total time: 5 min

Calories: 152 | Proteins: 1g | Carbohydrates: 5 g | Fat: 13g

**Ingredients**

- One and a half cup frozen strawberries
- One and a half cup frozen raspberries, plus more for garnish (optional)
- One cup frozen blackberry
- Two cup coconut milk
- One cup baby spinach
- Shaved coconut for garnishing purposes

**Steps of preparation**

- Combine all the ingredients (except coconut) in a mixer. Mix so that it gets creamy.
- Divide, if used, into cups and top with raspberries and coconut.

## 7. Keto Breakfast Cups

Servings: 12 cups | Total time: 40 min

Calories: 82 kcal | Proteins: 6g | Carbohydrates: 1 g | Fat: 2g

**Ingredients**

- Two pounds ground pork
- Two tablespoon freshly chopped thyme
- Two cloves of minced garlic
- Half teaspoon paprika
- Half teaspoon. ground cumin
- One teaspoon kosher salt
- Half cup ground black pepper.
- One cup chopped fresh spinach
- White cheddar shredded
- Twelve eggs
- One tablespoon freshly chopped chive

**Steps of preparation**

- Start by preheating the oven to 400 ° F. Mix the ground pork, garlic, paprika, thyme, salt and the cumin in a large dish. Now season with a salt and the pepper.
- Add just that small handful of pork per muffin container, and then push the sides to create a cup. Start dividing spinach and cheese similarly in cups. Crack the egg at the top of every cup and add salt and pepper for seasoning.

## 8. Keto Breakfast Blueberry Muffins

Servings: 12 muffins | Total time: 40 min

Calories: 181 kcal | Proteins: 4.5g | Carbohydrates: 25 g | Fat: 5.6g

**Ingredients**

- Two and a half cup almond flour
- One third cup keto friendly sugar
- One and a half teaspoon baking powder
- Half teaspoon baking soda
- Half teaspoon kosher salt
- One-third cup melted butter
- One-third cup unsweetened almond milk
- Three large eggs
- One teaspoon pure vanilla extract
- Two-third cup blueberries
- Half lemon zests

**Steps of preparation**

- Start by preheating the oven to a temperature of 350 ° and put in a muffin tray with cupcake liners.
- In a big container, stir together almond flour, Swerve, baking soda, baking powder, and salt. Gently stir in melted butter, eggs, and vanilla once mixed.
- Gently fold the blueberries and the lemon zest until uniformly spread. Scoop equivalent quantities of the mixture into each liner of cupcakes and bake until softly golden and a toothpick inserted into the middle of the muffin comes out clean, this will happen within 23 minutes. Let it cool slightly before serving.

## 9. Keto Thai Beef Lettuce Wraps

Serving: 4 | Total Time: 30 min |

Calories: 368 Kcal, Fat: 14.5g, Net Carbs: 3.1g, Protein: 53.8g

**Ingredients**

- Olive oil 1 tablespoon
- Ground beef 1.5lb.
- Beef stock 1 ½ cups
- Garlic 2 cloves, minced
- lime juice fresh ¼ cup
- Fish sauce 2 tablespoons
- Chopped parsley ½ cup
- Mint chopped ½ cup
- To taste salt & pepper

**Steps of Preparation**

- Heat the olive oil over medium to high heat in a skillet.
- In a skillet, brown the beef for eight to ten mins.
- Add beef to skillet.
- Cook till the stock has fully boiled off.
- Meanwhile, mix the garlic, fish sauce, and lime juice.
- Add beef to the lime mixture.

- Cook 2 to 3 mins.
- Garnish with chopped herbs.
- Assemble, the beef is scooped over the leaves of the cabbage or the lettuce.
- Serve.

## 10. Breakfast **Skillet Cilantro-Lime Chicken**

Serving 4 | Total Time: 30 min

Calories: Kcal 426, Fat: 16.4g, Net Carbs: 6g, Protein: 61.8g

**Ingredients**

- Olive oil 1 tbsp
- Chicken breasts 4 boneless skinless
- Kosher salt
- Ground freshly black pepper
- Unsalted butter 2 tbsp
- Garlic minced 2 cloves
- Medium limes 2 finely grated zest
- Lime juice freshly squeezed 1/4 cup
- Freshly chopped cilantro leaves & tender stems 1/3 cup
- (Optional) for serving cooked rice

**Steps of Preparation**

- Pat the chicken, thoroughly dry using paper towels. Season properly with pepper and salt. Steam 1 tbsp of the oil over medium to high shimmering steam in a ten-inch or bigger skillet. If possible, working in batches, add the chicken and sear to the bottom for 5 to 7 minutes, until deeply browned. Flip the meat, then sear for 5 to 7 mins before the other side is browned. Place the chicken into a plate; put aside.
- Reduce to medium heat. Attach the garlic, butter, and lime zest then cook for 1 minute, stirring frequently. Stir in the juice of the lime. Send the chicken back to the skillet and any leftover juices. Cover, heat is reduced as required to maintain a moderate simmer and cook till the meat is cooked through and record 165°F on thermometer instant-read, 2 to 3 min.
- Stir some of the sauce and the cilantro and pour over the chicken. When desired, eat with rice.

## 11. Breakfast keto Buffalo Chicken

Serving 4-6 | Total Time: 29 min

Calories: 295 Kcal, Fat: 12.6g, Net Carbs: 0g, Protein: 42.6g

**Ingredients**

- Boneless chicken breasts 2 1/2 pounds skinless
- Bottle hot sauce 1 (12-ounce)
- Ghee or unsalted butter 4 tbsp

**Steps of Preparation**

- In a 6-quarter or Electric Pressure Cooker, bigger Instant Pot put 2 1/2 pounds of chicken breasts boneless, skinless into one layer. Pour 1 (12-ounce) spicy chicken sauce bottle over it. Cube 4 tbsp of ghee or unsalted butter, then put the chicken on top.
- Lock the cover in place and ensure that the valve is shut. High pressure cooking to cook about 15 minutes. It's going to take 10 - 12 minutes to work up under pressure. Once the time for cooking is finished, let the pressure drop for 5 min naturally. Release the remaining pressure
- Move the chicken right away to a clean cutting plate. For slice the meat, using two forks, then move to a dish. Whisk the sauce once mixed and emulsified in a pressure cooker. Apply to chicken 1 cup sauce and flip to coat. Apply more sauce if appropriate and set aside any leftover sauce to consume or store.

## 12. Chocolate Breakfast Keto Protein Shake

Servings: 1 | Total time: 40 min

Calories: 445 kcal | Proteins: 31g | Carbohydrates: 7 g | Fat: 12g

**Ingredients**

- Three fourth cup almond milk
- Half cup ices
- Two tablespoon almond butter
- Two tablespoons unsweetened cocoa powder
- Two tablespoons keto-friendly sugar
- One tablespoon chia seed

- Two tablespoon hemp seeds
- Half table pure vanilla extract
- A Pinch of kosher salt

**Steps of preparation**

- Mix all ingredients together in a blender and process until smooth. Pour in a bowl and compote with a little more chia & hemp seeds.

## 13. Breakfast Bell Pepper Eggs

Servings: 3 yields | Total time: 20 min

Calories: 121 kcal | Proteins: 8.6g | Carbohydrates: 4 g | Fat: 7.9g

**Ingredients**

- One bell pepper
- Six eggs
- Pinch kosher salt
- Pinch of freshly ground black peppers
- Two tablespoon chopped chives
- Two tablespoon chopped parsley

**Steps of preparation**

- Warm a nonstick saucepan over medium heat then gently oil with a cooking mist.
- Place the bell pepper ring in the pan and simmer for 2 minutes. Swap the ring, then break the egg there in the middle of it. Add salt and pepper, then simmer until the egg is prepared to your preference for two to four minutes.
- Repeat the same procedure with other eggs and serve with the chives and the parsley.

## 14. Omelet-Stuffed Peppers

Servings: 4 | Total time: 1 hour

Calories: 380 kcal | Proteins: 26g | Carbohydrates: 4.5 g | Fat: 28g

**Ingredients**

- Two bell peppers
- Eight eggs

- One fourth cup milk
- Four slices of bacon cooked
- One cup shredded cheddar
- Two tablespoon finely chopped chives
- A pinch of Kosher salt
- Black pepper crushed

**Steps of preparation**

- Preheat the oven to 400 ° C. Now place the peppers sliced horizontally in a big baking sheet. Apply a very little water to the sheet and bake the pepper for five minutes.
- In the meanwhile, beat the eggs and milk together. Stir in sausage, cheese, and chips and add salt and pepper as required.
- When the peppers are baked, apply the egg mixture to the peppers. Place in the oven and cook for 35 to 40 minutes until the eggs have been set. Garnish with a little more chives and eat.

## 15. Keto breakfast Clouded Bread

Servings: 6 rolls | Total time: 35 min

Calories: 98 kcal | Proteins: 4g | Carbohydrates: 0.2 g | Fat: 9g

**Ingredients**

- Three large eggs
- One fourth teaspoon cream of tartar
- A Pinch of kosher salt
- Two oz. cream cheese
- One tablespoon Italian seasoning
- One tablespoon shredded mozzarella
- Two teaspoon tomato paste
- Pinch of kosher salt
- One teaspoon poppy seed
- One teaspoon sesame seed
- One teaspoon minced dried garlic
- One teaspoon minced dried onion

**Steps of preparation**

- Start by preheating the oven to 300 ° C and cover a wide pan with parchment paper.
- Separate the egg whites from its yolks in 2 small glass containers. Apply the cream of the tartar and the salt to the egg whites, then with a hand blender, beat until solid. It will happen within 2 to 3 minutes. Transfer the cream cheese to the egg yolks and now, using a hand blender, combine the yolks and the cream cheese until blended. Gently incorporate the egg yolk mixture in the egg whites.
- Divide the dough into portions of 8 mounds on a lined baking sheet, 4 "off from each other – Bake until it becomes golden, which will happen within twenty-five to thirty minutes.
- Instantly sprinkle each slice of bread with cheese and oven for two or three minutes. Let it cool a bit. Easy plain cloud bread is ready for you.
- Add 1 tablespoon of Italian seasoning, two tablespoons of shredded mozzarella or parmesan cheese, and two tablespoons of tomato paste to the egg yolk mixture. Add 1 tablespoon of Italian seasoning, two tablespoons of shredded mozzarella or parmesan cheese, and two tablespoons of tomato paste to the egg yolk mixture. Bake until it becomes golden, which will happen within twenty-five to thirty minutes.
- Add 1⁄8 teaspoon of kosher salt, 1 teaspoon of poppy seeds, 1 teaspoon of sesame seeds, 1 teaspoon of mashed dried garlic, then 1 teaspoon of chopped dried onion to the egg yolk mixture. (Or use 1 tablespoon with all bagel seasoning.) All bagel cloud bread is set.
- Add 11⁄2 teaspoons of ranch seasoning powder to the egg mixture. Bake until it becomes golden, which will happen within twenty-five to thirty minutes. Ranch cloud bread is ready to go.

## 16. Breakfast Jalapeño Popper Egg Cups

Servings: 12 cups | Total time: 1 hour

Calories: 157.2kcal | Proteins: 9.5 g | Carbohydrates: 1.3 g | Fat: 12.2 g

**Ingredients**

- Twelve slices bacon
- Ten large eggs
- One fourth cup sour cream

- Half cup shredded Cheddar
- Half cup shredded mozzarella
- Two jalapeños, one minced and one thinly sliced
- One teaspoon garlic powder
- A pinch of kosher salt
- Cooking spray
- Ground black pepper

**Steps of preparation**

- Preheat the oven to 375 ° C. Cook the bacon in a wide medium saucepan until it is well golden brown and still stackable. To drain, put aside on a paper towel-lined dish to drain.
- In a large plastic container, stir together eggs, cheese, sour cream, jalapeno minced, and garlic powder. Season to taste with salt & pepper.
- Use a nonstick cooking spray to oil the muffin tin. Fill each well along with one slice of bacon, then add the egg mixture into each muffin tin until around two-thirds of the way to the tin's top Cover each muffin with a slice of jalapeno.
- Bake for a period of 20 minutes just until the eggs are no longer sticky. Cool briefly before withdrawing the muffin tin.

## 17. Keto Zucchini Breakfast Egg Cups

Servings: 18 cups | Total time: 35 min

Calories: 17 kcal | Proteins: 1 g | Carbohydrates: 1.3 g | Fat: 1 g

**Ingredients**

- Cooking spray
- Two zucchinis peeled
- One fourth lb. ham
- Half cup cherry tomatoes
- Eight eggs
- Half cup heavy cream
- A pinch of Kosher salt
- A grounded black pepper

- Half teaspoon dried oregano
- One Pinch red pepper flakes
- One cup shredded cheddar

**Steps of preparation**

- Start by preheating the oven to 400 ° F and oil the muffin tray with a cooking mist. To form a crust, line inside and underside of muffin tin with both the zucchini strips. Sprinkle with the cherry tomatoes and the ham each crust.
- In a medium container, stir together eggs, whipping cream, oregano & red pepper flakes and add salt and pepper. Pour the egg mixture over the ham and tomatoes and cover with the cheese.
- Bake for 30 minutes until eggs are ready.

## 18. Breakfast Brussels Sprouts Hash

Servings: 4 cups | Total time: 40 min

Calories: 181 kcal | Proteins: 3 g | Carbohydrates: 13 g | Fat: 14 g

**Ingredients**

- Six slices bacon
- Half chopped onion
- One lb. Brussels
- An inch of Kosher salt
- Black pepper grounded
- One fourth teaspoon crushed red pepper flakes
- Two minced cloves garlic
- Four large eggs

**Steps of preparation**

- Cook bacon until crispy in a large frying pan. Switch off the heat and move the bacon to a paper towel tray. Hold much of the bacon fat in the pan, cut some black specks from the pan.

- Turn the heat down to low and transfer the onion and Brussels to the pan. Cook, stirring regularly before vegetables start to turn soft and turn golden. Season to taste with salt, pepper & red pepper flakes.
- Transfer 2 tablespoons of water in the mixture and cover the pan. Cook till the Brussels are soft, and the water gets evaporated for about five minutes. (If all the water is gone until the sprouts are soft, add a little more water to the pan and cover for a few more minutes.) Put the garlic to the pan. Cook until fragrant for almost 1 minute.
- Cut four holes in the hash using a wooden spoon, to expose the base of the pan. Break an egg into each gap and add salt and pepper for each egg. Replace the lid and cook it until eggs are ready to your taste, which is around 5 minutes for the egg that is runny
- Sprinkle the cooked bacon bites over the whole pan and serve hot.

## 19. Best Breakfast Keto Bread

Servings: 1 bread | Total time: 40 min

Calories: 165 kcal | Proteins: 6 g | Carbohydrates: 3 g | Fat: 15 g

**Ingredients**

- One fourth cup butter, melted and cooled
- One and a half cup ground almond
- Six large eggs
- Half teaspoon cream of tartar
- One tablespoon baking powder
- Half teaspoon kosher salt

**Steps of preparation**

- Start by preheating the oven to 375 ° F and then line the 8″-x-4 "loaf on a baking sheet. Completely separate egg whites from egg yolk.
- In a wide container, mix egg whites with tarter cream. Using a hand blender, keep whipping until strong peaks are created.
- Shake the yolks with melted butter, baking powder, almond flour, and salt in a separate big bowl using a hand blender. Fold in 1/3 of egg whites when completely blended, then fold in the remainder.

- Load the batter into the loaf pan and make flat layer. Then Bake for 30 minutes or until the surface is softly golden, and the toothpick comes out clean. Enable to cool for 30 minutes before cutting.

## 20. Bacon Breakfast Avocado Bombs

Servings: 4 bombs | Total time: 25 min

Calories: 251 kcal | Proteins: 6 g | Carbohydrates: 13 g | Fat: 18 g

**Ingredients**

- Two avocados
- One-third shredded Cheddar
- Eight slices bacon

**Steps of preparation**

- Steam the broiler and line up a narrow baking sheet with foil.
- Cut each avocado into half and scrape the pits. Take the skin off from each of the avocados.
- Cover two-thirds of the cheese, and substitute with the other thirds of the avocado. Cover 4 pieces of bacon in each avocado.
- Put the bacon-wrapped avocados upon this lined baking sheet and broil till the bacon is crisp, approximately 5 minutes. Turn the avocado really carefully and proceed to cook till crispy all around, approximately five minutes per side.
- Break half lengthwise and serve instantly.

## 21. Breakfast Ham & Cheese keto Egg Cups

Servings: 12 cups | Total time: 35 min

Calories: 108 kcal | Proteins: 10.4 g | Carbohydrates: 1.2 g | Fat: 5.9 g

**Ingredients**

- Cooking spray
- Twelve slices of ham
- One cup shredded cheddar
- Twelve large eggs
- A pinch of Kosher salt

- Ground black pepper
- Parsley, for garnish

**Steps of preparation**

- Preheat the oven to 400o and oil the 12-cup muffin tray with a cooking mist. Top each cup with just a piece of ham and top with cheddar. Break an egg inside each ham cup and add salt and pepper.
- Bake until the eggs are roasted thru, 12 to 15 minutes.
- Garnish with parsley, serve.

## 22. Keto Breakfast Peanut Fat Bombs

Servings: 12 bombs | Total time: 1 hour 40 min

Calories: 247 kcal | Proteins: 3.6 g | Carbohydrates: 3.3 g | Fat: 24.4 g

**Ingredients**

- Eight oz. cream cheese
- A pinch of kosher salt
- Half cup dark chocolate chips
- Half cup peanut butter
- One fourth cup coconut oil

**Steps of preparation**

- Line a narrow baking sheet with a sheet of parchment paper. In a medium container, mix cream cheese with peanut butter, 1/4 cup of coconut oil, and some salt. Using a hand blender, beat the mixture until it becomes thoroughly mixed, approximately for 2 minutes. Put the bowl in the freezer until it is lightly firmed, for 10 to 15 minutes.
- When a peanut butter mixture is formed, use a tiny cookie scoop to produce spoonful-sized balls. Put in the refrigerator for 5 minutes to harden.
- In the meantime, produce a chocolate drizzle by mixing chocolate chips and the leftover coconut oil in a large mixing bowl and microwave it for 30 seconds until completely melted. Drizzle over the balls of peanut butter and then put in the refrigerator for 5 minutes.
- Keep wrapped in the refrigerator to stock.

## 23. Breakfast keto Paleo Stacks

Servings: 3 | Total time: 30 min

Calories: 229 kcal | Proteins: 3 g | Carbohydrates: 11 g | Fat: 18 g

**Ingredients**

- Three sausage patties
- One mashed avocado
- A pinch of kosher salt
- Ground black pepper
- Three large eggs
- Hot sauce as required

**Steps of preparation**

- Heat the breakfast sausage.
- Mash the avocado onto the breakfast sausage and add salt and pepper.
- Spray a medium pan over medium heat with only a cooking spray and then spray the interior of the mason jar cap. Place the mason jar lid within middle of the pan and break the egg inside. Add salt and pepper and cook for 3 minutes until hot, then remove the cover and continue to cook.
- Place the egg on top of the mashed avocado. Season with chives and sleet with the hot sauce you want.

## 24. Breakfast keto quick chaffles

Servings: 2 yields | Total time: 25 min

Calories: 115 kcal | Proteins: 9 g | Carbohydrates: 1 g | Fat: 8 g

**Ingredients**

- Four eggs
- 8 oz. shredded cheddar cheese
- Two tablespoon chives
- A pinch of salt and pepper

- 4 eggs for toppings
- Eight bacons
- Eight cherry tomatoes diced
- Two oz. baby spinach

**Steps of preparation**

- Organize the bacon slices in a big, unheated pan and set the temperature to moderate flame. Golden brown the bacon for 8-12 mins, turning often, until crispy to bite.
- Put aside on a paper towel to drain when you're cooking.
- Put all of the waffle ingredients in a mixing container and blend well.
- Lightly oil the waffle iron and afterward uniformly spoon the mixture over the bottom of the tray, spreading it out gently to achieve even outcomes.
- Shut the waffle iron and cook for roughly. 6 minutes, depending on capacity of the waffle maker.
- Crack an egg in the bacon fat in the cooking pan and cook slowly until finished.
- Serve each tablespoon of scrambled egg and bacon pieces along with some baby spinach and some sliced cherry tomatoes.

## 25. Keto breakfast with fried eggs, tomato, and cheese

Total Time: 15 mins |Serving 1

Calories: Kcal 417, Fat:33g, Net Carbs:4g Protein:25g

**Ingredients**

- Eggs 2
- Butter ½ tbsp
- Cubed cheddar cheese 2 oz
- Tomato ½
- Ground black pepper & salt

**Steps of Preparation**

- Heat butter over medium heat in a frying pan.

- Season the diced side of the tomato with salt & pepper. Put the tomato in a frying pan.
- Break the eggs in the same pan. Leaving the eggs to scramble on one side for eggs sunny side up. Rotate the eggs for a couple of mins and cook for one more minute for eggs fried over quickly. Cook for a few more minutes for tougher yolks. Season with salt & pepper.
- On a plate, Put the eggs, tomatoes, and cheese to eat. Scatter with dried oregano eggs and tomatoes for some additional flavor and taste.

## 26. Keto eggs Benedict on avocado

Total Time: 15 mins |Serving 4

Calories: Kcal 522, Fat:48g, Net Carbs:3g Protein:16g

**Ingredients**

Hollandaise

- Egg yolks 3
- Lemon juice 1 tbsp
- Salt & pepper
- Unsalted butter 8½ tbsp

Eggs benedict

- Pitted & skinned avocados 2
- Eggs 4
- Smoked salmon 5 oz

**Steps of Preparation**

- Take a mason jar or other microwave-safe containers that will fit easily inside the immersion blender. Put the butter and then melt for around 20 seconds in the microwave.
- In butter, incorporate the yolks of egg and lemon juice. The hand blender is Placed at the container bottom and combine until a creamy white coating is created. Raise the blender and lower it slowly to create a creamy sauce.
- Place a saucepan over the stove with water and boil. Decrease the heat to low.

- Crack the eggs, one at a time, in a cup, and then carefully slip each into the bowl. Stirring the water in a circle can keep the egg white from displacing too much from the yolk. Cook 3-4 mins, depending on the yolk quality you like. To retain excess water, remove the eggs with a spoon.
- Break the avocados in two and remove the skin and stones. Create a slice of each half around the base, so it rests equally on the dish. Cover with one egg every half, then finish with a hollandaise sauce generous dollop. Load some smoked salmon.
- This dish must be consumed promptly and should not preserve or reheat. Hollandaise sauce Leftover can be preserved for up to 4 days in a fridge.

## 27. Keto quick low carb mozzarella chaffles

Total Time: 8 mins |Serving 4

Calories: Kcal 330, Fat:27g, Net Carbs:2g Protein:20g

**Ingredients**

- Melted butter 1 oz.
- Eggs 4
- Shredded mozzarella cheese 8 oz
- Almond flour 4 tbsp

**Steps of Preparation**

- Heat the waffle maker.
- Put all of the ingredients in a mixing bowl and beat to blend.
- Lightly oil the waffle iron with the butter, then spoon the mixture uniformly over the bottom, spreading it out to achieve an even outcome. Cover the waffle iron, then cook depending on the waffle maker, for approx. 6 mins.
- Release the cap softly when you feel it's done.
- Serve with favorite toppings.

## 28. Nut-free keto bread

Total Time: 50 mins |Serving 20

Calories: Kcal 105, Fat:8g, Net Carbs:1g Protein:6g

**Ingredients**

- Eggs 6
- Shredded cheese 12 oz
- Cream cheese 1 oz
- Husk powder ground psyllium 2 tbsp
- Baking powder 3 tsp
- Oat fiber ½ cup
- Salt ½ tsp
- Melted butter 1 tbsp

Topping

- Sesame seeds 3 tbsp
- Poppy seeds 2 tbsp

**Steps of Preparation**

- To 180 ° C (360 ° F), preheat the oven.
- Whisk eggs. Attach the cheese and the other ingredients, except the butter, and stir properly.
- Grease a buttered bread pan (8.5 " x 4.5 "x 2.75," non-stick or parchment-papered). Spread the dough with a spatula in the bread-pan.
- Sprinkle with poppy and sesame seeds over the rice. 35 Mins to bake the loaf.
- Let cool down the bread.

## 29. Simple keto breakfast with fried eggs

Total Time: 10 mins |Serving 1

Calories: Kcal 425, Fat:41g, Net Carbs:1g Protein:13g

**Ingredients**

- Eggs 2
- Butter 1 tbsp
- Mayonnaise 2 tbsp
- Baby spinach 1 oz
- Ground black pepper & salt
- Coffee or tea 1 cup

**Steps of Preparation**

- Heat butter over med heat in a frying pan.
- Crack the eggs into the pan right away. For sunny side up eggs, -leaving one side of the eggs to fry. Cooked over quick for eggs-flip over the eggs after a couple of mins and cook for 1 more minute. Only stop the cooking for a few more mins for stronger yolks. Season with pepper and salt
- Serve a dollop of mayonnaise with baby spinach.

**2.30. Keto taco omelet**

Total Time: 20 mins |Serving 2

Calories: Kcal 797, Fat:63g, Net Carbs:8g Protein:44g

**Ingredients**

Taco seasoning

- Onion powder ¼ tsp
- Ground cumin ½ tsp
- Paprika powder ½ tsp
- Garlic powder ½ tsp
- Chili flakes ¼ tsp
- Salt ½ tsp
- Ground black pepper ¼ tsp
- Fresh oregano ½ tsp

Omelet

- Ground beef 5 oz
- Large eggs 4
- Olive oil 1 tbsp
- Avocado 1
- Shredded cheddar cheese 5 oz
- Diced tomato 1
- Fresh cilantro 1 tsp

- Sea salt ½ tsp
- Ground black pepper ¼ tsp

**Steps of Preparation**

- Combine all Taco Seasoning products.
- In a large non-stick pan, add the ground beef. Apply the seasoning mixture(taco), blend well, and fry till completely cooked. Set aside in the bowl and remove it from heat.
- Beat the eggs in a mixing bowl and brush until they are soft.
- Reduce heat and add the olive oil in the saucepan. And add the eggs. Push the edges into the center, enabling the uncooked pieces to spill to the side, while the edges become solid. Cook a couple of mins, keep the inside a little runny.
- At ground beef, pinch lime.
- Break avocado half. The pit is Removed and suck the flesh out. Split into fragments.
- Spread ground beef over the omelet. Apply 2/3 of the grilled diced cheese and tomatoes.
- Remove the omelet cautiously from the pan. Add more avocado, cheese, and cilantro. Season salt & pepper. Serve.

## 30. Keto dosa

Total Time: 25 mins |Serving 2

Calories: Kcal 356, Fat:33g, Net Carbs:4g Protein:12g

**Ingredients**

- Almond flour ½ cup
- Shredded mozzarella cheese 1½ oz
- Coconut milk ½ cup
- Ground cumin ½ tsp
- Ground coriander seed ½ tsp
- Salt

**Steps of Preparation**

- Mix All ingredients in a bowl.

- Heat a non-stick skillet and oil lightly. The use of a non-stick skillet is very important to avoid the dosa from adhering to the pan.
- Pour in and spread the batter, by the pan moving.
- Cook on low heat the dosa. The cheese starts melting and crisping away.
- Once all the way through, it is cooked, and the dosa has turned golden brown on a side using the spatula fold it.
- Serve with chutney made from coconut.

For the Peanut Sauce:

- Peanut butter 1/2 cup
- Minced fresh ginger 1 tsp
- Minced fresh garlic 1 tsp
- Minced jalapeño pepper 1 Tbsp
- Sugar-free fish sauce 1 tbsp
- Sugar rice wine vinegar 2 tbsp
- Lime juice 1 tbsp
- Water 2 tbsp
- Erythritol granulated (sweetener) 2 tbsp

**Steps of Preparation**

For the Chicken:

- In a big bowl, Mix the fresh lemon juice, fish sauce, soy sauce, Rice vinegar, avocado oil, cayenne pepper, ginger, garlic, ground coriander & sweetener, and whisk.
- Apply pieces of chicken and stir to thoroughly coat the chicken only with marinade.
- Cover & chill up to twenty-four hrs., or for at least 1 hr.
- Remove 1/2 hr. before cooking from the freezer & heat the grill.
- Grill the chicken on med heat for around 6 to 8 mins each side.
- Remove it from the grill, add peanut sauce & serve.
- Chopped up cabbage, diced peanuts, minced scallions & minced cilantro are optional garnishes.

For the Sauce with Peanut:

- Mix all the ingredients from the sauce in a mixer & mix till smooth.
- Before serving, taste and set sweetness& saltiness to your choice.

## 31. One-Skillet Chicken with Lemon Garlic Cream Sauce

Total Time: 30 mins |Serving 4|

**Ingredients**

- Skinless &boneless chicken thighs 4
- Salt & pepper
- Chicken broth 1 cup
- Lemon juice 2 tbsp
- Minced garlic 1 tbsp
- Red pepper flakes ½ tsp
- Olive oil 1 tbsp
- Finely diced shallots ⅓ cup
- Salted butter 2 tbsp
- Heavy cream ¼ cup
- Chopped parsley 2 tbsp

**Steps of Preparation**

- The thighs or chicken breasts are pounded into 1/2-inch thickness using a mallet. Sprinkle both sides of the chicken with a pinch of salt & pepper.
- Mix the chicken broth, juice of lemon, red pepper flakes, & garlic into a two-cup measuring cup.
- Place a rack in the bottom 3rd of your oven & preheat to 375of.
- Heat the olive oil on med-high heat in the big oven-safe pan. Apply the chicken & let it to brown for 2 to 3 mins each side. Unless the chicken isn't fully cooked, don't worry, finish it in your oven. Take the chicken off to a plate.
- Decrease the flame-med, apply the shallots & the chicken broth combination to the pan. Drag the bottom of the skillet with a whisk, so that all brown pieces are loosened. Kick up the

heat back to med height and let the sauce come to low heat. Continue cooking the sauce for 10 to 15 mins, or till the sauce stays about 1/3 cup.

- Take from the flame whenever the sauce has thickened, then apply the butter & whisk till it fully melts. Apply the heavy whipping cream with the pan off flame, whisk in to mix. Place the pan on the flame for only thirty sec, Do NOT let the sauce boil. Take away from heat, apply the chicken back into the skillet & sprinkle the chicken over the sauce. Put the pan 5 to 8 mins in the oven, or till the chicken is fully cooked. Season with minced parsley or basil & serve hot with extra slices of lemon.

## 32. Low Carb Chicken Enchilada (Green) Cauliflower Casserole

Total Time: 45 mins |Serving 1

Calories: Cal 311, Fat:18g, Net Carbs:4g Protein:33g

**Ingredients**

- Frozen cauliflower florets 20 oz
- Softened cream cheese 4 oz
- Shredded cooked chicken 2 cups
- Salsa Verde ½ cups
- Kosher salt 1/2 tsp
- Ground black pepper 1/8 tsp
- Cheddar cheese shredded 1 cup
- Sour cream 1/4 cup

**Steps of Preparation**

- Place the cauliflower in a safe microwave plate and bake for 10 to 12 mins or till the pork is soft.
- Before microwave for the next thirty sec, add the cream cheese.
- Stir in the chicken, green salsa, pepper, salt, sour cream, cilantro& cheddar cheese.
- Bake for twenty mins inside an ovenproof baking dish in a preheated oven at 190 °, or you could have a 10-minute microwave on high. Serve warm.

## 33. Chicken crust pizza guilt-free

Total Time: 40 mins |Serving 8

**Ingredients**

- **For Crust**
- Fresh chicken breast 1.5 lbs.
- Minced garlic 2-3 cloves
- Blend Italian spice 1.5 tsp
- Shredded parmesan cheese 1/3 cup
- Shredded mozzarella cheese 1/3 cup
- Large egg 1
- **For toppings**
- Pasta sauce 3-4 tbsp
- Veggies
- Shredded mozzarella cheese 1/2 cup
- Shredded parmesan cheese 1/2 cup

**Steps of Preparation**

- Oven preheated to 400 ° c.
- Split the raw chicken into one "cubes & place it in small batches in a food processor to create some kind of handmade ground chicken.
- Place the raw ground chicken & the garlic, Italian spices, cheeses & egg in a bowl. Mix well.
- Line a baking sheet with a bakery release paper. Place the raw chicken combination ball on paper.
- Move out that much plastic wrap to covering the full pan or sheet and put it on top of the chicken combination ball. Push the chicken combination until it fills the pan or sheet.
- Pushed into two baking sheets for a lighter, crispier crust.
- Bake for almost 15 to 25 mins at 400 °, or till the crust becomes golden & to the desired crispness. Thicker crusts would be more about 20 to 25 mins & thin crusts take to cook in 10 to 15 mins.
- Take from the oven allow it to cool for around five mins.
- Distribute the sauce & top with the mozzarella. Apply the toppings & finish with the parmesan.
- Cook for 10 to 15 mins at 400 °, or till cheese seasoning has browned slightly.
- Cut, serve & enjoy this high protein meal that's free of guilt, low carb!

# 34. Asparagus stuffed chicken with parmesan

Servings: 3 | Total time: 30 min

Calories: 230 kcal | Proteins: 62 g | Carbohydrates: 10 g | Fat: 31 g

**Ingredients**

- Chicken Breasts 3
- Garlic paste 1 teaspoon
- Asparagus 12 Stalks
- Cream Cheese 1/2 cup
- Butter 1 tablespoon
- Olive Oil 1 teaspoon
- Marinara Sauce 3/4 cup
- shredded Mozzarella 1 cup
- Salt and Pepper

**Steps of Preparation**

- To start cooking the chicken, swirl the chicken (or split it in half without slicing it all the way around. The chicken breast can open like a butterfly with one end already intact in the center). Remove the asparagus stalks and set it aside.
- Rub salt, some pepper, and garlic all across the chicken breasts (both in and out). Divide the cream cheese between all the chicken breasts and then spread to the inside. Now place four stalks of asparagus and afterward fold one side of that same breast over another, wrapping it in place with the help of a toothpick to ensure that it doesn't get open.
- Now preheat the oven, then set it to a broiler. Then Add butter and the olive oil to a hot saucepan and put the chicken breasts in it. Now took the breasts on either side for almost 6-7 minutes (the overall period would be 14-15 minutes based on the size of the breast) until the chicken will be almost cooked through.
- Now top each breast with almost 1/4 cup of marinara sauce and also top with shredded mozzarella. Put in the oven and bake

# Chapter 3: Keto lunch recipes for women over 50

For women over 50 trying the keto diet, these simple keto lunch recipes are great and will help to get a balanced fat ketosis.

## 1. Keto avocado salad served with Blackened shrimp

Servings: 2 yields | Total time: 20 min

Calories: 420 kcal | Proteins: 49.5 g | Carbohydrates: 21 g | Fat: 18.5 g

**Ingredients**

- One teaspoon crushed basil
- One teaspoon black pepper
- One teaspoon cayenne
- Half kilogram peeled large shrimp
- Two minced cloves of garlic
- Two teaspoons paprika
- One teaspoon dehydrated thyme
- One teaspoon salt
- Two bunches of Asparagus
- One teaspoon of olive oil

- Four cups lettuce leaves
- One Avocado, diced
- One fourth red onion, cut
- One handful of basil leaves
- One third cup greek yogurt
- One teaspoon lemon pepper
- One teaspoon lemon extract
- Two tablespoons of water
- Salt as required

**Steps of preparation**

- In a narrow container, transfer shrimp and all other ingredients, and evenly coated it. Heat a big on medium flame and add some olive oil. Sauté the shrimp or prawns and the Asparagus, keep on turning seldom until they change color.
- Now combine the lettuce leaves, the avocado, the onion slices, and the basil leaves in a glass bowl. Now add the shrimp or prawns and avocado. Add some dressing.
- For the preparation of dressing, mix yogurt with the lemon pepper, the lemon juice, and the water and salt. Mix them well.

## 2. Keto Easy Egg Wrap lunch

Servings: 2 yields | Total time: 5 min

Calories: 411 kcal | Proteins: 25 g | Carbohydrates: 3 g | Fat: 31 g

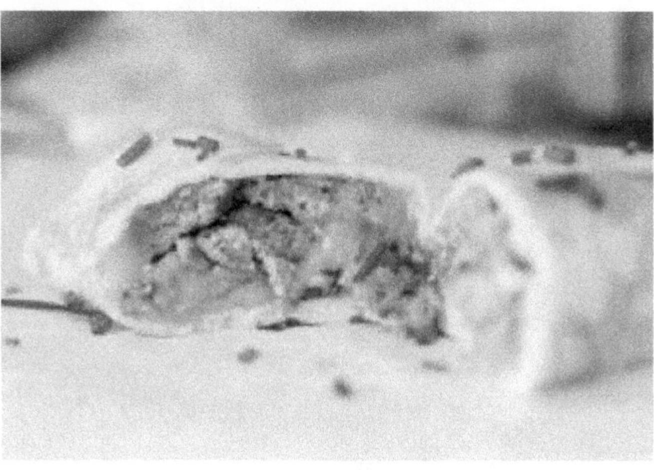

**Ingredients**

- Two Eggs
- Boiled turkey
- Mashed Avocado,
- Crushed Cheese
- Half teaspoon pepper,
- Half teaspoon paprika,
- Hummus
- A pinch of salt
- A pinch of cayenne pepper

**Steps of preparation**

- Heat a shallow skillet over a medium heat. Use Butter or oil to grease.
- Break one egg in a dish and blend well and with a fork.
- Drop it in a hot skillet and tilt it to spread the egg into a wide circle at the bottom of the pan.
- Let it simmer for 30 seconds.
- Switch sides gently with a huge spatula and let it cook for the next 30 seconds.
- Remove from heat and replicate the process for as number of eggs as you like to make.
- Let the egg wraps cool down slightly (or completely), cover with the fillings as needed, wrap and serve it hot or cold.

## 3. Keto California Turkey and Bacon Lettuce Wraps with Basil-Mayo

Servings: 4 | Total time: 45 min

Calories: 303 kcal | Proteins: 11 g | Carbohydrates: 25 g | Fat: 20 g

**Ingredients**

- One iceberg lettuce
- Four slices of deli turkey
- Four slices bacon
- One diced avocado
- One thinly diced tomato
- Half cup mayonnaise
- Six basil leaves
- One teaspoon lemon extract
- One chopped garlic clove
- Salt as desired
- Pepper as desired

**Steps of preparation**

- To prepare Basil-Mayo, mix the ingredients in a food processor and process till smooth. n Optionally, mince both the basil and the garlic and mix them all together. This can be done in a couple of days ahead.
- Place two wide leaves of lettuce on One slice of turkey and drench with Basil-Mayo. Put on a thin slice of turkey accompanied by bacon, including a couple of slices of avocado and the

tomato. Season gently with salt and pepper, and then curl the bottom up as well as the sides in and roll it like a burrito. Cut halfway through, and then serve it cold.

## 4. Keto Lasagna Stuffed Portobellos

Servings: 4 yields | Total time: 25 min

Calories: 482 kcal | Proteins: 28 g | Carbohydrates: 6.5 g | Fat: 36 g

**Ingredients**

- Four mushrooms
- Four Italian sausage
- One milk mozzarella cheese
- One chopped parsley
- One cup of whole milk cheese
- One cup marinara sauce

**Steps of preparation**

- Clean the mushrooms. Remove the branches using a spoon.
- Take the sausage out and push the mixture into 4 patties. Force each patty into each of the mushroom cups, towards the edges and also up the sides of the Pattie.
- Now put 1/4 cup of the ricotta in each of the mushroom caps and then press the sides of it, creating a hole in the middle.
- Spoon 1/4 cup of sauce of marinara onto each mushroom on the highest point of the ricotta base.
- Sprinkle 1/4 cup of sliced mozzarella cheese on the top.

- Bake in a 375-degree F preheated oven for almost 40 minutes.
- Garnish it with parsley and serve when warm.

## 5. Rapid Keto Sushi

Servings: 3 yields | Total time: 25 min

Calories: 353 kcal | Proteins: 18.3 g | Carbohydrates: 5.7 g | Fat: 5.7 g

**Ingredients**

- One nori wrapper
- One cup of sliced cauliflower
- Half avocado
- One and a half oz Cream Cheese
- One fourth cup cucumber
- One tablespoon coconut oil
- One cup of soy sauce

**Steps of preparation**

- Split about half the head of the cauliflower into the florets and spin in the processor until the rice is appropriately smooth.
- Heat the coconut oil in a medium-high pan and introduce the cauliflower rice.
- Then Cook for almost 5-7 minutes till the rice is finely golden brown and cooked completely. Put it in a separate bowl.

- Slice the avocado, the cream cheese, and the cucumber into thinly sliced pieces and put them aside with the prepared cauliflower rice.
- Place a long sheet of plastic wrap on a clear, flat surface and place the nori wrapping above the plastic wrap.
- Cover the cauliflower rice over all the nori wrapping as thinly or as dense as you want in an even coating. Leave some room around the corners and edges.
- For some keto sushi rice, apply the first coating of the avocado on the rice adjacent to you. Next, add a thin layer of some cream cheese straight to the avocado, and finally, add a layer of cucumber.
- For keto sushi cucumber, firs raise the plastic wrap on the side by using your palms to mask the ingredients.
- Steadily stretch the plastic wrap and the nori wraps over the avocado, the cucumber, and the cream cheese before you cover the whole.
- Using a sharp knife, split the sushi into eight parts. First, Begin in the center so that the rice is not pulled out along with the weight of the knife.

## 6. Chicken Piccata keto Meatballs

Serving: 3 | Total: Time 30 min

Calories: 323 kcal, Fat:21g, Net Carbs:2g Protein:26g

**Ingredients**

- Ground chicken 1 lb.
- Almond flour 1/3 cup
- Egg 1
- Kosher salt 1/2 tsp
- Ground black pepper 1/4 tsp
- Garlic powder 1/4 tsp
- Lemon zest 1/2 tsp
- Fresh chopped parsley 1 tsp
- Olive oil 2 tbsp

For the sauce:

- Dry white wine 1/2 cup
- Lemon juice 2 tbsp
- Drained & chopped capers 2 tbsp
- Lemon zest 1/4 tsp
- Butter 1/4 cup

**Steps of Preparation**

- In a med bowl, mix the ground meat, almond meal/flour, egg, pepper, salt, powder of garlic, zest of the lemon as well as parsley together & stir thoroughly. Form into fifteen meatballs. Heat the oil of olive in a non-stick skillet & cook the meatballs till they become golden brown & fried through.
- In the same skillet as the meatballs were cooked, add the white wine & bring to a simmer, having to scrape all the meatballs off the skillet & into the white wine. Apply the juice of lemon & capers and reduce by around half (2 to 3 mins). Turn off the heat & stir in the zest of lemon & butter till melted as well as smooth. sprinkle with salt to taste

## 7. Keto Chicken Alfredo Spaghetti Squash

Servings: 4 | Total Time: 20 mins

Calories: 327 kcal |Fat:25g | Net Carbs:14g | Protein:12g

**Ingredients**

- 2 tbsp butter
- Minced Garlic 2 tsp
- Sage 1 tsp
- Flour 2tbsp
- Chicken broth 1 cup
- Half cream 1/2 cup
- Cubed cream cheese 4 oz
- Shredded parmesan cheese ½ cup
- Cooked & shredded chicken 1/2 cup
- Cooked spaghetti squash 2 1/2 cups
- Pepper, salt & parsley

**Steps of Preparation**

- Melt the butter over med-heat in a pan.
- Add the sage & garlic, then cook for around a min.
- Mix in the flour/meal & cook, constantly mixing for around a minute.
- Mix a half & half in a chicken broth.
- Mix in the parmesan cheese & cream cheese till smooth.
- Add the vegetable squash, cooked and shredded chicken, & cook till fully heated.
- Taste the alfredo vegetable squash with chicken, then top with pepper, salt & parsley.

## 8. Keto Paleo lunch Spice Chicken Skewers

Serving 2 | Total Time: 2 hours

Calories: 198 |Fat:5g | Net Carbs |1g Protein:35g

**Ingredients**

- Boneless & skinless chicken tenders 2 lb.
- Granulated erythritol sweetener 2 tbsp
- 5 spice powder 2 tbsp
- Rice wine vinegar unsweetened 1 tbsp
- Avocado oil 1 tbsp
- Sesame oil 1 tsp
- Gluten-free soy sauce 1 tbsp
- Skewers red bell pepper pieces 1 cup
- Skewers 12

**Steps of Preparation**

- Cut the chicken finely into pieces just around two inches long onto the diagonal.
- In a med bowl, mix the sweetener, five powder spice, rice wine vinegar, oil of avocado, oil of sesame, soy sauce & cayenne pepper & stir.
- Season & adjust sweetness/saltiness according to your preference.
- Apply the pieces of chicken, then mix well to coat.
- Marinate a chicken for one hr. or more, & up to twenty-four hrs.

- Heat the grill.
- Thread pieces of chicken & red bell pepper onto the skewers.
- Grill each side for 2 -3 mins or once the chicken is cooked through.
- When desired, garnish with lime slices & cilantro (fresh).

## 9. Keto Asian pork ribs

| Serving 4 | Total Time 1 hr.

Calories: 505 | Fat: 44g | Net Carbs: 1g | Protein: 25g

**Ingredients**

- Chopped pork spareribs into individual ribs 2 lb.
- Fresh diced ginger 1 tbsp
- Diced green onions 2 tbsp
- Szechuan peppercorns ½ tbsp
- 2-star anise
- Diced garlic cloves 3
- Gluten-free tamari sauce or coconut amino 2 tbsp
- Avocado oil 2 tbsp
- Salt & pepper to taste

**Steps of Preparation**

- To a big pot of boiling water, add flour, Szechuan peppercorns, star anise, & ribs. Bring to boil, then cook till the meat is soft, for 45 mins. Skim away any shaping foam.
- Drain from the pot & remove ribs. Remove the star anise & peppercorns.
- Apply the avocado oil to the frying pan, then add the ginger and garlic. Put in ribs & cook on the medium-high fire. Add the coconut amino or tamari sauce, then season, to taste, with pepper and salt.
- Stir-fry ribs over high heat until fully covered and browned with the sauce.

## 10. Keto slow cooker pork's rib (Asian)

Servings: 2 | Total Time:3hrs. 20 mins

Calories: 482 | Fat: 38g | Net Carbs: 4g | Protein: 25g

**Ingredients**

- Baby back pork ribs 450g
- Sliced medium onion 1/2
- Garlic paste 1 tbsp
- Ginger paste 1 tbsp
- Chicken broth 1&1/2 c
- Gluten-free tamari sauce or coconut amino 2 tbsp
- Chinese five-spice seasoning ½ tsp
- Sliced green onions 2

**Steps of Preparation**

- Place the pork ribs rack inside the slow cooker. The rack may need to be halved to fit.
- Include the onions, paste for garlic, paste for the ginger, and broth for the meat. If the ribs are not completely coated, add up a little bit of broth until covered.
- Cover & cook for three hours at low flame.
- To keep warm, remove ribs & wrap in foil. Place this apart.
- Shift the onions & products from the slow cooker into the stove to a clean pan. Using a hand blender, blitz well (or use a food processor to blitz and move to the stove in the pan) and apply the Chinese 5-spice & tamari. Reduce the paste to dense and jammy, over a relatively high flame.

- Taste the marinade and add in a bit of erythritol if you think it will improve from a little more sugar.
- Brush over the warm ribs with this marinade & garnish with onions.

## 11. Keto baked ribs recipe

Serving 2 | Total Time: 3hrs. 5 mins

Calories 580 |Fat: 51g |Net Carbs: 5g |Protein: 25g

**Ingredients**

- Baby back ribs 1 lb.
- Applesauce 2 tbsp
- Gluten-free tamari sauce or coconut amino 2 tbsp
- Olive oil 2 tbsp
- Fresh ginger 1 tbsp
- Garlic cloves 2
- Salt & pepper

**Steps of Preparation**

- Preheat the oven to 275 F- change it to the minimum temperature if your oven does not go down to this point.
- Season with salt & pepper over ribs & cover securely with foil. Put the product onto a baking dish and bake in the oven for three hours at low temp.

- Mix olive oil, applesauce, tamari sauce, ginger, and garlic in a blender until it creates a purée.
- Take the ribs out from the oven after three hours, then adjust the heat in the oven up to 450 F (230 C) or just as high as the oven can go.
- With care, open the foil so the ribs can rest on top of the foil. Coat the ribs well with the marinade, by using a brush. Put the ribs in the oven and bake for 5-10 mins till it becomes sticky with marinade.

## 12. Keto fried pork tenderloin

Serving 2 | Total Time: 20 mins

Calories: 389 Kcal | Fat: 23g |Net Carbs: 0g |Protein: 47g

**Ingredients**

- Pork tenderloin 1 lb.
- Salt & pepper>> to taste
- Avocado or coconut oil 2 tbsp

**Steps of Preparation**

- Break the pork tenderloin into two-three pieces to fit more conveniently into your frying pan.
- Apply the oil to the frying pan & fry the pork tenderloin first on one side, using tongs. Using tongs, flip the pork tenderloin until that side is fried, then cook the other side until both sides are browned.

- Continue to turn the pork every several minutes till the meat thermometer displays just below 145F (63C), internal temperature. Since you remove it from the frying pan, the pork will begin to cook a little.
- Let the pork rest for a couple of minutes then slice with a knife into one-inch-thick slices.

## 13. Cauliflower Grits with shrimps and Arugula

Servings: 4 yields | Total time: 30 min

Calories: 122 kcal | Proteins: 16 g | Carbohydrates: 3 g | Fat: 5 g

**Ingredients**

- One-pound peeled shrimp
- One tablespoon bell pepper crushed
- Two teaspoons garlic paste
- Half teaspoon cayenne pepper
- One tablespoon olive oil
- Salt and freshly ground black pepper
- One tablespoon butter
- Four cups riced cauliflower
- One cup milk
- Half cup crumbled goat cheese
- Salt and freshly ground black pepper
- One tablespoon olive oil
- Three diced garlic cloves

- Four cups arugula
- Salt and black pepper as desired

**Steps of preparation**

- Put the shrimp in a big plastic zip bag. In a medium container, mix the paprika with some garlic powder and the cayenne. Put the mixture to the shrimp bag and toss well until the spices are covered. Refrigerate when you're preparing the grits.
- Melt the butter in a medium pot over medium heat. Include the cauliflower rice and cook till some moisture is produced, that is 2 to 3 minutes.
- Mix in half milk and bring to boil. Allow it to boil, keep stirring regularly, until some milk is absorbed by the cauliflower for; it will happen in 6 to 8 minutes.
- Incorporate the leftover milk and boil until the mixture is dense and smooth, cook for 10 minutes. Mix with goat cheese and then season it with some salt and pepper. Keep it warm.

## 14. Keto Chipotle Pork Wraps

Servings: 2 yields | Total time: 15 min

Calories: 292 kcal | Proteins: 14 g | Carbohydrates: 37 g | Fat: 0 g

**Ingredients**

- Half Avocado
- Two tablespoons Mayonnaise
- One lime juice extract
- One clove of garlic minced
- Salt and pepper as required
- Water
- One Head Iceberg Lettuce
- Two cups Pork
- One Avocado

**Steps of preparation**

- Mash the avocado and sweep in the mayonnaise, garlic, lime juice, and some salt and pepper. If the aioli wants to be thin, then apply a little bit of water so that it can be quickly drizzled.

- Place the pork in the lettuce cups, cover with the sliced avocado, and drizzle it with the aioli and cover with cilantro and some lime.

## 15. Keto Italian Chicken Meal Prep Bowls

Servings: 2 yields | Total time: 15 min

Calories: 292 kcal | Proteins: 14 g | Carbohydrates: 37 g | Fat: 0 g

**Ingredients**

- One teaspoon salt
- half t teaspoon pepper
- Two teaspoon basil
- Two teaspoon marjoram
- Two teaspoon rosemary
- Two teaspoon thyme
- Two teaspoons paprika
- Two pounds boneless skinless chicken breasts cut into bite-sized pieces
- One and a half cup broccoli florets
- One small red chopped onion
- One cup tomato
- One medium zucchini chopped
- Two teaspoons minced garlic
- Two Tablespoon olive oil
- Two cups cooked rice

**Steps of preparation**

- Preheat the oven to 450F. Then Line the baking sheet of aluminum foil and put it aside.
- In a small container, add some salt, some pepper, marjoram, some rosemary, basil, thyme, and paprika.
- Put chicken and vegetables in the baking bowl. Spray all the seasoning and garlic equally over all the chicken as well as the vegetables. Then Drizzle with some olive oil.
- Now Bake for almost 15-20 minutes unless the chicken is properly cooked and vegetables are finely crispy.

- Broil the brown chicken for 1-2 minutes.
- Put 1⁄2 or 1 cup of the cooked rice of your preference in four different preparation containers.
- Segregate chicken and vegetables equally all over the rice.
- Cover them, and them keep in the refrigerator for 3-5 days, or you can serve them for dinner.

## 16. Cheeseburger Lettuce Wraps

Servings: 1 | Total time: 15 min

Calories: 556 kcal | Proteins: 33.6 g | Carbohydrates: 8.2 g | Fat: 42 g

**Ingredients**

- Two pounds minced beef
- Half teaspoon salts
- One teaspoon black pepper
- One teaspoon oregano
- Six slices of American cheese
- Two heads iceberg
- Two tomatoes diced
- One fourth cup light mayo
- Three tablespoons ketchup
- One Tablespoon relish
- salt and pepper as required

**Steps of preparation**

- First, heat the grill or the skillet over medium temperature.
- In a large container, add some ground beef, some seasoned salt, and pepper, and some oregano.
- Now Divide the mixture into six parts and then curl each of them into a ball. Squeeze each ball down to create a patty.
- Put the patties on the grill or the pan and then cook for almost 4 minutes from either direction or till cooked to desired taste. (when using a grill, just prepare 3 min at a time to avoid congestion).

- Put a piece of cheese on top of the grilled burgers. Put each cheeseburger on a broad lettuce leaf. Cover with spreading and one slice of tomato, some red onion, and whatever you want. Wrap the lettuce over the top then eat. Savor it!
- In a little pan, add all the components of the spread. Put it in the fridge before available for usage.

## 17. Classic Stuffed Peppers

Servings: 6 | Total time: 1 hour 20 min

Calories: 376 kcal | Proteins: 16 g | Carbohydrates: 52 g | Fat: 12 g

**Ingredients**

- Six bell peppers
- One-pound ground beef
- One minced onion
- Two minced garlic cloves
- Three fourth cup boiled rice
- One teaspoon paprika
- Half teaspoon oregano
- Half teaspoon mustard powder
- Half cup parsley
- Salt and black pepper
- Half cup Jack cheese

**Steps of preparation**

- Preheat to 375 ° F in the oven. Apply the marinara sauce to the center of a medium-sized skillet.
- Prune the base within each pepper a bit, so it lies flat. Break off the tops of each pepper and then detach the ribs and the seeds and then discard them.
- In a medium dish, combine beef with onion, paprika, oregano, garlic, rice, mustard pepper, and some parsley and salt
- Load the mixture of meat into each of the peppers, filling up to the top. Shift the peppers to the heated skillet and put them on the upper edge of the sauce.

- Garnish with one and a half teaspoons of cheese. Bake until the peppers are juicy, and the beef is thoroughly cooked for 25 to 30 minutes. Serve straight away with some scoop of sauce.

## 18. Chicken Lemon herb Mediterranean salad

Servings: 1 | Total time: 15 min

Calories: 336 kcal | Proteins: 24 g | Carbohydrates: 13 g | Fat: 21 g

**Ingredients**

- Two tablespoons olive oil
- One lemon juice extract
- Two tablespoons of water
- Two tablespoons of vinegar
- Two tablespoons of parsley
- Two teaspoons basil
- Two teaspoons of minced garlic
- Two teaspoons of oregano
- One teaspoon of salt
- One pepper
- One-pound boneless chicken thigh fillets
- Four cups Romaine lettuce leaves
- One diced cucumber
- Two tomatoes cubed
- One red onion cubed
- One diced avocado
- One-third cup rutted Kalamata olives

**Steps of preparation**

- In a big container, mix together all the marinade components. Add half of the marinade to a big, shallow pan. Refrigerate the leftover marinade for further use as a topping.

- In a bowl, add chicken to some marinade and marinate the chicken for 15-30 minutes (and for up to 2 hours in the fridge if time allows). When waiting for the chicken to marinate, arrange all the components of the salad, and combine in a big bowl of salad.
- When chicken is prepared, warm 1 tablespoon of olive oil inside a grill pan or grill above medium-high heat. Barbecue chicken from both sides until golden brown and cooked completely.
- Keep chicken to settle for 5 min; cut and place over the salad. Drizzle with the leftover unchanged dressing. End up serving with a lemon slice.

## 19. Keto BLT stuffed chicken salad avocados

Servings: 1 | Total time: 30 min

Calories: 267 kcal | Proteins: 14 g | Carbohydrates: 13.6 g | Fat: 17 g

**Ingredients**

- Twelve slices of turkey bacon
- One and a half cups of shredded rotisserie chicken
- Two tomatoes
- One and a half cups of cottage cheese
- One cup of finely chopped lettuce
- Three avocados

**Steps of preparation**

- Preheat the oven to the temperature of 400 degrees F.
- Place Twelve slices of the turkey bacon on a parchment lining the baking dish
- Bake for almost 10 minutes, then rotate, and bake for the next five minutes, then scatter the bacon over a few sheets of some paper towels to it cool off.
- In the meantime, quarter the tomatoes, scrape out all the pulp and the seeds with the help of fingertips, and break into tiny bits.
- Cut the Romaine into little bits
- In a big bowl, add meat, some cottage cheese, some romaine, some berries, turkey bacon, and combine together.
- Sprinkle with salt and pepper as desired.

- Half the avocados cut the pits and then season gently with some salt and pepper.
- Scoop 1/6 (roughly) of the chicken salad inside each avocado. Not a massive amount is going to fit into the hole produced by the seed, so you're going to add a good amount on upper edge of the avocado.

## 20. Cheesy taco skillet

Servings: 6 yields | Total time: 30 min

Calories: 241 kcal | Proteins: 30 g | Carbohydrates: 9 g | Fat: 20 g

**Ingredients**

- One-pound ground beef
- One diced large yellow onion
- Two diced bell peppers
- One diced tomato
- One shredded large zucchini
- taco seasoning
- Three cups pf baby kale
- One and a half cup of shredded cheddar cheese

**Steps of preparation**

- In a wide pan, gently cook ground beef and also well crumble.
- Drain the waste of fat.
- Include the onions and the peppers and cook till golden.
- Add some canned tomatoes, some taco seasoning, as well as any water required for taco seasoning to uniformly cover the mixture (up to 1 tablespoon - the tomato liquid may benefit)
- Apply the greens and make it absolutely wilt.
- Mix it finely.

## 21. Cauliflower Cheesy Breadsticks

Servings: 8 | Total time: 43 min

Calories: 102 kcal | Proteins: 7.1 g | Carbohydrates: 1.1 g | Fat: 7.7 g

**Ingredients**

- Four cups of diced cauliflower
- Four eggs
- Two cups of mozzarella
- Three teaspoon oregano
- Four minced cloves of garlic
- Salt and pepper as desired
- One cup of mozzarella cheese

**Steps of preparation**

- Start by Preheating the oven to a temperature of 425 ° F. Arrange Two pizza plates or a broad baking sheet with parchment paper on them.
- Try to make sure the florets of cauliflower are finely cut. Apply the florets to the processor and spin.
- In a microwaveable jar, put the cauliflower then cover it with a lid. Microwave it for a time of 10-minutes. Only let cauliflower cool until there was no steam rising from it anymore. Put in a wide bowl the microwave cauliflower and transfer oregano, 2 cups mozzarella, salt, garlic, and pepper to the whites. Mix in everything.
- Segregate the mixture into two and put each half on the ready baking sheets and form the breadsticks either into a pizza crust or in a rectangular shape.
- Bake the crust for around 25 minutes (no covering yet) till it is soft and brown. Don't be scared; the crust isn't soggy. Sprinkle with the leftover mozzarella cheese once golden and bring it oven and bake for the next five min just until the cheese is melted.
- Start Slicing and serving.

## 22. Loaded cauliflower

Servings: 4 | Total time: 15 min

Calories: 298 kcal | Proteins: 7.4 g | Carbohydrates: 1.1 g | Fat: 24.6 g

**Ingredients**

- One-pound cauliflower
- Four ounces of sour cream

- One cup of grated cheddar cheese
- Two slices of bacon
- Two tablespoons of chives
- Three tablespoons of butter
- One fourth teaspoon of garlic paste
- Salt and pepper as required

**Steps of preparation**

- Slice the cauliflower into the form of florets and transfer them to a suitable bowl within microwave. Add almost 2 teaspoons of water and soak with film that sticks. Microwave for another 5-8 minutes, before fully cooked and soft, based on the microwave. Dump the extra water and allow for a couple of seconds to stay uncovered. (Alternately, the traditional method, boil the cauliflower. Upon boiling, you can need to drain a little extra water out from inside the cauliflower.
- In a food processor, add the cauliflower and process it until soft. Introduce the butter, and sour cream, and garlic powder, then process to the texture of mashed potatoes. Remove the mashed cauliflower to a pot and mix much of the chives, leaving any later to apply to the end. add the rest of the sharp cheddar cheese and combine through hand. Sprinkle some salt and pepper as desired.
- Cover the filled cauliflower with the remainder cheese, leftover chives, and some bacon. To melt the cheese, place it in the microwave or place cauliflower for another few minutes under the broiler.

## 23. Keto Grilled tuna salad

Servings: 2 | Total time: 1 hour

Calories: 975 kcal | Proteins: 53 g | Carbohydrates: 9 g | Fat: 79 g

**Ingredients**

- Two large egg
- Eight ounces of asparagus
- One tablespoon of olive oil
- Eight ounces of fresh tuna

- Four ounces of spring mix
- Four ounces of cherry tomatoes
- Half red onion
- Two tablespoons of chopped walnuts
- Half cup of mayonnaise
- Two tablespoons of water
- Two teaspoons of garlic paste
- Salt and pepper were required

**Steps for preparation**

- Gather all of the things for preparation.
- Add the water, the garlic powder, mayonnaise, and salt, and the pepper together in a bowl to create the dressing. Mix until well blended and set it aside.
- Boil the eggs for 8-10 minutes or so. Peel and break in half until cooled.
- Clean and split the asparagus onto similar lengths. In a pan, cook the asparagus.
- Pour the olive oil between both sides of the tuna in the same manner and fry it on both sides for 3-5 minutes. To taste, sprinkle the tuna with the salt and the pepper.
- Put the leafy greens, the cherry tomatoes (sliced in half), onion, and the eggs on a tray.
- Slice into pieces of the cooked tuna and put it on top. On the top of the salad, pour the dressing sauce and scatter the sliced walnuts on top of that.

## 24. Creamy ketogenic taco soup

Servings: 4 | Total time: 35 min

Calories: 345 kcal | Proteins: 21 g | Carbohydrates: 5 g | Fat: 27 g

**Ingredients**

- Sixteen ounces of ground beef
- One tablespoon of olive oil
- One medium diced onion
- Three minced cloves of garlic
- One diced green bell pepper
- Ten ounces of canned tomatoes

- One cup of heavy cream
- Two tablespoons of taco seasoning
- Salt and pepper as required
- Two cups of beef broth
- One medium cubed avocado
- Four tablespoons of sour cream
- Four tablespoons of cilantro

**Steps of preparation**

- Gather all of the supplies. Dice the bell pepper and the onion long in advance.
- Add the olive oil, onion, and ground beef and garlic, to a small saucepan over medium heat. Sprinkle salt and pepper, season.
- Cook it until golden brown beef and transparent onion.
- Add some bell pepper, heavy cream, sliced tomatoes with green chili, and taco seasoning until the beef is golden brown.
- Simmer together properly to guarantee that all of the products contain the spices and seasoning.
- Transfer the water to the beef and then get the soup to a simmer. Decrease the heat to low and simmer for almost 10-15 minutes or until liquid is decreased, and soup is prepared according to the desired taste. If needed, try and add salt and pepper.
- Add the sour cream and the cilantro avocado to the portions and garnish. Add a squeeze of lime juice, too.

## 25. Keto fish cakes with dipping sauce

Servings: 6 | Total time: 15 min

Calories: 69 kcal | Proteins: 53 g | Carbohydrates: 2.7 g | Fat: 6.5 g

**Ingredients**

- One-pound raw white boneless fish
- One by four cup of cilantro
- Salt as required
- Chili flakes as required
- Two garlic cloves

- Two tablespoons of coconut oil
- Two ripe avocados
- One lemon juice extract
- Two tablespoons of water

**Steps of preparation**

- Put the fish, vegetables, garlic (if used), spice, chili, and fish in a processor. Blitz before everything is equally mixed.
- Apply the coconut oil to a wide frying pan over medium-high heat and stir the pan.
- Oil the hands and roll in Six patties of the fish combination.
- To the hot frying pan and add the cakes. Cook till lightly browned and fried thru, on both sides.
- While the fish cakes are frying, in a blender, incorporate all the dipping sauce components (starting with lemon juice) and mix thoroughly until it becomes fluffy. Taste the mixture and apply, if necessary, other lemon juice or salt.
- Serve hot with the dipping sauce when the fish cakes become baked.

## 26. Ketogenic Paleo Meat Ball for lunch

Servings: 3 | Total time: 30 min

Calories: 475 kcal | Proteins: 61.3 g | Carbohydrates: 5.6 g | Fat: 21.7 g

**Ingredients**

- One and a half pounds of ground beef
- Two tablespoons ghee
- One tablespoon apple cider vinegar
- Half teaspoon of pepper
- One teaspoon of salt
- Yellow minced onion
- Two minced garlic cloved
- One fourth cup of chopped rosemary

**Steps of preparation**

- Start by Preheating the oven to the temperature of 350 degrees ° C.

- Put all the meatballs supplies in a bowl and mix, and when well mixed, use the hands to combine it together.
- Line a parchment paper on baking tray and fold the mixture into tiny balls, utilizing approximately a tablespoon of mix per meatball.
- Now meatballs are wrapped and placed on the parchment. Bake for almost 20 minutes or until baked completely.
- Serve hot or allow it to cool and seal in the refrigerator in an airtight jar.

## 27. Ketogenic Mexican Shredded beef

Servings: 20 | Total time: 3-hour 20 min

Calories: 323 kcal | Proteins: 53 g | Carbohydrates: 7.3 g | Fat: 12.9 g

**Ingredients**

- Three and a half pounds beef short ribs
- Two teaspoons turmeric powder
- One teaspoon salt
- Half teaspoon peppers
- Two teaspoons cumin powder
- Two teaspoons coriander powder
- Half cup waters
- One cup cilantro chopped

**Steps of preparation**

- Combine the dried ingredients in a shallow pan.
- For a slow cooker, introduce short ribs and gently brush each bit in the seasoning mix.
- Scatter over the ribs with cilantro stems and additional garlic. Apply water carefully without scrubbing the spices off.
- On low heat, cook for 6-7 hours, or until it falls apart. After 6 hours, inspect the beef and cook further when it's not soft enough.
- Drain the cooking liquid in a medium pan if necessary and decrease it over a moderate flame for 15 minutes.

- Transfer the liquid back into another crockpot. Take off the steak and cut the beef utilizing two forks.
- Serve warm with guacamole, taco-like silverbeet leaves, corn, cucumbers, organic cilantro, and green beans.

## 28. Keto low carb pork & cashew stir fry

Total Time: 10 mins | Servings: 2 |

Calories: 403 kcal | Fat: 27g |Net Carbs: 12g | Protein: 28g

**Ingredients**

- Avocado oil 2 tbsp
- Shredded pork ½ lb.
- Sliced green bell pepper ½
- Sliced red bell pepper ½
- Sliced medium onion 1/4
- Cashews 1/3 c
- Fresh grated ginger 1 tbsp
- Minced cloves of garlic 3
- Chinese chili oil 1 tsp
- Sesame oil 1 tbsp
- Gluten-free tamari sauce or coconut amino 2 tbsp
- Salt>> to taste

**Steps of Preparation**

- Put avocado oil in a frying saucepan & cook the pork (if uncooked).
- Next, add onions, pepper & cashews, all sliced.
- Sauté until completely cooked pork. Then mix in ginger, garlic, tamari sauce, chili oil, sesame oil & salt to your taste.

## 29. Keto pork stuffed with sausages & cauliflower rice

Total Time: 30 mins | Serving 4

Calories: kcal 473 | Fat: 24g | Net Carbs: 3g |Protein: 57g

**Ingredients**

- Avocado oil 4 tbsp
- Minced garlic cloves 2
- Small cauliflower cut into small rice-like particles ¼
- Chopped onion 1 tbsp
- Chopped red bell pepper 1 tbsp
- Chopped sausage ½
- Green peas 1 tbsp
- Pork tenderloin 1&1/2 lb.
- Salt & pepper>> to taste

**Steps of Preparation**

- Preheat the oven before 400 F (200 C).
- Pour 2 Tsp of avocado oil over moderate temp in a wide skillet, then add garlic & onion. Cook them, till the onion is transparent, for a few minutes.
- Stir in the cauliflower, sausage, red pepper & roast for ten minutes. Season with salt & pepper.
- Slice the pork tenderloin to open it lengthwise but don't cut through. Using a meat pounder, pound meat if you've it.
- Cover with rice mixture halfway over the tenderloin. Wrap meat up & use twine to bind it together. (use cocktail sticks to protect the pork If you don't have twine.)
- In a separate frying pan, melt two tbsp of avocado oil. Crisp up the pork tenderloin gently on either side for a few minutes until it is brown.
- Place your filled pork tenderloin upon the baking tray and let them steam for at least thirty minutes uncovered. If you have got a meat thermometer, this should display 145 F.
- Let the meat sit for ten minutes before the strings are cut and sliced.

## 30. Keto pork tenderloin stuffed with cabbage

Total Time: 40 mins | Serving: 4

Calories: 207 kcal | Fat: 12g |Net Carbs: 2g |Protein: 24g

**Ingredients**

- Avocado oil 2 tbsp
- Diced onion ¼

- Diced cabbage 1 c
- Minced garlic cloves 2
- Salt & pepper>> to taste
- Pork tenderloin 1 lb.

**Steps of Preparation**

- Preheat the oven before 400 F (200 C).
- Apply the avocado oil over medium heat to a frying pan and sauté the cabbage, onions, garlic till cabbage is soft. Season to taste, with salt & black pepper.
- Lengthwise slit the tenderloin but do not cut into it all the way completely. Using it to hammer the pork tenderloin to a big flat slice (approx. 1/2-inch-thick), if you have got a meat pounder.
- Place the flat tenderloin over a cutting board & put the fried cabbage in the center.
- Roll up and cover the tenderloin with twine or use cocktail sticks to roast.
- Place it on a baking dish and take 40 mins. Testing the pork achieves an inner temp of 145 F.

## 31. Keto marinated pork tenderloin

Total Time: 20 mins | Serving 4

Calories: 258 kcal | Fat: 19g | Net Carbs: 1g | Protein: 24g

**Ingredients**

- Cut into 2 long pieces of pork tenderloin 1lb.
- Olive oil ¼ c
- Greek seasoning 2 tbsp
- Red wine vinegar 1 tbsp
- Lemon juice 1 tbsp
- Salt & pepper

for Greek Seasoning:

- Garlic powder 1 tsp
- Dried oregano 1tsp
- Dried basil 1tsp
- Dried rosemary ½ tsp

- Dried thyme ½ tsp
- Dried dill ½ tsp
- Cinnamon ½ tsp
- Parsley ½ tsp
- Marjoram ½ tsp

**Steps of Preparation**

- Mix the olive oil, vinegar, lemon juice & seasoning in a big zip lock container.
- Put the 2 pieces of pork tenderloin in the container and marinate in the fridge overnight.
- Place the pork over medium heat in a frying pan. Place the pork with one side and roast. Then by using tongs, turn the pork into a good browning on every side.
- Continue to turn the pork till the inner temp reaches 145 F/63 C (control using a meat thermometer).

## 32. Keto herbs pork tenderloin

Total Time: 20 mins | Serving 2

Total Time: kcal: 627 |Fat: 49g | Net Carbs: 4g |Protein: 44g

**Ingredients**

- Pine nut 2 tbsp
- Chopped garlic cloves 3
- Fresh basil leaves 1 c
- Fresh parsley ½ c + 2 tbsp
- Nutritional yeast 2 tbsp
- Olive oil 5 tbsp
- Juice of 1 lemon
- salt to taste

For the pork

- Pork tenderloin 14 oz
- Salt & ground black pepper
- Olive oil 1 tbsp

- Reserved herbs paste 3 tbsp

**Steps of Preparation**

- Begin by toasting pine nuts in a heavy, dry skillet to create the herb paste. Take out the crispy pine nuts and apply the garlic, basil, nutritional yeast flakes, fresh parsley, and olive oil to a mini food processor. Combine to make a perfect paste, scraping many times across the sides of the container. Season with salt & lemon juice to taste. Place on the side.
- Preheat oven to 410 ° F (210 ° C) for pork.
- Season the pork tenderloin on both sides with salt and freshly ground black pepper. In a non-stick pan, heat the olive oil & brown the tenderloin at both sides. Remove from heat and let it cool down a little bit. Using a palette knife or thin silicone spatula until cool enough to treat, then spread the stored herb paste over the pork tenderloin on both sides. Put tenderloin with a well-equipped cover in a casserole dish & cook in the oven for 12-15 mins or till cooked to your taste.
- Remove from oven and enable it to cool before sliced and served. Serve with some extra herbs paste if needed.

## 33. Keto basil pork Fettucine

Total Time: 15 mins | Servings: 3

Calories: 231 | Fat: 16g | Net Carbs: 5g |Protein: 16g

**Ingredients**

- 5 packs of fettuccine shirataki noodles of 3 oz
- coconut oil 2 tbsp
- Pork tenderloin ½ lb.
- salt & pepper>> to taste
- Sliced leek 1
- Chopped garlic cloves 2
- coconut cream 4 tbsp
- Fresh chopped basil leaves ¼ c
- Dash of chicken broth

**Steps of Preparation**

- To 400 F, preheat the oven.
- Rinse under cool, flowing water the shirataki noodles, and hold warm in a pot of softly simmering water upon a burner.
- Heat 1 tbsp of coconut oil in a wide saucepan and brown both sides of the pork tenderloin. Take the pork off the skillet & season with salt & black pepper. Shift the pork to a baking tray and put over it in the oven for ten min. Remove, and then let rest.
- Meanwhile, heat in the same pan the remaining coconut oil used for the pork & cook the leeks & garlic over medium heat until soft. For keeping the mixture moist, apply a splash of chicken broth. Apply the coconut cream & basil once wet.
- Drain the hot noodles and put them in a bowl. Spoon over sauce with leek. Cut the pork & put it on top of the sauce.

o

# Chapter 4: Keto Dinner Recipes for Women above 50

These are some keto dinner recipes for women above 50. These recipes are simple, easy, and fulfill all the requirements of the body by keeping you healthy and fit.

## 1. Creamy Tuscan garlic chicken

Servings: 6 | Total time: 25 min

Calories: 368 kcal | Proteins: 30 g | Carbohydrates: 7 g | Fat: 25 g

**Ingredients**

- One and a half pounds of boneless chicken breasts
- Two Tablespoons of olive oil
- One cup cream

- Half cup of chicken broth
- One teaspoon of garlic powder
- One teaspoon of italian seasoning
- Half cup of parmesan cheese
- One cup spinach chopped
- Half cup tomatoes dried

**Steps of preparation**

- Put olive oil in a wide skillet and cook chicken on medium-high heat for 3-5 minutes per side or until golden around each side and cook until the middle is no longer pink. Remove the chicken then put that aside on a tray.
- Transfer some chicken broth, heavy cream, Italian seasoning, garlic powder, and parmesan cheese. Mix over medium-high heat unless it begins to thicken. Include the spinach and the sundried tomatoes and boil before the spinach starts wilting. Add the chicken to the skillet and, if needed, pour over pasta.
- Serve with a lemon slice.

## 2. Avocado Greek salad

Servings: 4 | Total time: 15 min

Calories: 305 kcal | Proteins: 10 g | Carbohydrates: 12 g | Fat: 27 g

**Ingredients**

- One by four cup olive oil
- Two tablespoons vinegar
- One teaspoon garlic paste
- Two teaspoons dried oregano
- One fourth teaspoon salt
- One large sliced cucumber
- Four wedge cut tomatoes
- One green pepper sliced
- Half sliced red onion
- 200 g cubed creamy feta cheese
- Half cup olives
- One large diced avocado

**Steps of preparation**

- Mix together the spices of the dressing in the jar.
- In a bowl, combine all the ingredients of the salad. Toss the dressing. Season with some salt only if required (depending about how salty your feta cheese is). Sprinkle on additional oregano to use. Start serving with chicken, lamb, beef, fish; the choices are infinite!

## 3. Keto Eggs and Zoodles

Servings: 2 | Total time: 25 min

Calories: 633 kcal | Proteins: 20 g | Carbohydrates: 27 g | Fat: 53 g

**Ingredients**

- Nonstick spray
- Three zucchinis
- Two tablespoons olive oil
- A pinch of Kosher salt and black pepper
- Four large eggs
- Red-pepper flakes
- Basil
- Two thinly sliced avocados

**Steps of preparation**

- Preheat oven to 350 ° degrees F. Lightly oil a nonstick spray baking sheet.
- In a wide pan, mix the zucchini noodles with the olive oil. Season to taste with the salt and the pepper. Divide into Four even parts, move to the baking tray, and build a nest shape.
- steadily crack the egg in the center of each nest. Bake until eggs are ready, for 9 to 11 minutes. Season to taste with salt and pepper, garnish with red pepper flakes and basil. Serve with the slices of avocado.

## 4. Cheese and the Cauliflower 'Breadsticks

Servings: 4 | Total time: 20 min

Calories: 200 kcal | Proteins: 12 g | Carbohydrates: 9 g | Fat: 14 g

**Ingredients**

- One head cauliflower
- Two garlic cloves
- One third cup mozzarella cheese
- One third cup Parmesan cheese
- Two eggs
- One egg white
- One tablespoon thyme
- One tablespoon rosemary chopped
- A pinch of Kosher salt and black pepper
- Two tablespoons of olive oil

**Steps of preparation**

- Begin by preheating the oven to a temperature of 425 ° F. Cover a baking sheet of parchment paper.
- In a food processor bowl, mix the cauliflower with the garlic. Pulse until the finely chopped like a fine meal, for around three minutes. Move to a broad blending pot.
- Mix the mozzarella, eggs, thyme, parmesan, egg white, and rosemary in the cauliflower until well blended; add salt and pepper.

- Spread the cauliflower mixture in a 1/2-inch-thick ring upon the baking sheet. Brush the olive oil on the surface. Bake until the sides are crisp and light golden, for 25 to 30 minutes.
- Cool for five min before cutting and able to serve in the sticks.

## 5. Rainbow Dinner Keto Chicken

Servings: 4 | Total time: 45 min

Calories: 394 kcal | Proteins: 39 g | Carbohydrates: 23 g | Fat: 16 g

**Ingredients**

- Nonstick spray
- One-pound chicken
- One tablespoon sesame oil
- Two tablespoons soy sauce
- Two tablespoons honey
- Two diced red bell peppers
- Two diced yellow bell peppers
- Three sliced carrots
- Half broccoli
- Two diced red onions
- Two tablespoons of olive oil
- A pinch of Kosher salt and black pepper
- One fourth cup chopped parsley

**Steps of preparation**

- Begin by Preheating the oven to a temperature of 400 ° F. Spray a baking sheet slightly with a nonstick spray.
- Put the chicken upon this baking sheet. In a bowl, shake with the sesame oil and the soy sauce. Brush the paste uniformly with the chicken.
- Place the red bell peppers, the yellow bell peppers, the vegetables, the broccoli, and the red onion on a baking sheet. Sprinkle the olive oil all over the vegetables and stir gently to coat, now season with some salt and pepper.
- Bake until the vegetables are soft as well as the chicken is thoroughly cooked for 23 to 25 minutes. Pull the mixture from oven and season with parsley.

## 6. Keto Dinner Chicken Meatballs

Servings: 4 | Total time: 45 min

Calories: 205 kcal | Proteins: 20 g | Carbohydrates: 3 g | Fat: 13 g

**Ingredients**

- One tablespoon olive oil
- Half chopped red onion
- 2 tablespoon minced garlic
- One-pound ground chicken
- One fourth cup chopped fresh parsley
- One tablespoon mustard paste
- Three fourth teaspoon kosher salt
- Half teaspoon black pepper
- One can coconut milk

- One and ¼ cups fresh parsley chopped
- Four chopped scallions
- One garlic minced
- One lemon zest and juice
- A pinch of Kosher salt and black pepper
- A pinch of Red pepper flakes
- One recipe Cauliflower Rice

**Steps of preparation**

- Start by Preheating the oven to 375 ° F. Lay a baking sheet with an aluminum foil and coat this with a non - stick cooking spray.
- Heat the olive oil in a medium skillet over medium heat. Include the onion and sauté until soft, for about five minutes. Include the garlic and sauté until fragrant for around 1 minute.
- Move the garlic and the onion to a medium bowl and let it cool moderately. Stir in parsley, chicken, and the mustard, sprinkle in pepper and salt. Shape the mixture into 2 tablespoon spheres and shift to the baking sheet.
- Bake the meatballs unless solid and thoroughly cooked for 17 to 20 mins.
- In a food processor jar, mix parsley, scallions, garlic, coconut milk, lemon zest, and lemon juice and mix thoroughly, sprinkle with salt and black pepper.
- Cover with both the red pepper flakes as well as the remaining parsley. Serve the sauce over cauliflower rice.

## 7. Keto Dinner Pork Carnitas

Servings: 4 | Total time: 45 min

Calories: 205 kcal | Proteins: 20 g | Carbohydrates: 3 g | Fat: 13 g

**Ingredients**

- One sliced white onion
- Five minced garlic cloves
- One minced jalapeño
- Three pounds pork shoulder (diced)
- A pinch of salt and black pepper
- One tablespoon cumin
- Two tablespoons fresh oregano
- Two oranges
- One lime
- One-third cup of chicken broth

**Steps of preparation**

- Put the onion, garlic, the jalapeno, and the pork at the bottom of the slow cooker. Put cinnamon, oregano pepper, and cumin to taste.
- Put the oranges and lime zest all over the pork, and then halve them and drop the juice all over the pork. Spill the broth over the pork as well.
- Place the cover on the slow cooker and hold the heat down. Cook for almost 7 hours or till meat is soft and quick to break with a fork.

- Utilize two forks to crumble the beef. Pork may be presented immediately (we like it in tacos) or frozen in an airtight jar in a refrigerator for up to 5 days or in a freezer for up to 1 month.

## 8. Keto Butter Scallops Garlic and Steak

Servings: 4 | Total time: 45 min

Calories: 205 kcal | Proteins: 20 g | Carbohydrates: 3 g | Fat: 13 g

**Ingredients**

- Two beef tenderloin fillets
- A pinch of Kosher salt and black pepper
- Three tablespoons unsalted butter
- Eight to ten large sea scallops
- Three minced garlic cloves
- Six tablespoons cubed unsalted butter
- Two tablespoons parsley leaves chopped
- Two tablespoons fresh chives
- One tablespoon lemon juice
- Two teaspoons lemon zest
- A pinch of Kosher salt and black pepper

**Steps of preparation**

- Warm a cast iron pan on a medium-high flame for ten minutes.
- Use paper towels, pat all sides of steak dry; spice with some salt and pepper as you want.
- Melt 2 tbsp of butter. Put the steaks in the center of the pan and cook for around 4-6 mins until the thick crust has developed. Use tongs, flip and simmer for another five minutes or until done as desired; set the pan aside, cover it loosely.
- As the steak rests, clean the steak and heat the leftover one tablespoon of butter into it.
- Strip the short side muscle from of the scallops, clean with cold water, and dry completely.
- Season with salt and black pepper. Work in rounds, add the scallops to the pan in a single layer and fry, flip once, till golden brown and transparent in the middle, approximately three minutes per side. Put aside and leave it warm.
- Reducing overall heat to low for garlic butter sauce; add the garlic and simmer, stir constantly, until fragrant, for around 1 minute. Stir in butter, chives, lemon juice, parsley, and lemon zest, now season with salt and pepper.
- In the end, serve steaks and scallops directly with the garlic butter sauce.

## 9. Ketogenic Cauliflower Crispy Wrapped Prosciutto Bites

Servings: 8-10 | Total time: 45 min

Calories: 215 kcal | Proteins: 14 g | Carbohydrates: 5 g | Fat: 15 g

**Ingredients**

- One small head cauliflower
- Half cup tomato paste
- Two tablespoons white wine

- Half teaspoon black pepper
- Half cup grated Parmesan cheese
- Twenty slices prosciutto
- Six tablespoons olive oil

**Steps of preparation**

- Cut the bottom of the cauliflower and some green leaves. Split the cauliflower in half and slice the half into one-inch-thick strips. Split the slices into two or three bits, based on the size of the slice.
- Put to a boil a big pot of salted water. Blanch the cauliflower in water until it is almost soft, for 3 to 5 minutes. Remove the cauliflower and pat dry with the help of paper towels.
- In a small cup, combine the tomato paste with black pepper and white wine. Layer 1 tsp along each side of the cauliflower, then top with 1 tsp of Parmesan. Gently seal a prosciutto slice over each piece of the cauliflower, gripping gently at the end to secure
- Work in batches, cook two teaspoons of olive oil in a wide pan over medium heat. Bring the cauliflower then cook till the prosciutto is crispy and golden, three to four minutes per side. Then repeat with some extra oil and cauliflower until all the bits are fried. Let it settle slowly, then serve.

## 10. Ketogenic Fried Chicken Recipe

Servings: 12 | Total time: 12 min

Calories: 308 kcal | Proteins: 40.4 g | Carbohydrates: 0.7 g | Fat: 14 g

**Ingredients**

- Four ounces of pork rinds

- One and a half teaspoon thyme dried
- One teaspoon sea salt dried
- One teaspoon black pepper dried
- One teaspoon oregano dried
- Half teaspoon garlic powder dried
- One teaspoon paprika dried
- Twelve chicken legs and thighs
- One egg
- Two ounces mayonnaise
- Three tablespoons of mustard

**Steps of preparation**

- Start by preheating the oven at a temperature of 400 degrees Fahrenheit.
- Grind pork rinds in a powder form, leaving them in a few bigger pieces.
- Mix pork rinds with thyme, pepper, oregano, salt, garlic, and smoked paprika. Spread on a large plate into a thin sheet.
- In a big container, mix egg, mayonnaise, and Dijon mustard. Dip every piece of chicken in the egg-mayonnaise mixture, and then wrap in the pork rind blend until it is thinly coated.
- Put the chicken on a wire rack on a baking sheet and then bake for almost 40 minutes.

## 11. Greek Yogurt Chicken Peppers salad

Servings: 6 | Total time: 30 min

Calories: 116 kcal | Proteins: 7 g | Carbohydrates: 16 g | Fat: 3 g

**Ingredients**

- Two-third cup of Greek yogurt
- Two tablespoons mustard paste
- Two tablespoons vinegar
- A pinch of Kosher salt and black pepper
- One-third cup of chopped fresh parsley
- Half kg of cubed roseate chicken
- Two sliced stalks celery
- One bunch of sliced scallions
- One pint of cherry tomatoes
- Half diced cucumber
- Three bell peppers

**Steps of preparation**

- In a bowl, combine Greek yogurt, and rice vinegar, and mustard; add salt and pepper. Put some parsley.
- Include chicken, celery and three - fourths of the scallions, and cucumbers and tomatoes. Stir well and mix.
- Distribute the chicken salad between the bell peppers.
- Garnish the remainder scallions, some tomatoes, and cucumbers.

## 12. Easy chicken low carb stir fry recipe

Serving: 2 | Total Time: 12 mins

Calories: 219 | Fat:10g | Net Carbs:5.5g | Protein:19g

**Ingredients**

- Sesame oil 1 tbsp
- Boneless & skinless chicken thighs 2
- Minced fresh ginger 1 Tbsp
- Gluten-free soy sauce 1/4 cup
- Water 1/2 cup
- Onion powder 1 tsp
- Garlic powder 1/2 tsp
- Red pepper flakes 1 tsp
- Granulated sugar1 Tbsp
- Xanthan gum 1/2 tsp
- Bagged broccolis mix 2 heaping cups
- Chopped scallions 1/2 cup

**Steps of Preparation**

- Cut the chicken thighs into thin pieces/strips. Mix the chicken & chopped ginger in the edible oil in a big sauté pan for 2 to 3 mins.
- Apply the water, soy sauce, powder of onion, powder of garlic, red pepper flakes, sugar sub & xanthan gum. Remove well and simmer for five mins.
- Apply the slaw & scallions then coat – simmer for two min.

## 13. Keto Asiago Chicken with Bacon Cream Sauce

Serving: 4 | Total Time: 40 mins

Calories 581 kcal | Fat:38g | Net Carbs:8g | Protein:49g

**Ingredients**

- Chicken breasts 1.5 lb.
- Vegetable oil 1 1/2 tbsp
- Salt & pepper
- Minced garlic cloves 4
- Chicken stock 1 cup
- Cooked & chopped bacon 8 slices
- Sliced lemon 1/2
- Half & half 1 cup
- Shredded asiago cheese 1/2 cup
- Fresh chopped parsley 2 tbsp

**Steps of Preparation**

- Season the chicken nicely with salt & pepper on each side. Heat the vegetable fats in the big pan. Roast the chicken breasts over med-high heat-around two mins on per side to brown a bit. Do not cook the chicken thru-you will continue to cook it afterward. Take away the chicken from your Pan.
- Add chopped garlic to the same pan. Cook on med heat for around thirty sec, scraping the bottom of the skillet. Deglaze the skillet with a little chicken stock. Apply the leftover stock (total 1 cup).
- Apply half the bacon to the chicken broth.

- Return the chicken to the saucepan, on top of the bacon, as well as in the broth of the chicken. Prepare 5 slim lemon slices across the breasts of the chicken and cook, boiling at low heat, covered for around twenty mins, till the chicken is fully cooked & no longer pink in the middle.
- Take away the chicken from the pan after it is fully cooked. Remove the slices of lemon from the pan. It is much important to remove them. Do not abandon them in for the sauce, or else it'll be too sour. Put one half-and-a-half cup to the pan. Bring to the boil & stir well, scrap from the bottom. Apply 1/2 cup of Asiago shredded cheese & mix to melt totally, just around thirty sec.
- Spoon a little sauce on the chicken breasts to serve & toss with the leftover minced bacon & minced parsley.

## 14. Ketogenic Grilled Chicken Souvlaki with Yogurt Sauce

Serving 4 | Total Time: 2hour 10 mins |

Calories: 192 | Fat:7g | Net Carbs:2.5g | Protein:27g

**Ingredients**

- Chicken breast (cut in strips) 1 lb.
- Olive oil 3 tbsp
- Lemon juice 3 tbsp
- Red wine vinegar 1 tbsp
- Fresh chopped oregano 1 tbsp
- Minced garlic 4 cloves
- Kosher salt 2 tsp
- Ground black pepper 1/4 tsp
- Dried thyme 1/2 tsp

**For the yogurt sauce**

- Greek yogurt 3/4 cup
- Lemon juice 1 tsp
- Minced Garlic 1 tsp
- Fresh chopped oregano 1 tsp
- Kosher salt 1/2 tsp

- Granulated sugar 1/2 tsp

**Steps of Preparation**

- In a small non-reactive bowl, mix the oil of olive, juice of lemon, red vinegar, garlic, oregano, pepper, salt, & dried thyme.
- Fill the marinade with the chicken strips and combine well to cover.
- Cover in the freezer & marinate for two hours or longer.
- Take away the chicken from marinade & thread (when using) on skewers.
- Heat the grill & grill the chicken for around two mins each side, or when it is cooked thru.

For the yogurt sauce:

- Mix all the ingredients of the yogurt sauce & mix well. Season it with your preference.
- Serve the hot grilled chicken with them.

## 15. Low Carb Chicken Jalapeño Poppers

Serving 15 | Total Time: 30 mins

Calories: 111 | Fat:9g | Net Carbs:1g | Protein:1g

**Ingredients**

- Jalapenos large 15
- Sharp shredded cheddar cheese 1 cup
- Softened cream cheese 8 oz
- Shredded & chopped cooked chicken 2 cups
- Salsa Verde 1/3 cup
- Garlic powder 1/2 tsp
- Kosher salt 1/2 tsp
- Cajun seasoning 1 tsp
- Pulverized pork rinds 1 cup
- Cajun seasoning 1/2 tsp

**Steps of Preparation**

- Slice each pepper one/three off the top & scoop out in there.
- Put the peppers on a tray & microwave to soften for two mins.

- In a med bowl, mix cream cheese, cheddar cheese, chicken/turkey, salsa Verde, powder of garlic, salt & Cajun seasoning, then mix till it's blended & creamy.
- Spoon the blend within the jalapeños.
- Mix the pork rind powder & Cajun seasoning in a tiny bowl.
- Nicely roll the cream cheese part of the filled jalapeños into the rinds of Cajun pork till covered.
- Put on the baking sheet.
- Cook for twenty mins at 400, or till its color changes to golden brown & bubble.
- Cool before serving, for a minimum of five mins.

## 16. Lemon butter chicken

Total Time: 50 mins |Serving: 8

**Ingredients**

- Chicken thighs 8 bone
- Smoked paprika 1 tbsp
- Ground black pepper & kosher salt
- Divided unsalted butter 3 tbsp
- Minced garlic 3 cloves
- Chicken broth 1 cup
- Heavy cream 1/2 cup
- Freshly grated parmesan 1/4 cup
- Lemon juice 1
- Dried thyme 1 tsp
- Chopped baby spinach 2 cups

**Steps of Preparation**

- Oven Preheated to 205 degrees C.
- Top chicken thighs with salt, paprika & pepper.
- Melt two tbsp of butter on med-high heat in a big oven-proof pan. Put chicken, skin side down, & sear on each side till they become golden brown, approximately 2 to 3 mins each side; sink excess fat & set it aside.

- Melt the remaining tbsp of butter in the pan. Apply the garlic & cook till fragrant, constantly whisking, approximately 1 to 2 mins, mix in chicken broth, whipping cream, parmesan, juice of lemon, and thyme.
- Bring to a boil; lower the heat, mix in the spinach & boil till the spinach had also wilted & the sauce had already thickened slightly around 3 to 5 mins.
- Put in the oven & roast for around 25 to 30 min till fully cooked, trying to reach a core temp of 75 degrees C.
- Serve asap.

## 17. Keto Chicken Low Carb Stir Fry.

Servings: 4 | Total time: 22 min

Calories: 116 kcal | Proteins: 28 g | Carbohydrates: 9 g | Fat: 7 g

**Ingredients**

- One fourth Olive oil
- One-pound Chicken breast
- Half teaspoon sea salt
- One by four teaspoon Black pepper
- Four Garlic minced
- Six ounces of Broccoli
- One Red bell pepper
- One fourth cup Chicken bone broth
- One-pound Cauliflower rice
- One fourth Coconut aminos
- One teaspoon Toasted sesame oil
- One fourth cup green onions

**Steps of preparation**

- Heat 2 tablespoons of olive oil in a large pan over medium heat. Include the strips of chicken and add salt and pepper. Now cook for 4-5 minutes, turning once, until chicken is crispy and just cooked thru.
- Remove the chicken from the pan, set it aside, then cover to keep it warm.
- Apply the remaining two tbsp (30 ml) of olive oil in a pan. Include the crushed garlic and then sauté for around a minute until aromatic.
- Include the broccoli and the bell pepper. Cook for 3-4 minutes before the broccoli begins to turn bright green, and the peppers tend to soften.
- Add the broth of bone. To deglaze, scrape the base of the pan. Reduce to medium temperature. Cover the pan and simmer for 3-5 minutes, until the broccoli is crisp.
- Transfer coconut aminos to pan, scrape the bottom of the pan and deglaze again. Put the chicken back in the pan. Transfer the rice to the cauliflower. Heat up to medium-high again. Now Stir for 3-4 minutes, before the cauliflower is tender but not mushy, most liquid evaporates, and the chicken is fully cooked through.
- Remove from the heat. Cover in toasted sesame oil. Add salt and black pepper if necessary. Cover with green onion, as needed

## 18. Keto Tomato chicken zoodles

Servings: 4 | Total time: 20 min

Calories: 411 kcal | Proteins: 45 g | Carbohydrates: 11 g | Fat: 18.8 g

**Ingredients**

- Coconut butter ½ tsp
- Diced onion 1 medium
- Chicken fillets 450- 500 g
- Garlic clove, 1 minced
- Zucchinis two medium
- Crushed tomatoes 400 g
- Chop half 7-10 cherry tomatoes
- Cashews 100 g
- Salt

- Dry oregano & basil
- Black pepper

**Steps of preparation**

- Heat a wide pan over medium heat. Add the coconut butter and the sliced onion. Cook for about 30 seconds to about 1 minute. Be alert, so you don't roast the onions.
- Slice the chicken into 2 cm chunks.
- Apply chicken and garlic to the pan. Season with the basil, the oregano salt and black pepper. Cook the chicken for about 5-6 minutes each side.
- Spiralize the zucchini when the chicken is frying. Cut them short when they're wanted. Use the vegetable peeler to create the ribbons out from the zucchini.
- Add the crushed tomatoes and simmer for about 3-5 minutes.
- Cook the cashews in another pan until golden brown. Taste and adjust with paprika, some turmeric and salt.
- Now add the spiralled zoodles, some cherry tomatoes and sprinkle with extra salt as appropriate. Cook for the next 1 minute and then switch off the heat.
- Now serve chicken zoodles with crispy cashews and the fresh basil.

## 19. Tuscan garlic chicken

Servings: 6 | Total time: 25 min

Calories: 225 kcal | Proteins: 30 g | Carbohydrates: 7 g | Fat: 25 g

***Ingredients***

- *Boneless chicken breasts 1½ pounds*
- *Olive oil 2 Tablespoons*
- *Heavy cream 1 cup*
- *Chicken broth 1/2 cup*
- *Garlic powder 1 teaspoon*
- *Italian seasoning 1 teaspoon*
- *Parmesan cheese 1/2 cup*
- *Chopped spinach 1 cup*
- *Dried tomatoes 1/2 cup*

***Steps of Preparation***

- Put olive oil in a wide skillet and cook chicken on medium heat for about 3-5 minutes on every side or until it gets brown on each side and then cook until the middle is no longer pink. Remove the chicken and put it aside on a tray.
- Include some of the chicken broth, the garlic powder, the heavy cream, the Italian seasoning and also some parmesan cheese. Simmer over on a medium-high flame until it thickens. Include the spinach and the tomatoes and then cook before the spinach becomes soggy. Transfer the chicken onto the plate.
- Serve over pasta.

## 20. Turkey and peppers

Servings: 4 | Total time: 20 min

Calories: 230 kcal | Proteins: 30 g | Carbohydrates: 11 g | Fat: 8 g

**Ingredients**

- Salt 1 teaspoon
- Turkey tenderloin 1 pound
- Olive oil 2 tablespoons
- Sliced onion ½ large
- Red bell pepper 1
- Yellow bell pepper 1
- Italian seasoning ½ teaspoon
- Black pepper ¼ teaspoon
- Vinegar 2 teaspoons
- Crushed tomatoes 14-ounce
- Parsley and basil for garnishing

**Steps of preparation**

- Sprinkle outa 1/2 teaspoon of salt over the turkey. Heat 1 tablespoon of the oil in a wide non-stick pan over medium heat. Include almost half of the turkey and then cook until golden brown on the rim, for 1 to 3 minutes. Flip and continue to cook for 2 minutes. Now remove the turkey from the slotted spatula to the tray, cover with foil to keep it warm. Apply the remaining 1 tablespoon of oil to the pan, reduce the heat to low and then repeat with the remaining turkey for 1 to 3 minutes per side.

- Transfer the onion, the bell peppers and the remainder 1/2 teaspoon of the salt to the pan, cover and simmer, then remove the lid and stir often, until the onion and the peppers are softened and golden brown in the spots for almost 5 to 7 minutes.
- Replace the cover, raise the heat to almost medium-high, then sprinkle with Italian seasoning and pepper and roast with stirring constantly before the herbs are fragrant for around 30 seconds. Now add vinegar and then cook until almost fully evaporated, for around 20 seconds. Put tomatoes and bring to a simmer, stirring regularly.
- Transfer the turkey to the pan with any leftover juices and bring to simmer. Now reduce the heat to medium-low and then cook until the turkey is hot all through the sauce for almost 1 to 2 minutes. Serve topped with parsley and basil if it's used.

## 21. Ketogenic Ginger butter chicken

Servings: 4 | Total time: 20 min

Calories: 293 kcal | Proteins: 29 g | Carbohydrates: 9 g | Fat: 17 g

**Ingredients**

- Cubed chicken breast 1.5 pounds
- Garam masala 2 tablespoons
- Fresh ginger grated 3 teaspoons
- Minced garlic 3 teaspoons
- Greek yogurt 4 ounces
- Coconut oil 1 tablespoon
- Ghee 2 tablespoons
- Onion sliced 1
- Fresh ginger grated 2 teaspoons
- Minced garlic 2 teaspoons
- Can crushed tomatoes 14.5 oz
- Ground coriander 1 tablespoon
- Garam masala ½ tablespoon

- Cumin 2 teaspoons
- Chili powder 1 teaspoon
- Heavy cream ½ cup
- Salt
- Cilantro

**Instruction**

- Slice chicken into 2 inches pieces and put in a wide bowl with 2 teaspoons of garam masala, one teaspoon of fried ginger and one teaspoon of minced garlic. Attach the yogurt, whisk to mix. Transfer to the refrigerator and cool for at least 30 minutes.
- Place the onion, ginger, garlic, and spices and crushed tomatoes in a blender and blend until soft. Set it aside
- Heat 1 tablespoon oil in a wide pan over medium heat. Put chicken and marinade in the pan, fry three to four minutes per side. After browning, add in the sauce and simmer for 5 to 6 minutes.
- Mix in the heavy cream and ghee and proceed to cook for another minute. Taste the salt and apply the extra if necessary. Cover with cilantro and, if needed, serve with some cauliflower rice.

## 22. Keto BLT Lettuce Wraps

Total Time: 25 minutes | Servings: 4

Calories: Kcal 368 |Fat: 30.8g |Net Carbs: 15.8g |Protein: 11.6g

**Ingredients**

- From 1 med head butter lettuce 8 leaves, like Bibb or Boston
- Bacon 6 slices
- Mayonnaise 2 tbsp
- Fine chopped chives 1 tbsp
- Squeezed freshly lemon juice 1 tbsp
- Black pepper ground freshly 1/8 tsp
- Grape tomatoes half or pint cherry 1
- Diced avocado 1 med

**Steps of Preparation**

- Set up a rack in the bottom third of the oven and to 400 ° F heat it. Lined a baking sheet with an aluminum foil or parchment paper.
- Place the bacon in one layer onto the baking sheet. Bake 15 to 20 mins until crispy and rich golden-brown. From the oven, Remove and allow cool. Alternatively, in a shallow pot, mix the mayonnaise, lemon juice, chives, and pepper; set aside.
- Move the bacon to a cutting board until it's cold and chop it roughly. Load a single leaf of lettuce with tomatoes, avocado, and bacon. Drizzle with the dressing, then serve.

## 23. Chipotle Avocado Mayonnaise

Total Time: 5 minutes | Serving 1

Calories Kcal 188 | Fat: 18.9g | Net Carbs: 5.8g | Protein: 1.4g

**Ingredients**

- Medium avocados 2 ripe
- Chipotle chile canned finely chopped in adobo sauce 1 tsp
- Dijon mustard 1 tsp
- Lemon juice freshly squeezed 1 tsp
- Kosher salt 1/2 tsp
- Olive oil 1/4 cup

**Steps of Preparation**

- In a mini food processor or blender, place the chipotle chili, avocados, in adobo sauce, lemon juice, Dijon mustard, and kosher salt. Process till smooth, for 30 - 1 minute. Scrape the bowl or pitcher side. Switch on the machine and drizzle gradually into the oil. Blend, about 1 minute, till smooth & emulsified.

## 24. Keto Egg Dinner Muffins

Total Time:15 minutes | Serving 12 muffins

Calories: Kcal 227 | Fat: 7.3g | Net Carbs: 5.3g | Protein: 11.7g

**Ingredients**

- Olive oil or Cooking spray
- Sweet potato shredded 1 1/2 cups
- Cheddar cheese shredded sharp 1 cup
- Strips bacon sugar-free, crumbled 6 cooked
- Large eggs 10
- Kosher salt 1 teaspoon
- Black pepper freshly ground 1/4 tsp

**Steps of Preparation**

- Arrange a middle-rack in -oven and to 400 ° F heat. Coat a regular 12 well muffin tray generously with olive oil or cooking spray. Divide the sliced sweet potato, bacon, and cheese equally throughout the wells of muffins.
- In a big cup, put the eggs, half-&-a-half, pepper, and salt and whisk till the eggs are thoroughly integrated. Pour in the wells of the muffins, filling 1/2 to 3/4 complete each.
- Bake for 12 - 14 minutes, till the muffins, are set and brown slightly around edges. On a wire rack, place the pan and allow it to cool for 2 - 3 mins. Run the butter knife to the release of the muffins around cups each of them before extracting them. Serve cold or warm, before cooling or freezing, absolutely on a wire rack.

## 25. Prosciutto-Wrapped Avocado with Arugula and Goat Cheese

Total Time: 15 minutes | Servings 4

Calories: Kcal 295 | Fat: 23.1 | Net Carbs: 9.6g | Protein: 15.4g

**Ingredients**

- Goat cheese fresh 4 ounces
- Lemon juice freshly squeezed 2 tbsp
- Black pepper freshly ground 1/2 tsp
- Kosher salt 1/4 tsp
- Prosciutto 8 thin slices
- Arugula 1 1/2 cups
- Thinly sliced avocados ripe medium 2

**Steps of Preparation**

- In a shallow pot, mix the goat cheese, lemon juice, salt, and pepper until smooth. Place pieces of the prosciutto. Layer single slice of prosciutto with 2 - 3 tsp of goat cheese mixture. Split the arugula into the prosciutto, placing the greens on one end of each piece. Cover each pile of greens similarly with 2–3 slices of avocado. Operating with one prosciutto slice at a time, then wrapping up into a compact package beginning with the avocado from the end.

## 26. Garlic Butter Steak Bites

Total Time: 20 minutes | Serving: 2-4

Calories: Kcal 748 |Fat: 61.9g| Net Carbs: 1.4g |Protein: 44.4g

**Ingredients**

- Garlic 4 cloves
- Black pepper freshly ground 1/2 teaspoon
- Parsley leaves chopped fresh 1/4 cup
- Thick-cut strip steaks New York 2 pounds
- Kosher salt 1/2 teaspoon
- Unsalted butter 8 tablespoons

**Steps of Preparation**

- Mince 4 cloves of garlic. Place in a cup and apply 1/2 tsp of black pepper freshly ground. Cut until 1/4 cup of fresh parsley leaves is available, then move to a small pot. Cut 2 pounds of strip steak New York into 1-inch pieces, then apply 1/2 tsp of kosher salt to season.
- Melt 8 tbsp (1 stick) of unsalted butter over medium-high heat in a large skillet. Attach the steak cubes then sear till browned, tossing them halfway through, taking 6 - 8 mins. Add the pepper and garlic, and simmer for another 1 minute. Take off the heat and with the parsley garnish.

## 27. Pesto Chicken with Burst Cherry Tomatoes

Total Time: 25-30 minutes | Serving 4

Calories: Kcal 445 | Fat: 16.2g |Net Carbs: 8.2g |Protein: 63.6g

**Ingredients**

- Grape tomatoes or pints cherry 2

- Olive oil 1 tbsp
- Kosher salt 1/2 tsp
- Black pepper freshly ground 1/4 tsp
- Chicken breasts boneless, skinless 4
- Basil pesto 1/4 cup

**Steps of Preparation**

- Place a rack in the center of the oven and to 400 ° F heat the oven.
- Put the tomatoes on a baking sheet, which is rimmed. Remove the grease, season with pepper and salt, and mix. Spread out over a single sheet.
- Pat, the chicken, completely dries it with paper towels. Season with pepper and salt. Put the chicken on the baking sheet in the middle. Spread the pesto on each chicken breast (about 1 tbsp each), spread on a thin layer, so each breast is covered evenly and fully.
- Roast until caramelized the tomatoes have, and others have burst and cooked the chicken and registers 165 ° F, 25 - 30 mins, on a thermometer. Serve the drizzled chicken and tomatoes with pan juices.

## 28. Scrambled eggs with basil and butter

Total Time: 10 mins |Serving 1

Calories: Kcal 641 | Fat:59g |Net Carbs:3g | Protein:26g

**Ingredients**

- Butter 2 tbsp
- Eggs 2
- Heavy whipping cream 2 tbsp
- Ground black pepper & salt
- Shredded cheese 2 oz
- Fresh basil 2 tbsp

**Steps of Preparation**

- Melt butter over low heat in a saucepan.

- In a small cup, put cracked eggs, shredded cheese, cream, and seasoning. Offer it a quick whisk and apply it to the saucepan.
- Push from the side to the middle with a spatula before the eggs are scrambled. If you want fluffy and soft, mix on lower heat to desired consistency.

## 29. Keto seafood special omelet

Total Time: 20 mins |Serving 2

Calories: Kcal 872| Fat:83g |Net Carbs:4g| Protein:27g

**Ingredients**

- Olive oil 2 tbsp
- Cooked shrimp 5 oz
- Red chili pepper 1
- ½ tsp fennel seeds or ground cumin
- Mayonnaise ½ cup
- Fresh chives 1 tbsp
- Eggs 6
- Olive oil 2 tbsp
- Salt & pepper

**Steps of Preparation**

- Preheat the broiler.
- In olive oil, broil the seafood or shrimp mixture with the chopped garlic, chili, cumin, fennel seeds, salt & pepper.
- To cooled seafood mixture, apply mayo and chives.
- Whisk the eggs together, season with salt & pepper, and cook in a non-stick saucepan with butter or oil.
- When the omelet is nearly full, apply the seafood mixture. Fold. Reduce the heat and enable it to set fully. Serve.

## 30. Keto Fried eggs

Total Time: 10 mins |Serving 4

Per serving: Kcal 226, Fat:20g, Net Carbs:1g Protein:11g

**Ingredients**

- Butter 4 tbsp
- Eggs 8
- Salt & pepper

**Steps of Preparation**

- Heat coconut oil or butter over medium heat in a frying pan.
- Break the eggs directly into the saucepan. For sunny side up eggs, allow the eggs to be fried on one side. Cover the saucepan with a lid to ensure that they are fried on top. For eggs that are easily cooked, turn over the eggs after a few mins and then cook for another.
- Season with salt & pepper.

## 31. Keto egg butter with smoked salmon and avocado

Total Time: 20 mins |Serving 2

Calories: 1148, Fat:112g, Net Carbs:5g Protein:26g

**Ingredients**

- Eggs 4
- Sea salt ½ tsp
- Ground black pepper ¼ tsp
- Butter 5 oz
- Avocados 2
- Olive oil 2 tbsp
- Chopped fresh parsley 1 tbsp
- Smoked salmon 4 oz

**Steps of Preparation**

- Carefully put the eggs in a pot. Cover with colder water and place without the lid on the stove. Get the water to boil.
- Reduce heat and allow to simmer for 7-8 mins, from the warmed water. Remove the eggs and put them in an ice-cold bowl to cool.

- Peel and chop the eggs completely. Combine the eggs with the butter with the fork. Season with the pepper, salt, and other spices of your choosing
- Serve.

## 32. Ketogenic scallions egg muffins

Total Time: 25 mins |Serving 6

Calories: Kcal 336, Fat:26g, Net Carbs:2g Protein:23g

**Ingredients**

- Finely chopped scallions 2
- Chopped air-dried chorizo 5 oz.
- Eggs 12
- Salt & pepper
- Shredded cheese 6 oz

**Steps of Preparation**

- Preheat an oven to 175 ° C (350 ° F).
- Line a non-stick muffin tray with insertable baking cups/grease, a buttered silicone muffin tin.
- Apply the chorizo and scallions to the tin base.
- Mix the eggs with the pesto, pepper, and salt then incorporate the cheese and mix.
- Pour the batter over the scallions and the chorizo.
- Bake the muffin tin for 15–20 mins, depending on the scale.

## 33. Keto fried eggs with kale and pork

Total Time:20 mins |Serving 2

Calories: Kcal 1033, Fat:99g, Net Carbs:8g Protein:26g

**Ingredients**

- Kale ½ lb.
- Butter 3 oz
- Smoked pork belly 6 oz
- Frozen cranberries 1 oz
- Pecans 1 oz.

- Eggs 4
- Salt & pepper

**Steps of Preparation**

- Chop and Trim the kale into wide squares. Melt 2/3rd of the butter in the frying pan and cook the kale rapidly over high heat until the sides are slightly browned.
- From the frying pan, Remove the kale and put aside. Cook the bacon or pork belly in the frying pan until it is crisp.
- Reduce heat. The sautéed kale is Returned to the saucepan and add the nuts and cranberries. Remove until soft
- Turn the flame on the rest of the butter and fry the eggs. Add Salt and pepper. Put two fried eggs for each part of the greens and serve.

## 34. Keto Croque Monsieur

Total Time: 20 mins |Serving 2

Calories: Kcal 1083, Fat:92g, Net Carbs:8g Protein:54g

**Ingredients**

- Cottage cheese 8 oz
- Eggs 4
- Husk powder ground psyllium 1 tbsp
- Butter 4 tbsp
- deli ham 51/3 oz
- Cheddar cheese 51/3 oz
- Lettuce 3½ oz.
- Olive oil 4 tbsp
- Red wine vinegar ½ tbsp
- Salt & pepper

**Steps of Preparation**

- In a bowl, whisk the eggs. Blend in cottage cheese. Apply a psyllium husk powder ground when stirring in order incorporate it without lumps smoothly. Rest the mixture for five minutes before the batter has formed.
- Put the frying pan over med heat. Apply a large quantity of butter and cook the batter like tiny pancakes on either side for a few minutes, until they are brown.
- Create a sandwich between the two warm pancakes with cheese and sliced ham. Add finely diced onion on top.
- Wash and cut the lettuce. In a clear vinaigrette, add the oil, vinegar, salt, and pepper.

## 35. Veggie keto scramble

Total Time: 20 mins |Serving 1

Calories: Kcal 415, Fat:31g, Net Carbs:4g Protein:28g

**Ingredients**

- Butter 1 tbsp
- Sliced mushrooms 1 oz.
- Eggs 3
- Diced red bell peppers 1 oz
- Ground black pepper & salt
- Shredded parmesan cheese 1 oz
- Chopped scallion ½

**Steps of Preparation**

- Heat the butter over medium heat in a wide frying pan. Add the sliced mushrooms, diced red peppers, salt, and fry until tender.
- Put the eggs directly into the saucepan and quickly mix so that it is properly incorporated.
- Transfer the spatula to create big, soft curds over the bottom and side of the skillet. Cook until no clear liquid egg remains.
- Put the scramble with scallions and shredded parmesan on top.

## 36. Keto dinner chaffles

Time: 25 mins |Serving 4

Calories: Kcal 599, Fat:50g, Net Carbs:4g Protein:32g

**Ingredients**

- Eggs 4
- Shredded cheddar cheese 8 oz
- Chopped fresh chives 2 tbsp
- Salt & pepper

Toppings

- Eggs 4
- Sliced bacon 8
- Sliced cherry tomatoes 8
- Baby spinach 2 oz

**Steps of Preparation**

- Heat the waffle maker.
- Place the bacon slices in a big, unheated frying pan and raise the temperature to med heat. Cook the bacon for around 8-12 mins, regularly rotating, until it is crispy to taste.
- Set aside to cool as you cook the chaffles on a paper towel.
- Put all ingredients of your waffle in a mixing bowl & beat to blend.
- Grind the waffle iron lightly and spoon the mixture equally over the bottom surface, spreading it out to achieve an even outcome.
- Shut the waffle iron then cook according to the waffle maker for approx. 6 mins.
- Break the eggs in the bacon grease in the frying pan as the chaffles are heating, then cook softly until finished.
- Serve with scrambled egg and baby spinach, bacon strips, and cherry tomatoes on each chaffles side.

# Chapter 5: Keto snacks recipes for women above 50

## 1. Keto Tortilla Chips

Servings: 10 chips | Total time: 40 min

Calories: 198 kcal | Proteins: 11 g | Carbohydrates: 4 g | Fat: 16 g

**Ingredients**

- shredded mozzarella 2 cups

- almond flour 1 cups
- kosher salt 1 teaspoon
- garlic powder 1 teaspoon
- chili powder half teaspoon
- Black pepper

**Steps of preparation**

- Preheat the oven to 350 ° F. Place two big baking sheets of parchment paper.
- Melt mozzarella in a microwave safe jar, around 1 minute and 30 seconds. Include almond flour, cinnamon, garlic powder, chili powder and several cracks of black pepper. Use your hands to knead the dough a few times until the ball is smooth.
- Put the dough between the two sheets of the parchment paper and then roll it into a rectangle 1/8 "wide. Break the dough into triangles by using a knife.
- Scatter the chips on the lined baking sheets and cook until the sides are crispy and begin to be crisp, for 12 to 14 minutes.

## 2. Ketogenic Avocado Chips

Servings: 6 chips | Total time: 30 min

Calories: 171 kcal | Proteins: 7 g | Carbohydrates: 6 g | Fat: 16 g

**Ingredients**

- Ripe avocado 1 large
- Freshly grated parmesan 3/4 cup.
- Lemon juice 1 teaspoon
- Garlic powder half teaspoon

- Italian seasoning half teaspoon
- A pinch of kosher salt
- Black pepper

**Steps of preparation**

- Start by Preheating the oven to 325 ° f and then line two baking sheets with a parchment paper. In a medium dish, mash the avocado with a fork until it is smooth. Stir in Parmesan, some lemon juice, some garlic powder and also Italian seasonings. Season with salt and pepper.
- Put the heaping teaspoon-sized mixture scoops on the baking sheet, leaving around 3 "apart across each scoop. Deflate each scoop to 3 "wide with the wooden spoon or a cup. Now bake it until it is crispy and golden, for about 30 minutes, then let it cool to room temperature. Serve at room temperature.
- 

## 3. Ketogenic Nacho Cheese Crisps

Servings: 9 chips | Total time: 1 hr. min

Calories:99 kcal | Proteins: 6 g | Carbohydrates:1.3 g | Fat: 7 g

**Ingredients**

- Sliced cheddar 8-oz.
- Taco seasoning 2 tsp.

**Steps of preparation**

- Start by preheating the oven to 250° and then line a baking sheet with a parchment paper. Now cut slices of cheese into about 9 squares and then place them in a medium bowl. Now add the taco seasoning.

- Put cheese slices on the prepared baking sheet. Now bake them until crisp and golden brown, for about 40 minutes. Let them cool for 10 minutes and then remove from the parchment paper.

## 4. Ketogenic coconut vanilla Ice Cream

Servings: 3 | Total time: 10 min

Calories: 347 kcal | Proteins: 2 g | Carbohydrates: 3 g | Fat: 36 g

**Ingredients**

- Coconut milk 15-oz.
- Heavy cream 2 cup
- Swerve sweetener 1/4 cup
- Vanilla extract 1 tsp.
- A Pinch of kosher salt

**Steps of preparation**

- Start by chilling the coconut milk in the refrigerator for about 3 hours, preferably overnight.
- place the coconut cream in a big tub, leave the liquid in a can, using a hand blender to beat the coconut cream till it is very smooth. Set it back.
- Beat heavy cream in a separate wide bowl using a hand blender (or a stand mixer in a bowl) until soft peaks are created. Beat the sweetener and the vanilla.
- Fold the mixed coconut into the whipped cream, then move the mixture to the loaf tray.
- Freeze to a solid condition, around 5 hours.

## 5. Jalapeno popping Egg Cups

Servings: 12 cups | Total time: 45 min

Calories: 157 kcal | Proteins: 9.7 g | Carbohydrates: 1.3 g | Fat: 9.7 g

**Ingredients**

- bacon 12 slices
- large eggs 10
- sour cream 1/4 c.
- shredded cheddar half c.
- shredded mozzarella half c.
- sliced 2 jalapeños
- a pinch of kosher salt
- black pepper
- cooking spray

**Steps of preparation**

- Start by preheating the oven to 375° F. Cook bacon till it becomes slightly browned in a large pan over a medium flame, to drain, set it aside on a plate lined with paper towel.
- In a separate bowl, mix the eggs together with cheeses, minced jalapeño, sour cream, and garlic powder. Now season with salt and pepper.
- Grease a muffin tin through nonstick cooking spray. Put a slice of bacon and line each well, put egg mixture into every muffin cup. Garnish each muffin with a jalapeño slice.
- Now bake for almost 20 minutes, or till the eggs are no longer looking wet. Now Cool them slightly.
- Remove from the muffin tin and serve.

## 6. Ketogenic Bacon Guac Bombs

Servings: 1 | Total time: 45 min

Calories: 156 kcal | Proteins: 3.4 g | Carbohydrates: 1.4 g | Fat:15.2 g

**Ingredients**

- cooked 12 slices bacon
- mashed 2 avocados
- cream cheese 6 oz.
- 1 lime Juice
- minced garlic 1 clove
- minced 1/4 red onion
- jalapeno chopped 1 small
- cumin half tsp.
- Chili powder half tsp.
- A pinch of Kosher salt
- black pepper

**Steps of preparation**

- In a large bowl, put all the ingredients of the guacamole. Stir until it is mostly smooth and then season with the salt and pepper. Put gently in the refrigerator for almost 30 minutes.
- Put the crumbling bacon on a wide tray. Scoop the guacamole mixture with a little cookie scoop and put in the bacon. Roll to coat the bacon. Repeat before both guacamole and bacon are used. Store in the freezer.

## 7. Ketogenic TPW White Choc Truffles

Servings: 1 | Total time: 1 hour 15 min

Calories: 102 Kcal, | Fat: 7g | Protein: 7g | Carbohydrates: 3g

**Ingredients**

- Pea Protein 60g
- Chocolate Fudge 80g
- Syrup Honey flavor 10g
- dark chocolate 100g
- chopped salted peanuts 70g

**Steps of preparation**

- Mix the pea protein 80, the honey and the stuffed nuts in a wide bowl until mixed. If the mixture is too dry, apply some peanut butter. Apply more protein powder if the combination is too sticky.
- When your mixture is the consistency, you can accommodate, roll it into equal-sized balls (as large or small as you choose) and put it on a cling film or baking tray that is parchment lined. Refrigerate for an hour.
- When they're chilling, start to melt the chocolate in a heat-resistant container, either in a microwave or in a glass bowl over a boiling water pan.
- When melted, allow to cool moderately and cover with a cling film or with a baking sheet.
- Take the balls from the refrigerator and use a skewer coat in dark chocolate until each ball it is fully coated.
- Return to a baking tray and then sprinkle each truffle with salted chopped peanuts until coated.
- Return to the refrigerator for at least an hour to rest before dining.
- Remove and let it rest for a minute or two until you feed. Enjoy!

## 8. Brownie Fat Bombs

Servings: 1 | Total time: 45 min

Calories 118 Kcal | Carbs: 2g |Protein: 5g |Fat: 9g

**Ingredients**

- Smooth peanut butter 250g
- Cocoa 65g
- Zero syrup 2-4 tbsp
- Coconut oil 2 tbsp
- Salt ¼ tsp

**Steps of preparation**

- Simply transfer all the ingredients to the food processor, rubbing near the bottom, if necessary, until mixed into a dough.
- While using liquid sweetener or Zero Syrup or a coconut oil, refrigerate dough in refrigerator till the mixture is solid enough to scoop into a little scoop or spoonful of ice cream. Roll in the balls of your perfect size and serve and enjoy!

## 9. Cheesy Stuffed Mushrooms

Servings: 12 | Total time: 15 min

Calories: 72 Kcal, |Fat: 7g |Protein: 6g | Carbohydrates: 0g Fat: 5g

**Ingredients**

- Bacon 225g

- Mushrooms 12
- Butter 2 tbsp
- Cream cheese 200g
- Finely chopped 3 tbsp chives,
- Paprika powder 1 tsp
- Salt and pepper

**Steps of preparation**

- Start by preheating the oven to 200 ° F.
- Now fry the bacon until it becomes really crisp. Enable to cool and afterward toss into the crumbs – save the fat of the bacon.
- Take the stems from the shrooms and cut them finely. Fry in the bacon fat, add the butter if needed.
- In a dish, blend the bacon crumbs with the fried mushroom stems and the leftover marinade.
- Cover each of the mushrooms with a mixture and then bake for 20 minutes until it gets golden brown.

## 10. Keto Peanut Butter Granola

Servings: 12 | Total time: 40 min

Calories: 338 Kcal, | Fat: 30g | Protein: 9g | Carbohydrates: 9g

**Ingredients**

- Almonds 1 1/2 cups
- Pecans 1 1/2 cups
- Coconut 1 cup shredded
- Sunflower seeds 1/4 cup
- Swerve Sweetener 1/3 cup
- Vanilla 1/3 cup
- Peanut butter 1/3 cup
- Butter 1/4 cup
- Water 1/4 cup

**Steps of preparation**

- Preheat the oven to 300F and line a wide-rimmed baking tray with a parchment paper.
- Process the almonds and pecans in a processor until they match rough crumbs with some bigger parts. Now transfer them to a large bowl and then mix in a, sunflower seeds, shredded coconut, sweetener and some vanilla extract.
- Now melt the peanut butter and the butter together in a microwave safe jar.
- Pour the molten peanut butter mixture over the nut mixture and combine gently, stirring gently. Stir it in the water. Mixture is going to clump together.
- Now spread mixture uniformly on the prepared lined baking sheet for 30 minutes, by stirring halfway through. Now remove and let it cool off completely.

## 11. Ketogenic hot caramel chocolate

Servings: 1 | Total time: 6 min

Calories: 144 Kcal, | Fat: 14g | Protein: 14g | Carbohydrates: 4g

**Ingredients**

- Unsweetened almond milk 1/2 cup
- Heavy whipping cream 2 tbsp
- Cocoa powder 1 tbsp
- Salted caramel collagen 1 to 2 tbsp
- Liquid sweetener
- Whipped cream
- Caramel sauce

**Steps of preparation**

- Combine almond or the hemp milk and heavy cream in a pan over medium heat. Get it to a boil.
- In a mixer, incorporate the chocolate powder and the collagen. Put in the hot milk and mix until the milk is frothy.
- Top with thinly sweetened ice cream and a caramel sauce to top it off!

## 12. Ketogenic brownie bark

Servings: 12 | Total time: 45 min

Calories: 98 Kcal, | Fat: 8.3g | Protein: 2.4g | Carbohydrates: 4.3g

**Ingredients**

- Almond flour 1/2 cup
- Baking powder 1/2 tsp
- Salt 1/4 tsp
- Room temperature 2 leg whites
- Swerve sweetener 1/2 cup
- Cocoa powder 3 tbsp
- Instant coffee 1 tsp
- Butter melted 1/4 cup
- Heavy whipping cream 1 tbsp
- Vanilla 1/2 tsp
- Chocolate chips 1/3 cups

**Steps of Preparation**

- Start by preheating the oven to 325F and place parchment paper on a baking sheet. Lubricate the parchment paper with oil.
- In a small cup, mix together the flour, baking powder and the salt.
- Mix the egg whites in a large bowl until it becomes foggy. Mix in the sweetener, chocolate powder and some instant coffee until it becomes smooth and then mix in the melted butter, cream and the vanilla. Mix in a mixture with almond flour until it is well mixed.
- Now spread the batter on the lubricated parchment in a square of around 12 by 12 inches. Sprinkle some chocolate chips.
- Now bake for 18 minutes, until it is puffed and all set. Remove from the oven, turn the oven off and let it cool for 15 minutes.
- Using a sharp knife, cut through 2-inch squares, but do not detach. Return to a warm oven for about 5 to 10 minutes and toast lightly.
- Remove, let it cool fully, then divide into squares.

## 13. Ketogenic Homemade Nutella

Servings: 6 | Total time: 20 min

Calories: 158 Kcal, | Fat: 18.3g | Protein: 3.3g | Carbohydrates: 18 g

**Ingredients**

- Hazelnuts toasted 3/4 cup
- Coconut oil 2 to 3 tbsp
- Cocoa powder 2 tbsp
- Powdered swerve sweetener 2 tbsp
- Vanilla extract 1/2 tsp
- Pinch salt

**Steps of Preparation**

- Grind hazelnuts in a processor until finely ground and starts to clump together.
- Now add two tablespoons oil and keep on grinding until the nuts become smooth out. Add remaining of the ingredients and then blend until well mixed. in case of thick mixture, add one more tablespoon oil.

## 14. Ketogenic snickerdoodle truffles

Servings: 24 truffles yield | Total time: 20 min

Calories: 150 Kcal, | Fat: 14g | Protein: 3g | Carbohydrates: 13 g

**Ingredients**

- Almond flour 2 cups
- Swerve 1/2 cup
- Cream of tartar 1 tsp
- Ground cinnamon 1 tsp
- Salt 1/4 tsp
- Butter 6 tbsp
- Vanilla extract 1 tsp
- Swerve 3 tbsp
- Ground cinnamon 1 tsp

**Steps of preparation**

- In a large bowl, mix together the Swerve, the cream of tartar, the almond flour, cinnamon, and the salt. Now stir in melted butter and some vanilla extract till the dough is combined. Add a tablespoon of water in case of hard dough and stir together.
- Now scoop dough with rounded tablespoon and then squeeze in the palm and hold together, now roll into a ball. Transfer on a waxed paper which is lined on a cookie sheet, and then repeat.
- In a small bowl, mix together the cinnamon and the Swerve. Now roll the truffles in this coating.
- Serve.

## 15. Chocolate chip keto cookies

Servings: 20 | Total time: 30 min

Calories: 238 kcal | Proteins: 4.3 g | Carbohydrates: 8.18 g | Fat:21.5 g

**Ingredients**

- Almond flour 1 1/4 cups
- Unsweetened coconut 3/4 cups
- Baking powder 1 tsp
- Salt 1/2 tsp
- Butter softened 1/2 cup
- Swerve sweetener 1/2 cup
- Yacon syrup or molasses 2 tsp
- Vanilla extract 1/2 tsp
- Egg 1 large
- Chocolate chips sugar-free 1 cup

**Steps of preparation**

- Start by preheating the oven to a temperature of 325F and then line a baking sheet with the parchment paper.
- In a small bowl, mix together some almond flour, baking powder, salt and coconut.
- In a big bowl, add cream butter and the Swerve Sweetener along with molasses. Add in vanilla and egg, beat until well mixed. Now beat in some flour mixture till dough is well mixed completely.

- Mix in some chocolate chips.
- Now shape the dough into small balls and then place them 2 inches apart on the lined baking sheet. Press the ball to a 1/4 inch of thickness.
- Now bake 12 to 15 minutes, till just starts to brown.
- Let cool completely on the pan after removing from oven.
- Serve.

## 16. Keto Fat Bomb with jam and Peanut butter

Servings: 12 | Total time: 45 min

Calories: 223 kcal | Proteins: 3.8 g | Carbohydrates: 4.5 g | Fat:21.5 g

**Ingredients**

- Raspberries 3/4 cup
- Water 1/4 cup
- powdered Swerve Sweetener 6 to 8 tbsp
- grass-fed gelatin 1 tsp
- creamy peanut butter 3/4 cup
- coconut oil 3/4 cup

**Steps of preparation**

- Fill a muffin tin with 12 liners of parchment paper.
- Mix the raspberries and water in a small saucepan. Bring it to a boil and lower the heat and simmer for 5 minutes. Now mash the berries with your fork.
- Mix in 2 to 4 tbsp of powdered sweetener, based on how sweet you want. Mix in the peanut butter and gelatin and let it cool.
- Mix peanut butter and the coconut oil in a microwave safe jar. Cook on maximum for 30 to 60 seconds, once it has melted. Whisk the powdered sweetener in 2 to 4 tbsp, depending about how sweet you want it.
- Partition half of peanut butter mixture into 12 cups and put in the freezer for around 15 minutes. Divide the mixture of raspberry between the cups then top with the remaining mixture of peanut butter.
- Chill in refrigerator until becomes solid.

## 17. Classic Blueberry Scones

Servings: 12 | Total time: 40 min

Calories: 223 kcal | Proteins: 5.5 g | Carbohydrates: 7.21 g | Fat:12 g

**Ingredients**

- Almond flour 2 cups
- swerve sweetener 1/3 cup
- coconut flour 1/4 cup
- Baking powder 1 tbsp
- Tsp salt 1/4
- Eggs 2 large
- Heavy whipping cream 1/4 cup
- Vanilla extract 1/2 tsp
- Fresh blueberries 3/4 cup

**Steps of Preparation**

- Preheat the oven to 325F and cover a big baking sheet with a silicone lining or a parchment paper.
- In a big bowl, mix together the rice, coconut flour, the baking powder, sweetener, and salt.
- Mix in the eggs, whipped cream and vanilla and combine until the dough starts to combine. Include the blueberries.
- Assemble the dough together and now place on the prepared baking sheet. Put in a rugged rectangle measuring 10 x 8 inches.
- Using a sharp, broad knife to break into six squares. Then split each of these squares laterally into the two triangles. Gently raise the scones and then scatter them across the tray.
- Bake for almost 25 minutes until becomes golden brown. Remove it and leave it cool.
- Serve.

## 18. Chocolate coconut cups

Servings: 20 | Total time: 20 min

Calories: 223 kcal | Proteins: 5.5 g | Carbohydrates: 7.21 g | Fat:12 g

**Ingredients**

- Coconut butter 1/2 cup
- Kelapo coconut oil 1/2 cup
- Unsweetened coconut 1/2 cup
- Powdered swerve sweetener 3 tbsp
- Ounces cocoa butter 1 & 1/2
- Unsweetened chocolate 1 ounce
- Powdered swerve sweetener 1/4 cup
- Cocoa powder 1/4 cup
- Vanilla extract 1/4 tsp

**Steps of preparation**

- For candies, cover a mini muffin tray with a 20 mini paper lining.
- Mix coconut butter and the coconut oil in a small saucepan over low flame. Stir until melted and creamy, then mix in the shredded coconut and the sweetener until merged.
- Divide the mixture between the prepared muffin cups and then freeze until solid, for around 30 minutes.
- For chocolate coating, mix cocoa butter and the unsweetened chocolate in a bowl placed on a pan of simmering water. Stir until it has melted.
- Mix in the sifted powdered sweetener and now stir in cocoa powder until smooth.
- Now remove from the heat and whisk in the extract of vanilla.
- Put chocolate topping over the coconut candies and then let it cook for around 15 minutes.
- Candies can be kept on your kitchen countertop for up to one week.

## 19. Roll biscotti

Servings: 15 | Total time: 1 hr. 20 min

Calories: 123 kcal | Proteins: 4 g | Carbohydrates: 4 g | Fat:12 g

**Ingredients**

- Swerve Sweetener 2 tbsp
- Ground cinnamon 1 tsp
- Almond flour Honeyville 2 cups

- Swerve Sweetener 1/3 cup
- Baking powder 1 tsp
- Xanthan gum 1/2 tsp
- Salt 1/4 tsp
- Melted butter 1/4 cup
- Egg 1 large
- Vanilla extract 1 tsp
- Swerve Sweetener 1/4 cup
- Heavy cream 2 tbsp
- Vanilla 1/2 tsp

**Steps of preparation**

- In a small bowl, combine the sweetener and the cinnamon for filling. Set it apart.
- Preheat the oven to a temperature of 325F, cover the baking sheet with the parchment paper.
- In a big bowl, whisk together the starch, baking powder, the xanthan gum, sweetener, and salt. Stir in 1/4 cup of butter, the egg and the vanilla extract before the dough fits together.
- Turn the dough onto the lined baking sheet and then half it in two. Shape each half into a rectangular shape of around 10 by 4 inches. Making sure the scale and form of both halves are identical.
- Sprinkle with around 2/3 of cinnamon filling. Cover with one of the other parts of the dough, close the seams and then smooth the cover.
- Bake for almost 25 minutes or until gently browned and solid to the touch. Transfer from the oven and spray the remaining melted butter on it, then dust with the leftover cinnamon mixture. Allow it to cool for about 30 minutes and reduce the temperature to 250F.
- Cut log into around 15 slices with sharp knife.
- Place the slices back on the cut-side in the baking sheet and bake for another 15 minutes, then turn over and bake for the next 15 minutes. Turn the oven off and let it stay within until it's cold.

## 20. Garahm crackers

Servings: 10 | Total time: 1 hr. 5 min

Calories: 156 kcal | Proteins: 5 g | Carbohydrates: 6 g | Fat:13 g

**Ingredients**

- Almond flour 2 cups
- Swerve brown 1/3 cup
- Cinnamon 2 tsp
- Baking powder 1 tsp
- A pinch of salt
- Egg 1 large
- Butter melted 2 tbsp
- Vanilla extract 1 tsp

**Steps of preparation**

- Preheat the oven to 300F for crackers.
- In a big cup, stir together flour, cinnamon, baking powder, sweetener, and salt. Stir in egg, melted butter, molasses and vanilla extract before the dough falls together.
- Transform the dough into a wide sheet of parchment paper and pat into a rough rectangle. Cover with a sheet of parchment. Print out the dough to around 1/8-inch thickness as uniformly as possible.
- Cut the top of the parchment and now use a sharp knife to rank around 2x2 inches in squares. Move the whole piece of parchment to the baking sheet.
- Bake for 20 to 30 minutes, until brown and strong. Remove the crackers and let them cool for 30 minutes, then split up along the score. Return to the warm oven if it's so far cooled off, turn it on and adjust the temperature to no higher than 200F). Let it sit for yet another 30 minutes, then cool absolutely.

# Conclusion

This book explained keto diet in detail, which is a high-fat, low-carbohydrate diet similar to Atkins & low-carb diets. It involves substantially reducing the consumption of carbohydrates and replacing them with fat. After reading this book, you will several unique concerns and subjects that relate mainly or exclusively to women over 50 on keto diet. There are some key takeaways for women above 50 on keto Diet and the problems one has to be aware of. After reading this book, you will learn some easy, rapid and simple recipes for women above 50. These include the breakfast, lunch and the dinner keto-based recipes, which are low in carbohydrates. This book also presented some delicious snacks and smoothies too. Some exercise and gym friendly recipes are also presented.

# Intermittent Fasting for Women Over 60

*The Science-Based Program for Seniors to Conquer and Keep a Young Body, Reset Your Metabolism and Activate Autophagy Above 60's*

*[11 Anti-Aging Exercises Included]*

**By**

**Dora Gray**

# Table of Contents

# INTRODUCTION

What exactly does intermittent fasting refer to? Almost all of us are familiar with the word fasting. The reasons people fast vary from one group to another. For some, it is a religious practice; they sacrifice food to commit to prayer. Others have no reason; they just lack food. In past societies, people would go out to the fields to work, and eat only when they rested.

Intermittent fasting is not among the fasting practices described above. It is neither a religious practice, nor is it driven by the lack of time or food - it is a choice. It is best described as an eating pattern that alternates between eating periods and fasting periods, with each period lasting a predetermined amount of time. For example, the 16:8 method has a fasting period of 16 hours and an eating period of 8 hours.

Note that it is not a diet but an eating pattern. Less is said about the foods you should eat, but more emphasis is put on when you eat them. Does this mean you can eat whatever you want? Unfortunately not. Just like anything else in life, you're going to get out what you put in. Clean eating is one of the three factors in the tripod to fat burning success. Does this mean you must live on chicken and broccoli? No of course not. We are humans and I believe in enjoying life, but as you already know moderation is the key here.

It is important to know that IF isn't some program that popped up from somewhere, will trend for a while, and disappear like most weight loss programs do. It has been around for a long time and has been popular for many years (even if you are learning about it just now). It is one of the leading health and fitness trends in the world today.

# PART ONE

## Knowledge (The Science-Based Program for Seniors to Conquer and Keep a Young Body)

## How Fat is Stored & Burnt

Intermittent fasting has been tried and found to be a powerful fat burning and weight loss tool. But how exactly does it work? Before delving into how IF works it's important to understand some key factors:

- How the body stores energy
- How the body uses energy
- Your hormones role in this process

The body is either in a state of storing energy or burning energy. There is no middle ground.

What does this mean? Well basically if you're not burning glucose (sugar) you're storing it as either glycogen or fat. Does this mean you need to be constantly working out? Short answer- no. In fact, exercise is only 10% - 15% of the weight loss equation (more about that later). Your body burns energy in a variety of different ways. Even when you're stationary doing absolutely nothing your body expends energy as it completes functions required for living. This is what RMR or BMR refers to. However, even though your cells might be using glucose and burning energy, any excess will be stored. This would count as a state of storage.

Wait! If we're either storing sugar or burning it, logic would dictate less food and more exercise equals weight loss. It seems straight forward, right? If you're reading this you have most likely tried this approach to no avail. You either saw results in the beginning only to have them come to a grinding halt or you put it all back on when you returned to your normal lifestyle.

So, how do I lose weight then?? To get a better picture we need to understand two principles:

1. How glucose (sugar) is stored and burned, or used for energy.
2. Our hormone's role in this process

## *How is energy stored?*

The body can store energy in two ways; glycogen and fat.

Food (yum) is broken down into a variety of different macronutrients through digestion. These macronutrients are absorbed into the bloodstream and transported throughout the body to our cells to use for various functions. For example, Carbohydrates are broken down into Glucose (sugar), absorbed by the blood stream and sent to cells to use for energy. However, if there is excess glucose in the bloodstream (high blood sugar), it will be stored as glycogen through a process called Glycogenesis. The body can only store so much glycogen. Once these stores are full any excess glucose is stored as fat through a process called Lipogenesis.

## *How is energy used?*

When our cells require more energy than the bloodstream can provide (low blood sugar) glycogen is turned back into glucose through a process called glycogenolysis. Our glycogen stores are slowly emptied to raise our blood sugar levels back to normal. When these stores are empty, fat will be broken down for energy in a process called lipolysis. Now we're burning fat Wahoo!

Summary

- Excess glucose will be turned into glycogen for storage, triggered by high blood sugar
- Once glycogen stores are full, excess glucose will be turned into fat for storage
- When blood sugar levels drop, glycogen will be turned back into glucose and added to the bloodstream
- When glycogen stores are emptied, fat will be broken down and released into the bloodstream for energy

Now you have a rough idea of how and why the body stores and uses energy, we will look at some key hormones that control this process.

*Why Low-Calorie Diets Don't Work*

Have you ever tried lowering your calories to lose weight? Did it work long term? Could you keep the weight you lost off? If you're reading this book, my guess is that it didn't, and you're not alone. Data from the UK show 1 in 124 obese women get results using this method, meaning the nutrition guidelines some professionals are following have a 99.5% fail rate. A quick goggle of what happened to the contestants on the hit TV series "The Biggest Loser" should be enough to put you off this method. This show is a classic example of why moving more and eating less only works in the short term, if at all. There is a reason there are few reunion shows. So why are low calorie diets flawed?

A study on 14 contestants on the biggest loser show revealed some alarming results six years after filming had finished. The initial results were impressive but as the study showed, they were short lived. Below are results of some of the factors tested.

Weight

- Average weight before filming: 328 lb./ 148 kg
- Average weight after 30 weeks on the show: 199 lb./ 90 kg
- Average weight six years after final: 290 lb./131 kg

As you can see, contestants lost a massive amount of weight during filming, but struggled to maintain the weight loss over a long period of time.

One of the 14 who participated in the study managed to keep the weight off. That's over a 95% fail rate! So why is this?

Check out the results below showing contestants Resting metabolic rate (RMR).

## Resting Metabolic Rate

RMR reflects the amount of energy or calories the body burns to stay alive without movement.

In some places this is measured in BMR or basal metabolic rate.

RMR is responsible for around 70% of your entire metabolism which is why the results below are shocking.

- Average RMR before filming: 2,607 kcal burned / day.
- Average RMR after 30 weeks on the show: 1,996 kcal burned / day.
- Average RMR six years after final weigh-in: 1,903 kcal burned / day.

As you can see, even though contestants put around 70% of their initial weight back on, their RMR did not raise back to its levels pre- filming. It stayed around 700 calories lower a day! This means to lose the same amount of weight second time round; contestants would need to eat 700 less calories than they did on the show. Considering the original diet consists of 1200 - 1500 calories with 90 minutes of exercise six days a week. This would be near impossible.

So why did the contestants RMR stay so low even when they put the weight back on?

## *Metabolic adaptation*

I mentioned BMR (basal metabolic rate) and RMR (resting metabolic rate) earlier. These both refer to how much energy (calories) your body uses to live without action and make up roughly 70% of your entire metabolism. When you sit in caloric deficit, the bodies BMR/RMR will slowly drop as it enters starvation mode, meaning it will burn less calories. Basically, your metabolism slows down. This is an important reaction through times of famine. The body doesn't want to use its stored energy, and naturally uses incoming energy sparingly. This is not beneficial when the aim is everlasting, sustainable weight loss. When you start dieting in this manner and increase your exercise you will generally only see results at the start before your body's metabolism adjusts for the lack of food. Once it adjusts, your results become stagnant and often times after frustration people give up and all the weight comes piling back on. If you're lucky your RMR/BMR will rise with the weight gain, ensuring you only end up putting back on what you lost, but constant yo-yo dieting could lead to a lower metabolism meaning you will struggle to lose weight and could even end up the heaviest you've ever been!

So, if eating too little causes this, you're probably wondering how not eating at all over a period of time could be any better right? Keep reading to see why.

## Intermittent fasting vs Low calorie diets

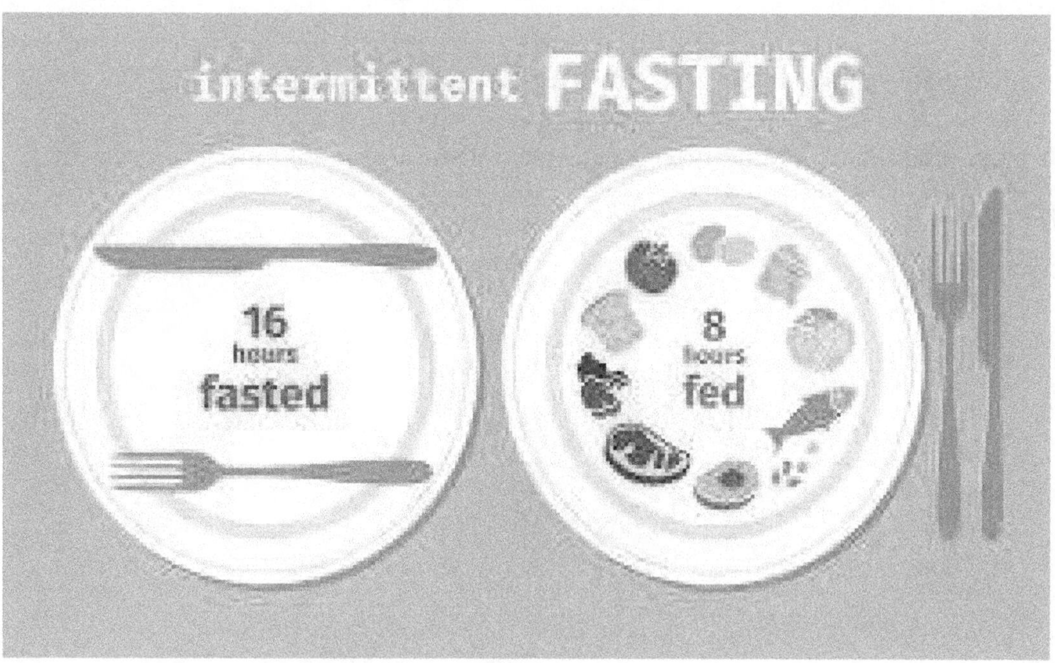


Low calorie diets simply don't cause the hormone adaptations fasting does. Remember those hormones we covered earlier in the book? They are the key to weight loss and your salvation. Remember how we need the help of hormones such as glucagon and HGH to stimulate the liver and fat cells to break down stored energy? As we now know they're triggered by low blood sugar levels. This is accomplished during the fasted period. Other hormones I haven't mentioned for simplicity's sake are also stimulated during this window to prevent metabolism drops associated with low calorie diets. Low calorie diets still include eating, and every time we eat our blood sugar levels are going to rise which triggers.........Insulin! As you now know, insulin is a storage hormone. So even though you might be consuming low calories, your lowered metabolism plus this little guy equals stored fat. Nothing turns off HGH like high blood sugar levels and insulin which ruins your chance to maintain muscle mass.

*Summary*

- Low calorie dieting could ruin your metabolism making maintainable weight loss near impossible
- Maintainable weight loss relies heavily on hormone adaptation
- Fasting stimulates key hormones for metabolism retention, muscle preservation, and fat burning

# WHAT YOU SHOULD WEIGH

Before you embark on a fasting program for weight loss, let me help you establish what you should weigh. For many people, women in particular, the figure we think of as "ideal" is far removed from what is realistic, or even healthy. I could go on and blame the media or the fashion industry. We all know that argument and, yes, it's partly true.

Ironically, where I learned about fasting in India, the thought of using fasting to get slim would be abhorrent, as being skinny is associated with poverty and lower social castes. Fasting should never be used to strive for a body that's slimmer than is healthy – the size zero craze being a case in point. The less body fat you have to lose, the more you need to ensure that fasting is not over- done since weight loss is a guaranteed side-effect.

## BODY MASS INDEX (BMI)

Healthy weight ranges are especially useful if you're already light for your frame

- you've probably heard of BMI, which gives an indication of how healthy your current weight is in proportion to your height. The formula for calculating BMI is:

BMI = weight (kg) ÷ height (m)2

(in other words, your weight in kilograms divided by your height in meters squared).

If math isn't your strong point, you can find out your BMI using an online calculator.

A healthy BMI is between 18.5 and 24.9. Although many celebrities have a BMI below 18.5, this simply isn't healthy. Some studies suggest that the ideal BMI is 23 for men and 21 for women - particularly if it's a long and healthy life you're after.

However, if your BMI is, say, 25 you won't become magically healthier by losing 450g (1lb) and dieting down to a BMI of 24.9. In fact, it's perfectly possible for someone with a BMI of 27 to be much healthier than someone with a BMI of 23. That's because BMI doesn't take your body fat, waist circumference, eating habits or lifestyle into account. An example of this could be a professional rugby player who's heavier than average simply because he or she is very muscular. There's nothing unhealthy about having lots of muscle, but the BMI scale might say he or she is overweight or even obese. In contrast, a chain-smoker who lives on diet drinks and never exercises can have a so-called "healthy" BMI. Who do you think is healthier?

A BMI of 30 or above is considered "obese". A 2008 study by researchers at the Mayo Clinic in the USA, involving over 13,000 people, found that 20.8 percent of men and 30.7 percent of women were obese according to the BMI scale. But when they used the World Health Organization gold standard definition of obesity - measuring body fat percentage - 50 percent of the men and 62.1 percent of the women were classified as obese. (In other words, you can have a healthy BMI and an unhealthy level of body fat.) What this means is that the athlete who's unfairly classed as "obese" is the exception rather than the rule. Unless you're an avid weight-lifter or sportsperson, or you have an extremely physical job, the BMI scale isn't likely to tell you that you need to lose weight if you don't. If your BMI is well over 25, don't worry. Medical experts agree that losing 5–10 percent of your starting weight is a sensible and realistic initial goal that will have lasting health benefits.

Therefore, when it comes to the BMI scale, it is worth calculating your BMI before deciding on a weight loss goal, especially if you only have a little weight to lose, but it definitely shouldn't be the only thing you think about.

## BODY FAT PERCENTAGE

What's great about monitoring your body fat percentage is that it gives you a better understanding of what's going on inside your body as you lose weight. Sustainable weight loss is best achieved through a combination of good nutrition and an active lifestyle. The thing is, when you start exercising more, you often gain muscle mass.

It can be demotivating to step onto the scales and see that your overall weight hasn't changed in spite of all your hard work. But because muscle is denser than fat, you can look slimmer and achieve health benefits without actually losing weight. To track changes in your body fat, you need to invest in body composition scales which enable you to track your progress by measuring changes in your muscle mass, body fat and hydration. Gyms often have high- quality versions of these scales if you don't want to buy your own.

Body composition scales are also helpful because if you notice that your muscle mass is decreasing as rapidly as your body fat, this suggests that you've cut your energy intake too dramatically. For most people, it's realistic to lose 450–900g (1–2lb) of body fat per week. If you're losing much more than this, the chances are you're eating into your muscle mass. Body composition scales can alert you to this before you've risked damaging your health.

In women, it's normal for hydration levels to fluctuate along with the menstrual cycle. Again, measuring weight alone doesn't enable you to track these changes. By using the body composition scales at a similar time of day, and recording changes throughout the month, you can get a clearer understanding of the times you're gaining body fat, and when it's simply a matter of fluid retention.

Sophisticated body composition monitors also enable you to track abdominal fat. Remember, not all fat is created equal, and abdominal fat is concentrated around your vital organs, posing the biggest health risk. You can be a "healthy" weight, and have high levels of abdominal fat – being aware of this can give you the motivation you need to address your eating habits and activity level.

The scales use a weak electric current to differentiate between fat, muscle, fluid and bone – we won't go into too much detail here as different brands have different features. As a guide, if you're an ordinary adult, and not an athlete or aspiring fitness model, you should be aiming for the following body fat percentages:

| AGE | MALE | FEMALE |
|---|---|---|
| 20-39 | 8-20% | 21-33% |
| 40-59 | 11-22% | 23-34% |
| 60+ | 13-25% | 24-36% |

# WHY TRADITIONAL DIETING MAKES YOU HUNGRY

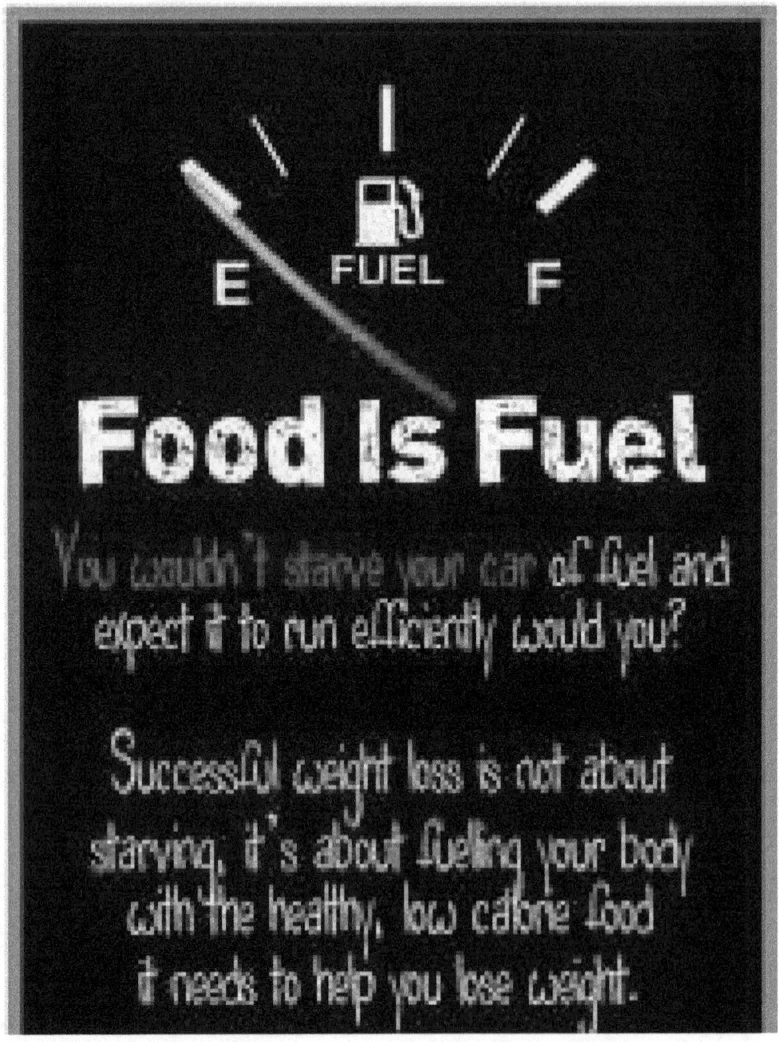


Going on a traditional diet without adequate energy intake for long periods of time can make your metabolic rate plummet and your appetite soar. Say you reduce your calories to below 1,000 a day for a number of weeks to fit into a party dress, the chances are you'll feel hungry and fed up much of the time, and as soon as the party starts, you'll dive head first into all the foods you've been avoiding, re-gaining that lost weight in no time! This, in a nutshell, sums up the seesaw of the diet industry.

The real trick is to keep your body feeling fuller for longer. I'm not talking about choosing one ready-meal over another, it's about understanding how to manage hunger so you naturally eat less most of the time. Please note, I don't say all of the time. Special events and over-indulging every now and then are good for the soul.

In tandem with a good diet overall, fasting can be used to retrain your hunger without the need for appetite suppressants or dodgy supplements. When you begin to fast, you will feel hungry at your usual meal times. However, if you choose not to eat at that time, the peaks and troughs of hunger start to level out. All this happens without a decrease in metabolic rate. It doesn't take a genius to recognize that if you feel hungry less often, you'll eat less and therefore lose weight. There's a biological explanation for this. Feelings of hunger and satiety (feeling full) are controlled by two main hormones produced within the body, ghrelin (even the word sounds hungry) and leptin. This dynamic duo of hormones has a powerful effect on how much food you eat and how much of what you've consumed you "burn off".

## *GHRELIN*

This hormone seems pretty straightforward. When your stomach's empty, it sends out some ghrelin to tell an area of your brain, the hypothalamus, that you ought to be eating. You then feel ravenous. But research published in the American Journal of Physiology suggests that ghrelin levels also rise in anticipation of eating - you get hungry partly because you're expecting a meal, not just because you have an empty stomach.

On a traditional diet, you get a peak of ghrelin before every meal - but because you don't eat as much as you'd really like to, you never feel fully satisfied. When you're fasting, your ghrelin levels still rise, but anecdotal evidence suggests that over time your body finds this sensation easier to get used to, probably because of the changes in your meal patterns. There's also a theory that a nutritionally poor diet (think additive-packed "diet" meals) sends ghrelin rocketing faster than a nutrient-dense plan like the ones I recommend.

## *LEPTIN*

This hormone is a little more complicated. You'll sometimes hear leptin referred to as a "master regulator" of fat metabolism. There are even whole diet books devoted to it.

Leptin is made by the fat cells - put simply, the more fat you have, the more leptin is produced. Like ghrelin, it sends a signal to the hypothalamus, but with the opposite effect. Leptin is supposed to maintain your body fat at a healthy level by telling you to stop eating when you start to gain too much fat. We all know it doesn't really work like that in practice - if it did, no one would be overweight. So, what happens?

Well, leptin also increases when you overeat - especially stodgy, carbohydrate-rich meals. This is because its release is triggered by insulin, which responds to an increase in blood glucose after a meal. So, if you're constantly eating without a proper break, your leptin levels will always be high. At first this is good - it should signal to your brain that it's time to put down that muffin - but it can lead to a very dangerous vicious circle. The theory is that, over time, too much leptin leads to the brain becoming resistant to its effects. As your brain stops recognizing what leptin is trying to tell it, you end up feeling hungry all the time, and are never satisfied by even the biggest meal.

## WHY MOST DIETS FAIL

This probably isn't the first book about weight loss you've ever read. I often say I've been down the diet road myself so many times that I could be a tour guide. If you're asking yourself why fasting is going to be any different, here are the facts you need to know:

- "Yo-yo" dieting is the bane of many people's lives, but even if you've lost and gained weight countless times, recent research has shown that it's possible to lose weight safely without messing up your metabolism.

- Burning off more calories than you eat is the only way to lose weight – and the simple truth is that you will lose weight if you manage to keep the number of calories you eat below the amount you burn off… boring but true.

There are hundreds of different ways to create a calorie deficit – as evidenced by the huge diet book, diet shake, diet bar and "miracle" weight-loss supplement industry. But there are two main reasons why diets never tend to live up to their expectations, especially as you get closer to your goal weight:

1 *Traditional diet misrepresent the calories in/calories out equation*.

We've all heard that 450g (1lb) of fat is roughly equal to 3,500 calories, so the traditional calorie-counting approach is to cut calories by 500–1,000 per day in order to lose 450–900g (1–2lb) per week. The trouble is, as you get slimmer you become lighter and that actually reduces the number of calories you burn at rest (your basal metabolic rate). So, in traditional weight-loss plans, weight loss is initially rapid but tends to slow down over time, even if you maintain that original calorie deficit. This can be very demotivating.

2 *It's sticking to your chosen approach that's often the hard part.*

Even if you get your calories exactly right, how boring does counting every calorie get? Demotivation - either as a result of not seeing the numbers on the scales going down as quickly as they were, or boredom - can lead to lapses, which slow down the rate of weight loss even further. When you go back to your old eating habits - surprise, surprise - you'll gain all the weight back, and a little more, as a result of the natural dip in basal metabolic rate (calorie burn) caused by your initial weight loss.

# PART TWO

## Action (Reset Your Metabolism)

# HOW FASTING MAKES A DIFFERENCE

## FASTING MAY BOOST METABOLIC RATE

You're probably thinking, "If I start starving myself, won't that be worse for my metabolism?" First of all, fasting is not starving yourself, and don't worry that eating less often will damage your metabolism. Losing weight naturally slows your basal metabolic rate (the number of calories you burn at rest) in proportion to the amount of weight you lose, no matter which method you use. This is because your daily energy (calorie) needs are directly related to your age, height, gender and weight, in particular your lean body mass (muscle). It doesn't mean that eating more often will fire up your metabolism.

You'll hear over and over again that after a night of sleep, your metabolism has ground to a halt and you need to eat breakfast to stoke your metabolic fire. The idea that "breakfast boosts metabolism" is simply not true – it hasn't been backed up by research at all. The breakfast myth is based on the "thermic effect of food". Around 10 percent of our calorie burn comes from the energy that we use to digest, absorb and assimilate the nutrients in our meals. Roughly speaking, if you eat a 350-calorie breakfast, you'll burn 35 calories in the process. But notice that you've eaten 315 extra calories to burn that 35. No matter what time of day you eat, you'll burn off around 10 percent of the calories in your food through the thermic effect of food. So, whether you eat your breakfast at 7am, 10am or never, if you eat roughly the same amount and types of food overall, its effect on your metabolism will be the same.

In fact, all the research on fasting seems to show that eating less often could actually boost your metabolic rate. In one British study conducted at the University of Nottingham, a two-day fast boosted participants' resting metabolic rate by 3.6 percent. In another study by the same research group, 29 healthy men and women fasted for three days. After 12–36 hours, there was a significant increase in basal metabolic rate, which returned to normal after 72 hours. The exact mechanisms for why this happens aren't clear.

## FASTING INCREASES FAT BURN

What is clear is that more of the calories you use for fuel during fasting come from your fat stores. Scientists can estimate what proportion of your energy is coming from fats and carbohydrates by measuring the amount of oxygen inhaled and the amount of carbon dioxide exhaled in your breath. The higher the proportion of oxygen to carbon dioxide, the more fat you're burning. As part of the same Nottingham study, findings proved that the proportion of energy obtained from fat rose progressively over 12–72 hours, until almost all the energy being used was coming from stored fat. This is incredible news really!

We're so often told to "breakfast like a king, lunch like a prince and dine like a pauper" with a view to becoming healthy, wealthy and wise. This is usually explained by telling us that breakfast kick-starts the metabolism - but it turns out that eating breakfast doesn't boost your fat-burning potential at all. In a small study on breakfast-eaters - published in the British Journal of Nutrition - a 700-calorie breakfast inhibited the use of fat for fuel throughout the day. Put simply, when we eat carbohydrates, we use it for fuel, and this prevents our bodies tapping into our stubborn stored fat. Constant grazing might be what's keeping fat locked away in your belly, bum or thighs - and fasting is one way to release it.

## FASTING MAINTAINS LEAN MUSCLE

The more muscle you have, the more calories you burn at rest. And before you say you don't want big muscles, another way to put that is: the less muscle you lose as you drop in weight, the less your basal metabolic rate falls as you move toward your goal weight. (Remember, your basal metabolic rate is the rate at which you burn calories, so it's really important in order to make staying in shape easier in the long term.) Besides, muscle takes up less room than fat. So, a person with good lean muscle mass will take a smaller dress size or use a narrower belt notch than someone who doesn't have it.

Fasting is better than plain old calorie restriction when it comes to maintaining lean body mass. This is largely because fasting triggers the release of growth hormone (GH), which encourages your body to look for other fuel sources instead of attacking its muscle stores. This is thought to be a survival advantage - back when humans were hunter gatherers it wouldn't have made sense for our muscle mass to reduce when food was scarce - we needed strong legs and arms to hunt down our dinner!

In one study carried out by researchers at Intermountain Medical Center in the USA, participants were asked to fast for 24 hours. During this time, GH levels rose by a whopping 1,300 percent in women and 2,000 percent in men.

Many other studies have investigated the effects of fasting on GH. Like other hormones, GH levels rise and fall throughout the day and night. They tend to be highest at the beginning of a good night's sleep, when our stomachs are empty but our bodies are hard at work repairing in preparation for a new day. Larger or more frequent bursts of GH are released when we continue to fast and also when we take part in vigorous exercise.

GH acts by sending a signal to our fat cells to release some of their contents into the bloodstream. This enables us to use more fat for fuel, instead of burning mainly carbohydrates for energy. GH is also thought to maintain concentrations of another hormone, insulin-like growth factor (IGF-1), which helps our muscles to build more protein.

This is totally different to what happens when you simply cut calories without changing how often you eat. When you hear people saying you should eat little and often to maintain your blood glucose levels, what they're telling you to do, in actual fact, is to avoid this state. This is because whenever you top up your blood glucose levels through eating, your body releases insulin to compensate, and GH levels never get a boost when insulin is around.

It's important to note that more isn't necessarily better when it comes to GH – what's key is resetting the balance between GH release (which happens in the fasted state) and insulin release (which happens in the fed state, however small your meal) in order to stimulate fat loss without losing lean muscle. You never need to fear growing giant muscles as a result of fasting – GH is released in waves and goes back to normal levels quickly as soon as your body has released enough fat to burn.

As mentioned earlier, if you're already slim, it's especially important not to overdo it when fasting. Research published in the academic journal Obesity Research shows that within just two days of complete fasting, there's a dramatic increase in the use of muscle for fuel in people who are already a healthy weight. This is because they have less fat available to burn overall. Perhaps the advice for people who are already svelte but who want to fast for health benefits is to fast little and often rather than to eat little and often.

## FASTING PATTERNS GIVE YOU ENERGY WHEN YOU NEED IT

Alongside maintaining your muscle mass to reduce the dip in your metabolic rate that happens as you lose weight, fasting may help with stubborn weight in other ways.

There's a theory that the reduction in calorie burn typically seen after following a calorie-restricted diet may be related more to changes in activity level than to basal metabolic rate. When you're only eating, say, 1,200 calories day after day, it may be difficult to maintain the energy levels and motivation to exercise. But following an intermittent fasting pattern means that you can concentrate your workouts around the times when you're eating. More energy means a tougher workout – and more calorie burn overall.

## COMMON QUESTIONS AND ANSWERS

**Q** Isn't "not eating" dangerous?

**A** It's very important to establish that fasting is not starvation, which, of course, is dangerous. What I'm talking about is the health benefits of increasing the gaps between meals or eating less from time to time.

Some people who are fully signed up to the merry-go-round of traditional dieting will argue that not eating is likely to induce a low-blood-sugar or "hypo" episode. Feeling faint, clammy and unable to concentrate are typical symptoms, happily offset by a visit to the vending machine or, for the health- aware, a snack such as an oatcake or nuts and seeds. I'm not suggesting that snacking should be outlawed – most of the time, I'm more than happy to tuck right in. But fasting challenges the assertion that we can't survive, or even thrive, without five mini-meals a day.

I accept that challenging the blood-sugar story isn't going to win me any popularity prizes. However, the reality of what science is telling us today is that there's no medical consensus on the concept of low blood sugar. The vast majority of us are perfectly capable of regulating our blood glucose level and, although we may feel ravenous between meals, going without food for a few hours won't cause the blood glucose to plummet and, even if it does, our self-preserving mechanisms will kick into action long before we pass out. What this means is that insulin's countermeasure, glucagon, will kick in, releasing those locked-up glucose stores into the blood and bringing the glucose level back within its normal range.

A few words of warning, though… Diabetic "hypos" are a different thing altogether, of course, and can be very dangerous, but they are drug- induced. For people diagnosed as diabetic but who are not yet on insulin medication, fasting has proved promising. In a year-long study on intermittent fasting, the group who fasted every other day stayed off diabetes medication for significantly longer.

**Q** Won't I feel light-headed and really hungry on a fast?

**A** You might be worried that your blood sugar levels will dip too low between meals and that you'll feel faint and weak. But when you're not eating, other hormonal signals trigger your body to release glucose or make more. In one Swedish study by researchers at the Karolinska Institute, students who'd reported that they were sensitive to hypoglycemia (low blood sugar) felt irritable and shaky during a 24-hour fast, but there was actually no difference in their blood sugar levels – it may all have been in their minds.

It's true that your brain requires about 500 calories a day to keep the grey matter ticking over effectively. The brain's preferred fuel is glucose, which your liver stores around 400 calories-worth of at a time. In a longer fast, the body is forced to increase its production of ketone bodies, which act as a glucose-substitute for your brain. But in the short term, so long as you eat well before and after your fasting period, your body is perfectly able to produce enough glucose to keep your brain happy.

**Q** Hang on a minute… My trainer told me that six small meals will fire up my metabolism and stop me feeling peckish. Who's right?

**A** This is one of those fitness and nutrition "truths" that has been repeated so many times, people are convinced that it's a fact. In one small study at the US National Institute on Aging, researchers found that people who ate only one meal a day did tend to feel hungrier than those who ate three. But beyond eating three meals a day, meal frequency doesn't seem to make a difference to hunger or appetite, so it comes down to what's actually easiest for you. A study published by the International Journal of Obesity showed that people who are overweight tend to snack more often.

**Q** Can fasting change my shape?

**A** For many women, that last bit of surplus weight is carried around the hips and thighs and it simply won't shift. To solve this problem, I suggest looking to the true body professionals.

According to noted intermittent-fasting expert Martin Berkhan, there's a good reason for this. All the cells in our body have "holes" in them known as receptors. To switch activity on and off in those cells, hormones or enzymes enter the receptors. Fat cells contain two types of receptor - beta 2 receptors, which are good at triggering fat burning, and alpha 2 receptors, which aren't. Guess which is mostly found in the fat stores of your lower body? Yes, our hips and thighs have nine times more alpha 2 receptors than beta.

**Q** What about belly fat?

**A** All over the Internet you'll see promises that you can get rid of belly fat in a matter of days by taking supplements. We all know that this is simply not true. Stubborn fat around the middle is linked to a number of factors - including stress, alcohol, lack of exercise and a diet high in refined carbohydrates.

Every time you eat something sweet or a refined carbohydrate such as biscuits or white bread, your blood sugar levels rise quickly, causing your pancreas to release the fat-storing hormone, insulin. If you spend the day going from sugary snack to sugary snack, and especially if you wash everything down with a couple of glasses of wine, your body ends up storing more of the calories you eat and you end up with that dreaded "muffin top"!

Stress + refined carbohydrates + alcohol = a recipe for belly fat, especially if you're unlucky enough to be genetically predisposed to weight gain around the middle.

**Q** How does fasting help torch belly fat?

**A** To burn belly fat, free fatty acids must first be released from your fat cells (this is called lipolysis) and moved into your bloodstream, then transferred into the mitochondria of muscle or organ cells, to be burned (a process known as beta-oxidation).

Glucagon (another pancreatic hormone that has pretty much an equal and opposite effect to insulin) rises around four to five hours after eating, once all the digested nutrients from your last meal have been stored or used up. The purpose of glucagon is to maintain a steady supply of glucose to the brain and red blood cells, which it achieves by breaking down stored carbohydrates and leftover protein fragments in the liver. It also activates hormone-sensitive lipase, which triggers the release of fat from the fat cells, allowing other cells to be fueled by fat as opposed to glucose.

When you're fasting, belly fat can be turned into energy to keep your organs working effectively and, for example, to provide power to the muscles that hold you upright, as well as fueling muscle movement.

In contrast, when you're constantly grazing, your body doesn't need to release glucagon. Instead, the pancreas pumps out insulin, which also acts to maintain blood glucose levels within a narrow range. Insulin encourages the fat cells to keep their fat tightly locked up. Not only that, but any spare glucose that isn't required for energy and cannot be stored can actually be converted into fat.

**Q** What else can I do to help get rid of belly fat?

**A** Endurance exercise selectively reduces abdominal fat and aids maintenance of lean body mass, so it's great to do in combination with intermittent fasting. Choose a fasting method that will enable you to take regular exercise – gentle activity such as walking will help, but high-intensity training is even better.

Also, a very small recent study, carried out at the University of Oklahoma in the USA, found that quality protein intake was inversely associated with belly fat, so make sure you fuel up on lean proteins (which your fasting plans are rich in), when you are eating.

**Q** What about losing that last 4.5kg (10lb)?

**A** This is often the hardest weight to shift. Not only that, it tends to creep back over a matter of weeks after you've finally reached your target weight. A familiar story is the strict diet we follow to get into beach-body shape in time for a holiday: in all the years I've helped people to lose weight, I've lost count of the number of times I've heard people telling me that all their hard work was undone by two weeks of sun, sea and sangria!

Remember that losing weight is all about creating a calorie deficit. Here, fasting is acting in two different ways. First, fasting helps maintain calorie burn – so in theory you can eat more overall and still lose weight. Second, fasting might just be easier to stick to than a boring calorie-counting diet. And when it comes to beach bodies, remember that old saying "a change is as good as a rest". If you're bored of the approach you've taken to weight loss up to now, a short blast of fasting can help you achieve your goal weight without damaging your metabolism.

# FASTING AND CANCER

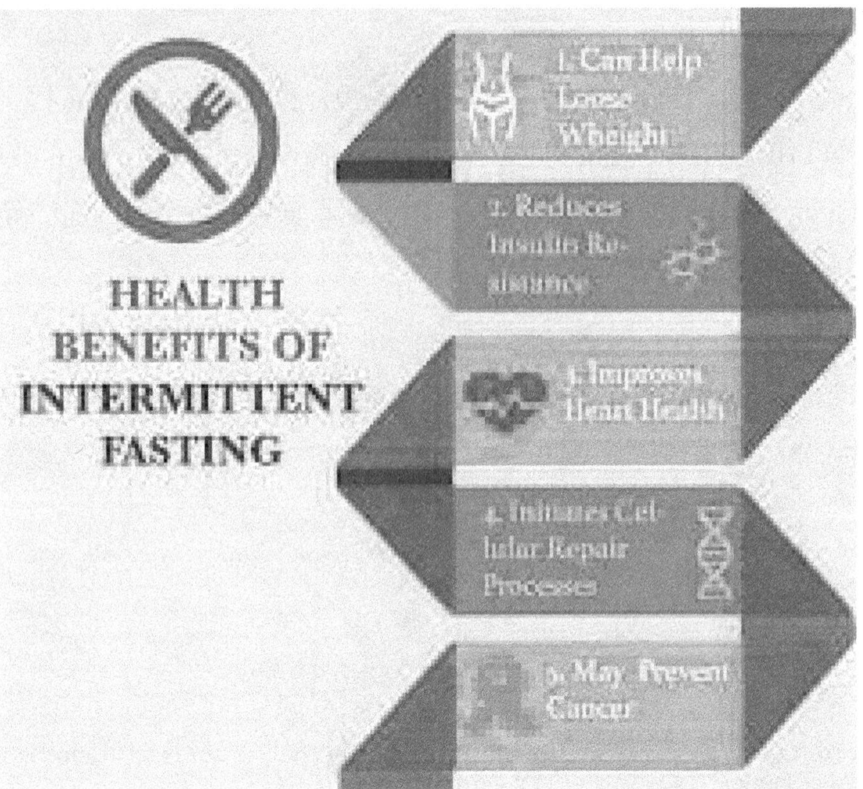


Fasting is considered to be an alternative or complementary treatment for cancer in certain sectors of complementary medicine, and has been popularized by a naturopathic doctor called Max Gerson. However, my focus is not on fasting as a stand-alone treatment but rather on exciting evidence about fasting in cancer prevention and the encouraging results from trials involving fasting during cancer treatment, particularly chemotherapy.

There's evidence that intermittent fasting, and calorie restriction more generally, fights the growth and spread of cancer cells in animals. Often when we read about research on animals, it seems so compelling that we want to see if the same thing will work for us. However, research is so much less likely to be done on humans as, rightly or wrongly, ethics committees are often reluctant to approve the same types of study that are done on animals. As discussed above, in experiments on laboratory animals, diets with 25 percent fewer calories have shown a positive link with longer, healthier life spans. So far there's little empirical study evidence to show the same effect in humans, yet anecdotal evidence is growing that restricting calories, and fasting, activates cell-protecting mechanisms. Research is also underway to find out whether alternate-day fasting can help reduce the risk of breast cancer.

In studies on mice with cancer, fasting appears to improve survival rates after chemotherapy. Hearing of the effects of these animal studies by Valter Longo, ten cancer patients took it upon themselves to try fasting before chemotherapy. The results were published in the medical journal Aging. Of these ten, the majority experienced fewer side-effects as a result of fasting than those eating normally, and the authors concluded that fasting for two to five days before chemotherapy treatment appeared to be safe. This work has yet to be taken to a truly meaningful empirical testing on humans, but it's understandable that cancer patients are excited by the potential of calorie restriction and fasting, not least by it helping the body to mitigate the effects of cancer treatment and specifically chemotherapy.

## DETOXING

Personally, I no longer like the word "detox". It's been used and abused by marketeers in their quest to sell, sell, sell fancy products, when, in fact, detoxing is something that the body does naturally every hour of the day. However, until someone comes up with a better word, "detox" will have to do.

## HOW WE BECOME TOXIC

A toxin is anything that has a detrimental effect on cell function or structure. Toxins are materials that our bodies cannot process efficiently. Over time they build up and, as a result, our systems function below par, leaving us drained, tired and frequently ill. People become "toxic" in many ways - through diet, lifestyle and the environment, as a natural by-product of metabolism, and through genetic lineage. Stress and harmful emotions can also create a kind of toxic environment.

Toxins include, but are not limited to:

- Food additives, flavorings and colorings.
- Household and personal cleaning chemicals, which are both inhaled and absorbed via the skin.
- Agricultural chemicals, such as pesticides, fungicides and herbicides.
- Heavy metals, which occur naturally but are poisonous.
- Oestrogens, which enter the environment due to human usage of the contraceptive pill and HRT.
- Xeno-oestrogens, which are chemicals that mimic oestrogen.

...And here are the most common ways people become toxic on the inside:

- Eating a poor diet. This includes low-fiber foods, fried foods and foods tainted with synthetic chemicals. Unlike live foods (fresh fruits and vegetables), these lack the enzymes that assist proper digestion and assimilation, and the fiber or bulk that assists proper elimination. They're also void of essential vitamins, minerals and other basic nutrients.

- Eating too much. Over-eating puts a great amount of stress on our digestive system. The body must produce hydrochloric acid, pancreatic enzymes, bile and other digestive factors to process a meal. When we over-eat, the digestive system finds it hard to meet the demands placed upon it. The stomach bloats as the digestive system goes into turmoil. Foods aren't broken down properly and tend to lodge in the lower intestine. Vital nutrients are then not absorbed.
- Inadequate water intake. When the body isn't receiving enough water, toxins tend to stagnate, hindering all digestive and eliminative processes.
- Exposure to synthetic chemicals in food and environmental pollutants. A clean, strong system can metabolize and excrete many pollutants, but when the body is weak or constipated, they're stored as unusable substances. As more and different chemicals enter the body, they tend to interact with those already there, forming second-generation chemicals that can be far more harmful than the originals.
- Being stressed. Stress hinders proper digestion, absorption and elimination of foods.
- Overuse of antibiotics. Antibiotics have a damaging effect on the intestines, especially if they're taken for extensive periods of time. Reducing the use of unnecessary antibiotics will also help minimize the very real danger of bacterial resistance.
- Lack of exercise. This lowers metabolic efficiency, and without circulatory stimulation, the body's natural cleansing systems are weakened.
- Eating late at night. The human body uses sleep to repair, rebuild and restore itself. In essence, the body uses the sleeping hours to cleanse and build. When a person goes to sleep with a full stomach, the body isn't at rest but is busy digesting and processing food. In addition, the body requires gravity to assist the passage of food from the stomach down the digestive tract.

**Q** If the body detoxes itself anyway, why bother to do anything further?

**A** Just as your home or office can become dusty and dirty, so your body can become clogged up with toxins and waste matter from the environment. A healthy body is able to disarm toxins by breaking them down, storing them in fat tissue or excreting them. However, here's the crux – many, if not most, people are depleted in the nutrients needed to detox optimally, and chronic health problems, sluggishness and weight gain are common results.

If you've never given your digestion much thought, don't beat yourself up about being neglectful. Unlike the head or the tips of the fingers, the gut contains very few nerve endings. What this means is, we're not so aware when things aren't working well. When you have a headache, you feel every throbbing pulse and do something about it. In contrast, gut problems go unresolved and uncared for over long periods.

The good news is, when you improve digestion, a whole range of seemingly unrelated health issues can improve. For example, it's not only the job of the white blood cells (the leukocytes) to defend your body since the digestive system forms the basis of your immune system with the action of beneficial bacteria. Improving the ecology of the gut can be achieved with a juice fast and healthy diet.

USING A JUICE FAST TO DETOX

A juice fast stands head and shoulders above other fasting techniques in its self-healing effect and is often mentioned in the context of detoxing the body.

Juice fasting is based on consuming juices and broths only, whereas intermittent fasting adds lean protein and fat for the feeling of fullness. Studies have shown that eating as little as 10g (¼oz) of essential amino acids (found in high-quality proteins) can switch off autophagy. Therefore, a juice fast is best placed to give your body a good "spring clean" because juices are typically very low in protein.

The simple act of juicing a fruit or vegetable will help you absorb more of the nutrients from it. The caveat here is that you should make the juice fresh rather than drink pasteurized fruit juice from a carton or bottle. The process of juicing eliminates a lot of the fiber that needs to be digested. Cutting out the bulk and drinking only the juice means that you can very effectively hit your antioxidant targets in one small cup. Juice provides tiny "particles" of nutrients that are readily absorbed into the bloodstream.

Fresh juices provide a highly effective fast-track and – importantly – easy delivery mechanism for the body to absorb and process key vitamins, minerals and plant chemicals (phytonutrients) that are so beneficial to our health. A fresh juice contains a concentration of nutrients that have been separated from pulp, making it easier to consume what's required to assist the healing process. In essence, a fresh juice should be considered more of a body tonic than a tasty drink.

**Q** Will I get withdrawal symptoms on a juice fast?

**A** The folklore of fasting is littered with stories about the dramatic side-effects of a juice fast. This is usually because the contrast between the diet and lifestyle before and after is simply too great. Or, in some cases, the enterprising individual has decided to "retox", that is go on an almighty bender before entering detox – not a good idea.

One of the most dramatic side-effects I ever witnessed was when a client was coming off a 20-year-long diet cola habit during a juice-fasting retreat. Her symptoms were akin to what you'd expect from coming off a class-A drug. The rest of the detox group watched mesmerized at her descent from bubbly, bouncy guest on arrival to a sweating, vomiting, pale-faced shadow of her former self after just 24 hours of juicing. Even I was a little worried. Luckily, her troubled time was followed by a rapid and dramatic improvement two days later, at which point she declared that she felt "reborn" and would never touch a drop of cola again.

So, learn from my diet cola story and start with a transition diet. Fasting can be a challenge physically and psychologically. I recommend having at least three days on the Countdown Plan to prepare. Juice fasting should be undertaken for between one and five days for optimum results – usually once or twice a year. Any longer requires more management and should only be considered when there are adequate reserves (body fat) or if there's a specific medical condition. Some people find that weekend-long juice fasts four times a year are helpful.

**Q** What are the most common side-effects of a juice fast?

**A** Let me be frank – a juice fast isn't a good idea for a romantic break or naughty weekend away. During a juice fast the capacity of the eliminative organs – lungs, liver, kidneys, and skin – is greatly increased, and masses of accumulated metabolic wastes and toxins are quickly expelled. It's like pressing the accelerator button on your body's waste disposal unit. As part of the eliminative process, your body will be cleansing itself of old, accumulated wastes and toxins. This typically throws up symptoms such as offensive breath, dark urine, increased faecal waste, skin eruptions, perspiration and increased mucus. As I said, it's not exactly romantic!

Your digestive system is the star of a fasting program. Poor digestion can be a hidden cause of weight gain, or more accurately, water retention. For example, if your body's responding to an allergy or intolerance, it will often retain water. So, when fasting, there's often a "quick-win" water loss that equates to an extra kilo being lost.

**Q** What about fiber?

**A** The process of juicing extracts the pulp (fiber) of the fruits and vegetables so on a juice fast it's a good idea to restore some bulk to maintain a healthy transit of waste matter through the gastrointestinal tract. Psyllium husks, a soluble form of fiber, do just the trick as, when taken with adequate amounts of fluids, they absorb water to form a large mass. In people with constipation, this mass stimulates the bowel to move, whereas in people with diarrhea it can slow things down and reduce bowel movements.

Some recent research also shows that psyllium husks may lower cholesterol. It's thought that the fiber stimulates the conversion of cholesterol into bile acid and increases bile acid excretion. In addition, psyllium husks may even decrease the intestinal absorption of cholesterol.

Psyllium comes from the plant Plantago ovata and is native to India. It is readily available in health food shops and online stores, either as husks or in powdered form. In non-fasting, normal dietary conditions, whole grains provide dietary fiber and similar beneficial effects to psyllium, so a supplement isn't needed unless recommended by your health care practitioner.

**Q** Can colon cleansing help?

**A** Your bowels are not just "poo pipes". Toxins and metabolic wastes from the blood and tissues are discharged into the intestinal canal to be excreted from the body. Not surprisingly, one of the long-established techniques to support the body's elimination organs during a fast is colon hydrotherapy or enemas. This is a technique that involves taking in water into the large intestine, also known as the bowel, to assist the removal of waste.

Colon hydrotherapy is not a new procedure. Enemas and rituals involving the washing of the colon with water have been used since pagan times. The first recorded mention of colon cleansing is on an Egyptian medical papyrus dated as early as 1500BCE. Ancient and modern tribes in the Amazon, Central Africa and remote parts of Asia have used river water for bowel cleansing, usually as part of magic-medical rites of passage performed by priests or shamans. Colon-cleansing therapies were an important part of Taoist training regimens and these therapies still form one of the fundamental practices of yoga teaching. Hippocrates, Galen and Paracelsus, who are recognized as the founding fathers of Western medicine, described, practiced and prescribed the use of enemas for colon cleansing. In Europe and the USA, colon-cleansing treatments were popular in the early decades of the 20th century and were often performed on patients by doctors practicing in sanatoria (health spas) and hospitals. From the 1920s to the 1960s, most medical practitioners were in favor of regular enemas, and these were often used as part of hospital treatment.

# PART 3

# REJUVENATION

# FASTING AND MOTIVATION

The final motivator, when thinking about incorporating fasting with exercise, is that it could give you more energy to train. There are lots of arguments over whether diet or exercise is more important when it comes to losing weight.

You may be familiar with the saying "you can't out-train a bad diet". While it's probably true that exercise alone isn't going to get you the body you want if you pay no attention to what you eat, dieting without exercise isn't a good idea either. After all, exercise comes with an impressive array of health benefits itself from heart and lung health, to stress relief, to maintaining strong bones.

When it comes to muscle strength and the way you look, exercise is the clear winner over diet. Researchers at Ann Arbor University in Michigan looked at how women's bodies responded to diet alone versus exercise alone. They found that, as expected, diet was more effective at reducing body weight, but exercise was more effective when it came to losing fat and maintaining muscle.

The thing is, getting the motivation to exercise can be hard when you're "on a diet" because you're always eating less than you're burning off and you often feel like you just don't have the energy. The good thing about fasting is that the gaps between meals are longer so when you do eat, you get to eat more. This means that you can time your exercise around the times when you've eaten and are feeling energetic. You're more likely to work harder!

## MEDITATION

For those with ambition above and beyond the physical benefits of fasting, getting into the fasting state of mind can be helped by meditation, and if you have the time and inclination at least once in your life, a week's retreat can take the fasting experience to another level.

Meditation can be viewed in scientific terms for its effects on the mind and the body. During meditation, a marked increase in blood flow slows heart rate, and high blood pressure drops to within normal ranges. Recent research indicates that meditation can also boost the immune system and reduce free radicals - in effect, a slowing down of the ageing process.

There's much talk about the power of meditation and how you can use your mind to manifest great piles of money. But, becoming more aware of your mind is not just about manipulating it or attempting only to have positive thoughts - rather, it's about the ability to direct your attention toward or away from the mind at will.

My most intensive fast was on a 10-day silent meditation retreat during my time in India. One evening, five days into the experience when I was seriously doubting my judgement about freezing my butt off in a cold cave in the Himalayas, I had what I've come to realize was a "breakthrough" moment. In spiritual terms I'd describe it as a moment of grace. With a raw, pure energy of infinite magnitude, my mind flashed through formative experiences - good and bad - that had shaped my life. As my mind was swept along on this emotional rollercoaster, my body conveniently left the room, leaving me nowhere to run or hide… or at least that was how it felt!

Even more strangely (and I realize I may lose a few of you here!), during this experience it felt like my spine had dissolved to be replaced by a light-filled serpent. I was left astounded, uplifted and more than a little confused. Given that I was in the middle of a silent retreat, I couldn't even talk to anyone about what I had experienced.

It felt like all the vertebrae in my spine had dissolved at once, to be replaced with an energy much like an electric current. Even more bizarre was the fact that this energy surge was joined by an unshakable vision of a cobra-like snake replacing my spinal column.

Seeking answers, the day I left the meditation retreat I went straight to an Internet café. Within a few minutes I'd discovered that Hindu mythology describes the "serpent power" that lies coiled at the base of the spine as a kind of universal energy. Reportedly, this energy is awakened in deep meditation or enlightenment.

However, let me offer a word of caution before your expectations are set on a one-way ticket to nirvana. If, like many of us, you're the kind of person who never switches off, who even on holiday has the day scheduled from dawn till dusk, the mind experience that can accompany fasting may pass you by altogether. If you want to know yourself better, fasting in a gentle, supportive and quiet environment can help you accomplish a gentle re-boot both physically and mentally, and possibly a little spiritually too. Fasting needs some willpower in the beginning and patience as you move forward. Creating the right environment to enter the fasting state of mind, both inside and outside the body, is really helpful.

When I first started to meditate, I tried too hard. Furiously studying the science of the mind or contorting your face into Zen-like expressions won't work. The only way to experience meditation is actually to experience it. It can be maddening. You'll be trying to meditate for hours and then, just when you're ready to give up, you might get a flash of something akin to what you were aiming for. Yet, in that momentary shift you might see how you could choose to do a few things differently, or how some really small things have a huge impact on you, and how easy it would be to make a few minor changes. Many great thinkers have talked about breakthroughs and inspiration. The most famous of all was probably Albert Einstein, who said that no problem can be solved from the same level of consciousness that created it.

So, if you do manage to get your mind to stop its usual chatter through meditation, try asking yourself a question when all is calm. For example, if you always react to something uncomfortable by quashing the emotion with food, then meditation can create a gap to ask why. Sometimes there's a clear answer to that question, and sometimes there isn't. Usually, it takes a bit of time.

## YOGA

Yoga is often lumped together with meditation since the kind of person who likes yoga is often into meditation, and vice versa. For people with a poor attention span, yoga can be a good way of getting into a calm state without the need ever to sit cross-legged.

There are many forms of yoga and it's a case of having a go and seeing which suits you best. Regardless of which tradition you choose, good yoga teachers can make you walk out of the class feeling a foot taller and ready to take on the world. My advice would be:

- If you're gentle by nature, try Hatha.
- If you're into precision and detail, go for Iyengar.
- If you like the spiritual side of yoga, opt for Sivananda.
- If you want yoga to help you sleep, try Yin.
- If you're fit and physical, Ashtanga or Vinyasa "flow" yoga will be more your bag.
- If you really want to sweat, try Bikram, or "hot yoga". It's not for the faint hearted and has some medical contra-indications, but it's considered seriously addictive by devotees.

## SELF-CONTROL

If you're into popular psychology or consider yourself a "Tiger Mum" (or Dad), you might well have come across the famous longitudinal "Stanford University Marshmallow Study", first started in the 1960s by Stanford psychology researcher Michael Mischel. The purpose of the original experiment was to find out at what age children develop the ability to wait for something they really want, and subsequent studies over many years tracked the effects of deferred gratification on a person's future success. Mischel's experiment went like this:

# NUTRITIONAL RULES FOR FASTING

## EAT WELL

The problem with most fasting information is that it only focuses on the fasting bit, not on what you need to eat. If you're eating fewer calories, what you do eat becomes even more important. Why? We need nutrients for the glands and organs of the body to thrive and burn fat. Restricting nutrients by living on processed foods can deprive the body of the essential vitamins, minerals, fats and proteins it needs to maintain a healthy immune system, recover from injury or illness, keep muscles strong and maintain the metabolism. That's why this book includes these nutrition rules and practical fasting plans and recipes to help guide you.

## RULE 1: ONLY EAT "REAL" FOOD

This means no fake food and no diet-drinks. If you grew up in the UK, chances are you'll have fond memories of bright orange corn snacks and fizzy drinks that turned your tongue red or blue. It's to be hoped that now you're "all grown up 'n' stuff", you eat lots of rocket and Parmesan salads, roasted artichoke and monkfish. If only that was the case for all of us. Celebrity chefs may make out that this is the norm but it just isn't. Most people still eat a diet full of processed, refined, low-fiber, nutrient-deficient foods.

Not all processed food is bad, though. In fact, some of it's great. Canned food without added sugar or salt and freshly-frozen fruit and veg are just a couple of examples of stellar staples for your larder. It's the low-calorie, low-fat, oh-so-easy snacks and meals that you need to watch out for since they're often loaded with chemicals and hidden sugars.

In many low-fat products the fat is simply replaced by processed carbohydrates in the form of sugar. Read the label of your regular low-fat treats (apart from dairy products where low fat is fine) and I'll bet you'll see words ending with "-ose". Various forms of sugar, be it sucrose, maltose, glucose, fructose, or the vaguely healthy-sounding corn syrup, are all bad news for weight gain, especially around the middle.

Heavily processed foods can also be high in chemicals. There's a real and present danger that chemicals in the environment may have a blocking effect on hormones that control weight loss. When the brain is affected by toxins, it's possible that hormone signaling is impaired. The reason why we're unsure as to the extent of the problem is that it's impossible to test for the thousands of chemicals that are contributing to the "cocktail" effect on the body. Err on the side of caution and control what you can. Keep foods "real"!

But what makes up a real-food diet?

## *PROTEIN*

Protein is made up of amino acids, often called the "building blocks of life", and we need all of them to stay alive and thrive. Proteins from animal sources - meat, dairy, fish and eggs - contain all the amino acids and are therefore classed as "complete" proteins. Soya beans also fall into this category. Once and for all, eggs are healthy. Eggs have had a tough time of it over the years. First the salmonella scare, then the unfair link to cholesterol. Eggs are low in saturated fat and if you eat eggs in the morning, you're less likely to feel hungry later in the day.

Vegetable sources provide incomplete proteins. If you're vegetarian or vegan, you'll get your protein from nuts, seeds, legumes and grains but you need a good variety of these to ensure that you get the full range of essential amino acids.

## *TOP TIP:*

- Include more beans and lentils in your meals. Examples include kidney beans, butter beans, chickpeas or red and green lentils. They're rich in protein and contain complex carbohydrates, which provide slow and sustained energy release. They also contain fiber, which may help to control your blood fats. Try adding them to stews, casseroles, soups and salads.

## *CARBOHYDRATES*

Carbs are one of the most controversial topics in nutrition and weight loss. For years we've been told that we eat too much fat, and that saturated fat is the main cause of heart disease. But recently, some experts have challenged this view, suggesting that carbohydrate is responsible for the obesity epidemic and a whole host of diseases. Should we cut carbs, avoid fat or simply reduce our food intake and exercise more?

When the body is starved of carbohydrates it looks for energy in its glycogen stores. Water binds to every gram of glycogen so it's easy to get dramatic weight loss – the only problem is that it's mostly water weight! Along with those glycogen stores you'll begin to lose fat but not at a rate higher than a healthier (and easier) weight-loss method.

The truth is there are healthy fats and healthy carbohydrates. Avoiding carbs altogether is unnecessary and potentially dangerous. The key is in recognizing that not all carbs are created equal. Low glycemic index (GI) carbohydrates, found in fiber-rich fruits, beans, unrefined grains and vegetables, are important for good health and can actively support weight loss – for example, through reducing appetite and energy intake.

However, high-GI refined carbohydrates, such as those found in soft drinks, white bread, pastries, certain breakfast cereals and sweeteners, not only make it harder to lose weight but could damage long-term health. Studies show that eating a lot of high-GI carbohydrates can increase the risk of heart disease and Type-2 diabetes.

*TOP TIP:*

- Eat bulky carbs to become slim. When you choose "big" foods like fruits, vegetables, salads and soups, which are bulked up by fiber and water, you're eating a lot of food that fills you up, but not a lot of calories.

## *FAT*

Since fat is the greatest source of calories, eating less of it can help you to lose weight. However, fat is actually a vital nutrient and is an important part of your diet because it supplies the essential fatty acids needed for vitamin absorption, healthy skin, growth and the regulation of bodily functions. In fact, eating too little fat can actually cause a number of health problems.

The right kinds of fat, in the right amounts, can also help you to feel fuller for longer, so try not to think of fat as your mortal diet enemy, but rather a useful ally in the pursuit of your healthier lifestyle! Adding a little fat to your meals helps your body absorb nutrients and enhances the flavor of your food, so recipes have been created with this in mind. Choose monounsaturated fats or oils (e.g., olive oil and rapeseed oil) as these types of fats are better for your heart. Coconut oil can be a good choice for cooking as it's heat-stable.

*TOP TIPS:*

- Increase essential fats – aim for at least two portions of oily fish a week. Examples include mackerel, sardines, salmon and pilchards. Oily fish contains a type of polyunsaturated fat called omega 3, which helps protect against heart disease. If you don't eat fish, use flaxseed oil in salad dressing and snack on walnuts.

- If you use butter, stick to a thin scraping on bread and just a smidgen for flavor in cooking.
- Choose lean meat and fish as low-fat alternatives to fatty meats.

- Choose lower-fat dairy foods such as skimmed or semi-skimmed milk and reduced-fat natural yogurt.
- Grill, poach, steam or oven bake instead of frying or cooking with oil or other fats.
- Watch out for creamy sauces and dressings - swap them for tomato-based sauces. Add herbs, lemon, spices and garlic to reduced-fat meals to boost flavor.

- Use cheese as a topping, not a meal - in other words, no macaroni cheese! Choose cheese with a strong flavor, such as Parmesan or goat's cheese so that you only need to use a small amount.

## RULE 2: CUT OUT SUGAR

Too much sugar makes you fat and has an ageing effect on the skin. Sugar links with collagen and elastin and reduces the elasticity of the skin, making you look older than your years. The recipes I provide use low-sugar fruits to add a little sweetness - and the occasional drizzle of a natural sweetener such as honey is fine - but, in general, sugar is bad news and best avoided.

*TOP TIP:*

- Stick to dark chocolate if you need a chocolate "fix" (which simply is the case sometimes!), as most people need less of it to feel satisfied.

## RULE 3: WATCH THE ALCOHOL

Over the years the alcohol content of most drinks has gone up. A drink can now have more units than you think. A small glass of wine (175ml/5½fl cup) could be as much as two units. Remember, alcohol contains empty calories so think about cutting back further if you're trying to lose weight. That's a maximum of two units of alcohol per day for a woman and three units per day for a man. For example, a single pub measure (25ml/¾fl oz) of spirit is about one unit, and a half pint of lager, ale, bitter or cider is one to one-and-a-half units.

*TOP TIP:*

- If you're out for the evening, try out some healthy soft drinks such as tonic with cordial, or an alcohol-free grape juice as a tasty substitute to wine. Alcohol-free beers are also becoming increasingly popular and are available in most pubs and bars.

## RULE 4: EAT FRUIT, DON'T DRINK IT

If you consume around 1 liter (35fl oz/4 cups) fruit juice, remember you'll be imbibing 500 calories. That's fine if you're juice fasting, but too much if it's simply a snack. You could tuck into a baked potato with tuna and two pieces of fruit for the same number of calories.

*TOP TIPS:*

- Choose herbal teas (especially green tea, which may aid fat loss).

- Feel free to have a cup or two of tea or coffee. A small amount of milk is allowed but keep it to a splash when you're fasting.

- Sip water throughout the fast, aiming for a fluid intake of around 1.2–2 liters (40–70fl oz/4¾–8 cups) a day. This will not only help to keep hunger pangs at bay, it will also keep you hydrated.

# RULE 5: AVOID THE PITFALLS

## *TOP TIPS:*

- Top up before you fast. When you first start fasting, you may feel hungry during the times when you'd normally have a meal and you may also feel slightly light-headed if you have sugary foods as your last meal. This isn't a sign that you're wasting away or entering starvation mode, and these feelings of hunger will usually subside once that usual meal time has passed. Try to get your carbohydrate intake from fruit, vegetables and whole grains and eat a good amount of protein, which will fill you up for longer. Following the fasting plans will make this as straightforward as possible.

- Stock up for quick meals. Make sure you always have ingredients in your fridge and cupboards for meals that can be put together quickly, such as stir- fries, soups and salads.

- Don't polish off the kids' plates. Eating the children's leftovers is a fast track to weight gain for parents. Put the plates straight into the sink or dishwasher when the children have finished their meal, so you won't be tempted!

- Downsize your dinner plate. Much of our hunger and satiation is psychological. If we see a huge plate only half full, we'll feel like we haven't eaten enough. But if the plate is small but completely filled, we'll subconsciously feel that we have eaten enough.

- Beware of the Frappuccino effect. Black coffee only contains about 10 calories but a milky coffee can contain anything from 100 calories for a standard small cappuccino to a whopping 350+ calories for a Grande with all the trimmings. Much like the plate size, shrink your cup size and shrink your waist line. Don't be afraid to ask for half the milk - spell it out: "Don't fill up the cup." I do it all the time and the best baristas get it right first time!

- The sandwich has become the ubiquitous carb-laden "lunch on the go". Lose the top piece of bread to cut your refined carbohydrates and instead fill up with a small bag of green salad leaves and healthy dressing.

- Don't try to change everything at once. Bad habits are hard enough to break as it is. Focus on breaking one at a time.

- If you're a parent, choose your meal skipping wisely. I've tried fasting with a toddler who doesn't understand why Mummy isn't eating and will, quite literally, shove a fistful of tuna pasta into my mouth.

- Get the portions right. If you're restricting the number of meals you're having, it makes sense that the portion sizes need to be bigger than they would be if you were eating five mini-meals a day. Use the recipe section as a guide to how big your portions should be.

# PART 4

# ANTI-AGING EXERCISES

# FITNESS RULES FOR FASTING

## WHY EXERCISE?

That old adage, "Daily exercise maketh for a healthy life and lively mind", is all well and good, but the saboteurs of all good intentions, Temptation, Procrastination and Distraction, tend to make exercise an erratic achievement for most people.

Exercise is especially challenging if you're juggling the demands of parenthood. Even though I know I'll feel much better afterwards, some days if my husband didn't proverbially kick me out of the door with my running togs on, I myself would most likely fall victim to the three scourges. Whether it's the long-drawn-out bedtime rituals of frisky toddlers or the clearing up of spaghetti-smeared kitchen walls, parenting saps desire to do anything at all in the evening other than collapse on the sofa with a glass of wine in hand to watch the latest Scandinavian import TV series. Or maybe that's just me.

But really, do we have to exercise? It's a question I'm often asked on retreat. Many people think that exercise is just about burning off calories, but there's so much more to it than that. Along with helping you to achieve and maintain your ideal weight, physical activity can do the following:

- Reduce your risk of heart disease, stroke, type-2 diabetes and some cancers.

- Help keep your bones strong and healthy.

- Improve your mood, reduce feelings of stress and help you sleep better.

- Give you strength and flexibility - attributes that seem to translate as much mentally as they do physically.

I also believe that on top of all these worthy benefits, exercise adds life to your years.

Sometimes it's a simple matter of making exercise more important to you. Also, if you're paying up front for an exercise class, you may find it's harder to miss. My days are dramatically improved by 30-60 minutes of exercise, whether it's running with my dog on the beach or Pilates with the girls. Exercise provides variety, buzz, a glow, a sense of achievement and perspective, plus it helps offset any guilt about enjoying that glass of Sauvignon at the end of the day!

## HOW MUCH EXERCISE DO YOU NEED?

In 2010 the World Health Organization (WHO) issued global recommendations on the amount of physical activity we need to stay healthy. They recommend that adults (aged 18-64) should build up to at least 2½ hours of moderate intensity aerobic activity, 1¼ hours of vigorous intensity activity, or a combination of the two each week. We should also incorporate two sessions of muscle-strengthening activities, such as weight training, every week. Although we can meet these recommendations by doing just five 30-minute workouts a week, less than a third of British women are active enough for health. And the benefits don't stop at 30 minutes. WHO stresses that additional benefits can be achieved if we double these minimum recommendations.

Focus is often placed on structured physical activity, such as hitting the treadmill or a spin class, but this is far from being the only factor when it comes to the calorie-burn equation. We've all heard the advice about getting off the bus a stop early, or taking the stairs instead of the lift, but in reality, how useful is this? Well, just think about it… as technology progresses we're at our computers for longer and longer periods each day, we shop online rather than going to the high street, we catch up with friends over Skype or Facebook rather than meeting them in the flesh, we watch TV to relax at the end of a busy day and sometimes we're just so busy that we don't think we can allow ourselves an extra five minutes to walk rather than take the car… the thing is, if you're looking to lose weight, the total energy you burn off has to be higher than the amount you eat and every little step helps.

Collectively, unstructured activities are referred to as non-exercise activity thermogenesis (NEAT) and include all activity-related energy expenditure that's not purposeful exercise. NEAT is actually pretty cool since some of us actually alter NEAT levels according to what we eat without even thinking about it. In other words, one of the secrets of the naturally slim is that they fidget and move more if they over-eat. In fact, one of the ways I was taught to help identify different body types during my training in India was to notice how much of a fidget people were when I was consulting with them! Without fail, those who had "ants in their pants" were the naturally slender types. So, if you're more of a couch potato, walking off dinner is clearly a very good idea! A basic pedometer can track how far you walk each day, and trying to

beat yesterday's step count can be addictive. The next generation of activity monitors track every move you make, and some even help you to understand your sleep patterns.

## WHAT COUNTS AS EXERCISE?

Physical activity doesn't just mean sweating it out at the gym – any movement that gets you slightly out of breath, feeling warm and a little bit sweaty, and that makes your heart beat faster, counts (yes, I know what you're thinking and that kind of workout counts too). You can choose from sport, active travel, structured exercise or housework. Even small changes are beneficial and you'll get more benefit from a brisk walk every day than from dusting off your gym membership card once a month. If you've never been very active, it's not too late to start. The key to developing an active lifestyle that you can keep up long term is to find an activity you enjoy.

## FINDING INSPIRATION

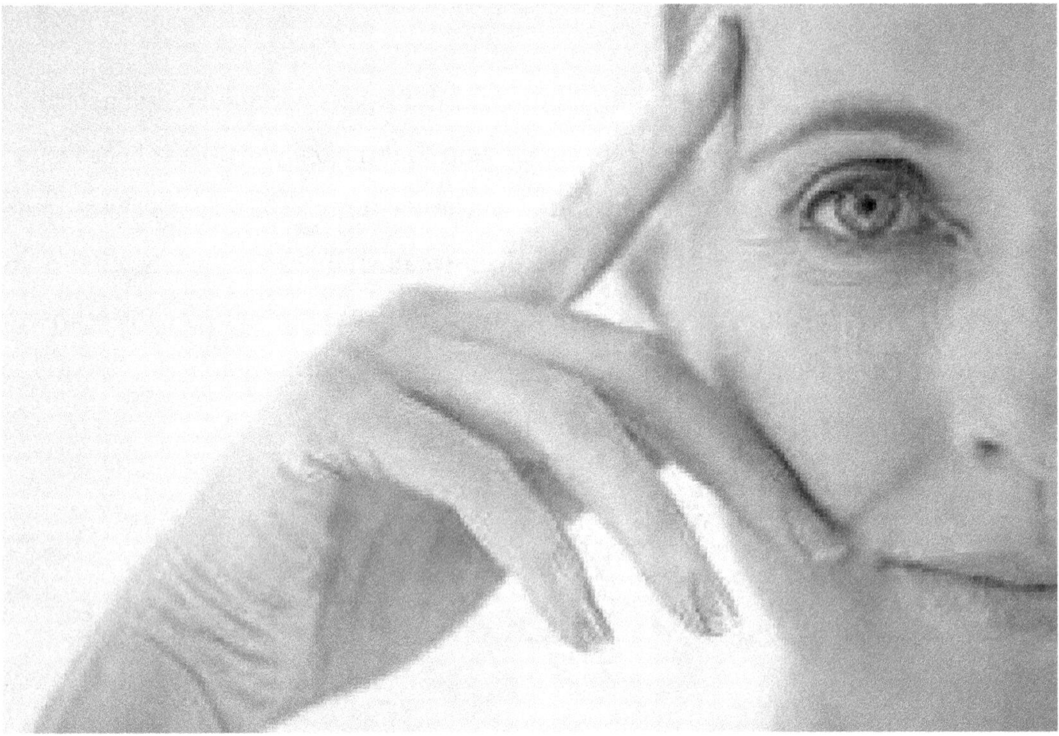

I've found that nothing works better than a bit of inspiration when it comes to changing habits. Over the last two decades, charity events such as marathons, 10km runs, cycle sportive and adventure racing have helped to motivate people to train with a goal in mind. Who would have thought that tens of thousands of women wearing sparkly bras would happily do the "Moonwalk" through the night in London and Edinburgh, kept going only by a sense of camaraderie and a shared purpose to raise money for breast cancer research?

Gyms, too, have revolutionized – it's no longer just about feeling the burn. Classes such as Zumba®, salsa and hula hooping, where having a laugh is every bit as important as burning off calories, have become part of many people's fitness regimes. "Outdoor gyms", like those run by military fitness types, have got all shapes, sizes and ages into the mud and pushing out the press-ups of a Sunday morning. For those willing to go even further, road-or mountain-biking, kitesurfing and triathlon provide accessible competitive events that you can now do much more easily at your own level.

## *TOP TIPS:*

- Book an active holiday to get yourself started.
- Sign up for a charity run or hike.
- Achieve inner calm with yoga or sweat it out in a Bikram studio.
- If dancing's your thing, try Sh'Bam™, the latest craze to follow Zumba®.
- If you have kids, encourage them to play active games and join in too.
- Work off job frustrations with a boxing or martial arts class.
- Treat yourself to a one-to-one with a personal trainer.
- Volunteer for a local conservation project or do some heavy-duty gardening.
- Get back to what you were good at in school – badminton and netball are popular team sports that stand the test of time.
- Improve your commute to work by walking or cycling.

# SIMPLE RULES FOR EXERCISE

## *RULE 1: TAKE THE FIRST STEP*

As the saying goes, "Every journey starts with a single step". If there's anything preventing you from taking that first step, take some time to think about how you can overcome this. From there, set yourself a realistic activity goal for the week. Make sure you write it down and, even better, tell a loved one that you're thinking/going to do it - it makes it more real to share your conviction.

## *RULE 2: TAKE IT FURTHER*

The next step is to monitor your progress - an activity diary is an ideal way to do this - and plan to add a little more each week. Keep setting new goals and challenging yourself. Variety is also vital as you can get into a rut with your exercise program just like with anything else. Follow the lead of international sport coaches who insist on variety to keep minds fresh and stimulated, or sign up to a sport where you'll be under the watchful gaze of a coach.

## *RULE 3: TAKE CARE*

If you're new to exercise, or haven't done any for some time, you should always check with your doctor before starting a new exercise program. The benefits of activity almost always outweigh the risks, but if you have a health

condition or are just starting out, your doctor will be able to advise on any activities that you should avoid or take extra care with.

## *RULE 4: GO FOR THE BURN*

You'll get the best benefits from a structured exercise plan, especially if you do some of your training at a high intensity and include some weights. But if you're not quite ready for that, fitting extra movement into your day is a good way to get started. If you take the stairs instead of the lift, get off the bus or train one stop early and are generally more active without actually working out, you could lose at least 6kg (1st) in 12 months, so long as you don't eat more to compensate! If you're already exercising regularly, instead of just focusing on doing more exercise, take every opportunity to do things the active way.

When you're fasting, a great way to boost your calorie burn is to focus on increasing your NEAT. Together with the advice below on exercising, this will make sure you're doing everything you can to achieve the best shape possible.

| ACTIVITY | TIME NEEDED (MINUTES) |
|---|---|
| 1. Skipping | 8 |
| 2. Jogging | 12 |
| 3. Gardening (weeding) | 14 |
| 4. Swimming (leisurely pace) | 14 |
| 5. Cycling (light effort) | 14 |
| 6. Scrubbing the floor (vigorous effort) | 15 |
| 7. Vacuuming | 18 |
| 8. Dancing | 19 |
| 9. Playing with children | 21 |
| 10. Walking the dog | 24 |
| 11. Food shopping (at the supermarket) | 28 |
| 12. Driving a car | 32 |
| 13. Computer work | 43 |

You might be disheartened when the running-or step-machine tells you you've burnt 87 calories when you've been sweating for at least 15 minutes. After all, it

doesn't even add up to a skinny cappuccino. Don't despair! You burn fat even after exercise because you primarily use carbohydrate fuel during the exercise, which takes time to replace, so in the meantime, your body burns fat for energy. In other words, your metabolism is raised for a little while after your workout.

# EXERCISING AND FASTING

The obvious second part to the puzzle is exercise. Exercise has many wonderful benefits. It can help with depression and anxiety, while also helping you to attain your aesthetic goals. Exercise is also going to play a part in the balancing of the hormones mentioned earlier. Exercise promotes the production of HGH, but will also help drain glycogen stores quickly.

## *What is the best exercise when fasting?*

It is popular belief that long drawn-out cardio at a steady pace is the best way to burn fat. In my experience, this is not the case. Although it has its benefits, when it comes to burning fat and the IF lifestyle, I've had far more success with HITT training for both female and male clients.

## High Intensity Interval Training (HITT)

If burning fat is your mission, I recommend HITT training. Fast paced workouts that can be done in 30 minutes make this ideal for someone with a busy lifestyle. HITT can be done with bodyweight exercises, barbells, kettlebells and dumbbells. I usually look to use exercises that use more than one muscle group. For example, a row rather than a bicep curl. The name of the game is short bursts at near maximum effort. Below are some guidelines you can play with. They are meant as guidelines, not gospel!

- 20 second exercise – 10 second rest (Advanced)
- 10 second exercise – 20 second rest (Intermediate)
- 10 second exercise – 30 second rest (Beginner)

Rounds:

- 8+ (Advanced)
- 3-6 (Intermediate)
- 1-3 (Beginner)

Number of exercises:

- 7+ (Advanced)
- 5-6 (Intermediate)
- 3-5 (Beginner)

## Example workouts

### *Beginner*

- Squat
- Running on the spot

- Star Jumps

*Intermediate*

- Burpees
- Weighted squat
- Press Up
- Medicine Ball Slam
- Battle Ropes

*Advanced*

- Burpee/ High Jump
- Box Jump
- Kettlebell Swing
- Clean & Press
- Battle Ropes
- Kettlebell Row

## EXERCISE AND THE 16/8 FAST

**THE 16:8 DIET**

| | DAY 1 | DAY 2 | DAY 3 | DAY 4 | DAY 5 | DAY 6 | DAY 7 |
|---|---|---|---|---|---|---|---|
| MIDNIGHT – 8 AM | FAST | FAST | FAST | FAST | FAST | FAST | FAST |
| 12 PM | First meal | First meal | First meal | First meal | First meal | First meal | First meal |
| 4 PM | Last meal by 8PM | Last meal by 8PM | Last meal by 8PM | Last meal by 8PM | Last meal by 8PM | Last meal by 8PM | Last meal by 8PM |
| 8 PM – MIDNIGHT | FAST | FAST | FAST | FAST | FAST | FAST | FAST |

But what about exercising while fasting? As you'll know from the "Fit You and Your Life to Fasting" chapter, the 16/8 fasting pattern is often used by people who are looking to get into their best shape ever, and workouts are usually done in a fasted state.

However, it's important to remember that most of the studies on exercise while fasted were done on men, and we know that women's bodies may respond differently. This means that, when it comes to the 16/8 fast, the rules for men and women are slightly different.

# EXERCISE AND THE 5/2 FAST

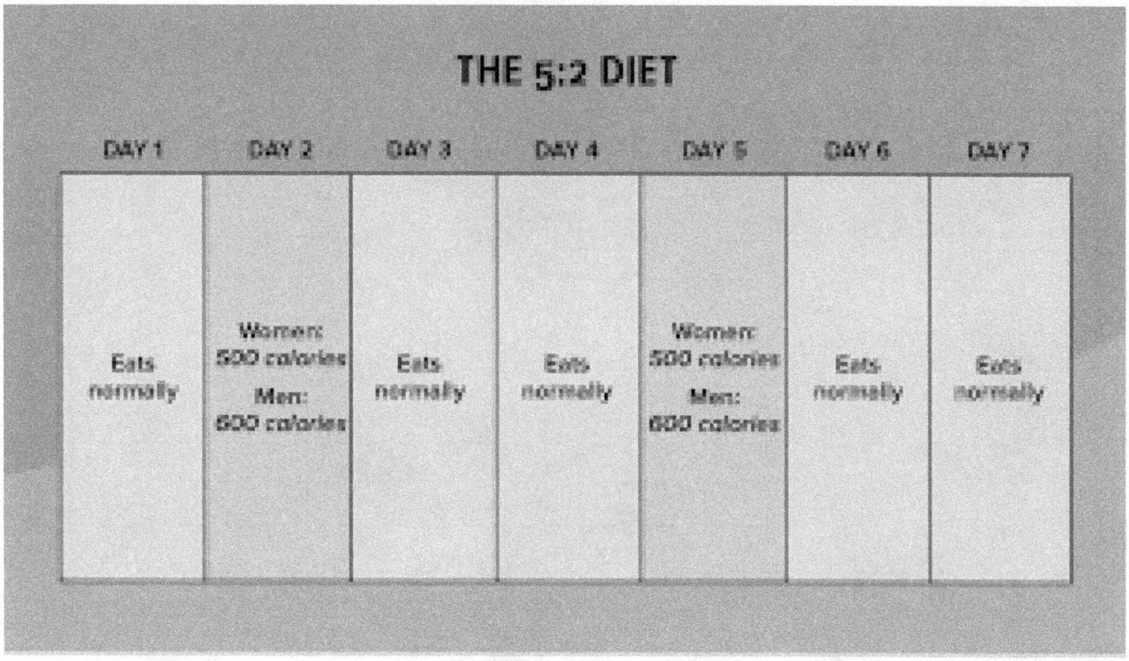

**THE 5:2 DIET**

| DAY 1 | DAY 2 | DAY 3 | DAY 4 | DAY 5 | DAY 6 | DAY 7 |
|---|---|---|---|---|---|---|
| Eats normally | Women: 500 calories<br>Men: 600 calories | Eats normally | Eats normally | Women: 500 calories<br>Men: 600 calories | Eats normally | Eats normally |

If you're going to do the 5/2 fast, it's best to avoid prolonged or hard exercise on your 500-calorie days. However, it's fine to do this sort of exercise a couple of hours after your first meal the following day. And do make sure that if you're exercising the day before your 500-calorie day, you end the day with a proper meal.

Although you'll be going for periods of the day without food, the fasting plan covers all your nutritional requirements. To ensure that you're getting everything your body needs to fuel an active lifestyle, I encourage you to eat more during your eating "windows" if you feel hungry. Keep healthy snacks to hand so that you're not tempted by junk food if hunger pangs strike.

## Recovery, Rest & The Importance of Sleep

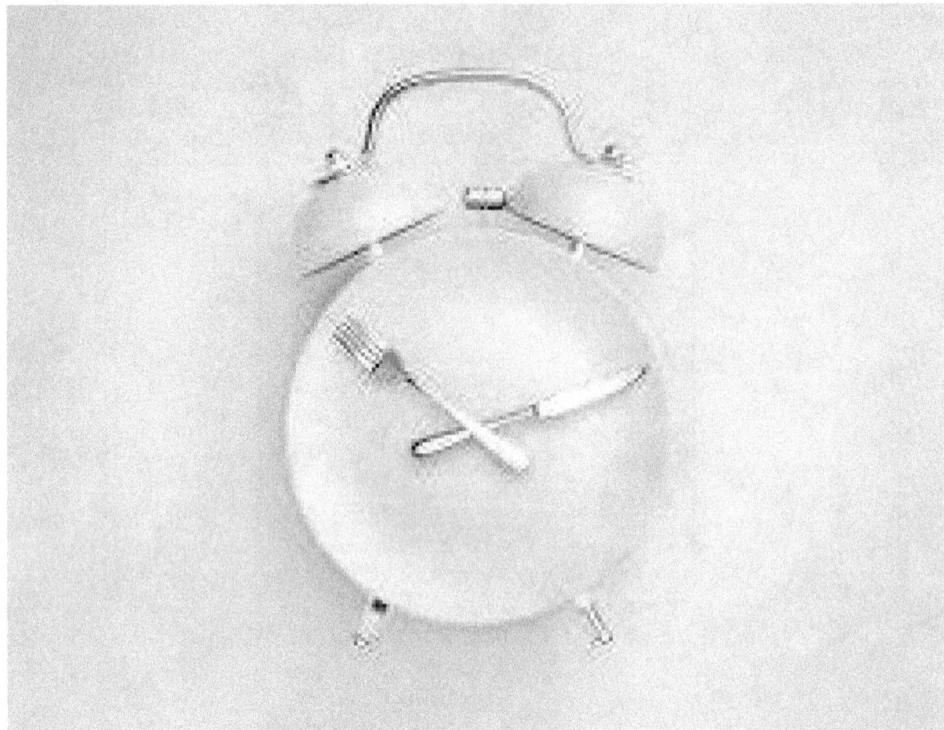

As promised, here is the third (perhaps most important) part of the weight loss puzzle which is often neglected. Sleep! Getting proper sleep can skyrocket your results - here's how.

Our body primarily enters an anabolic (building) type phase during sleep. Our body goes to work repairing damage, replacing cells, and believe it or not, burning fat. Shawn Stevenson explains this in his book "Sleep Smarter:

21 Essential Strategies to Sleep Your Way to A Better Body Better Health and Bigger Success". This book has outlined key hormones you should know about for weight loss, but there are many more. Some help initiate repair and growth and some help keep us awake and/or alert. One of the big factors dictating the creation and release of these hormones is quality sleep. Stevenson cites studies showing sleep deprivation can be linked to high levels of hormones such as cortisol and insulin (Remember what too much insulin does?). He also mentions hormones correlated with fat burning that are only secreted during sleep and darkness. Remember how HGH helps burn fat? Quality

sleep is linked to the creation of this hormone. If you're not getting quality sleep at the right times, all the exercise and healthy eating may not yield the results you were hoping for. If you've ever dieted before while thrashing yourself in the gym only to see little to no results, you know how frustrating this is! Perhaps proper sleep was the missing piece you needed!

## 4 tips to sleep better at night

### *TIP 1 – Get more sun*

Our body's circadian system or "body clock" plays a huge role in the production of hormones. This is heavily influenced by sunlight. Stevenson explained Light, specifically morning sunlight, signals your glands and organs it's time to wake up, queuing them to produce day time hormones (most of these helping keep you alert and awake). If our bodies get inefficient sunlight in the morning and then too much artificial light at night (such as TV, laptops and smart phones) our circadian clock gets jumbled. This can cause our glands to produce hormones that prevent us sleeping. Lack of quality sleep is going to hinder the production of hormones such as HGH and could even spike the creation of hormones such as insulin. If this happens, we won't burn fat over night!

### *TIP2 – Avoid screens before bedtime*

If you are someone who watches TV until 11pm or falls asleep to YouTube on your phone, the quickest way to improve sleep would be to stop using your devices at least an hour before bedtime. Remember how our body clock is impacted by sunlight? It's also impacted by artificial light. Our eyes are a major light sensor and the blue light produced by our favorite screens stimulate our body to produce day time hormones which are primarily for keeping us awake and active. With these bad boys circulating our body, falling asleep will be hard and our body won't produce those sweet anabolic hormones we need to repair and lose weight. Some of which Stevenson cited as only being produced in the dark. Interesting!

NOTE: My clients often argue that watching TV or some other device helps them go to sleep and without it they toss and turn. The information above is to achieve quality sleep and even though you might feel that way, I find in most cases this is simply because the client has made this a habit.

I encourage you to find other activities to replace your device, rather than lying in the dark stressing about not going to sleep.

## *TIP 3 – Sleep in darkness*

Although this might seem apparent after the first two tips, some of my clients neglect this tip when not told. We can't control lights outside, such as street lamps and annoying security lights, but these could still affect our sleep on the molecular level, interrupting repair and leaving us tired the next day. Black out your windows with heavy duty curtains to stop pesky outside lights ruining your healing process!

P.S If it wasn't obvious turn out lamps, nightlights as well.

## *TIP 4 – Quality not Quantity*

One of the most beneficial points I took away from Stevenson's book was that there is a sweet time window during the night where sleep is the most beneficial. During this window, our body produces the best number of hormones needed for repair and fat loss. He explained this was roughly between 10pm and 2am leaving every hour out of this window as a bonus. He also noted this could vary depending on time of year and what time zone you are in but suggested getting to bed as soon as possible after dark falls.

Improving your sleeping habits is key to weight loss, building muscle and living a healthier life in general. This important factor is often neglected in weight loss programs perhaps being the missing piece you needed! Quality sleep is going to ensure proper adaptation of key hormones for fat burning and might even be more important than increasing your exercise in the gym. Set a consistent bed time and make sure to get to bed about 30 to 60 minutes prior.

# FASTING SAFELY

By now I hope that you have an open mind to the many benefits of fasting and that you're excited about giving it a go. If you've read this book and are still trying to decide if, when, or how to give fasting a try, remember that you'll only ever truly "get it" by trying it for yourself.

Before you launch headlong into your new fasting lifestyle, here are a few words of caution. Although fasting has been around for millennia, the science on how and when to fast is in its early stages. For example, there's very little research on how fasting affects fertility.

There are some people who should avoid fasting completely, some who should seek medical advice first, and some situations where it might not be right for you. Fasting isn't something that you should just jump into, and it doesn't suit everyone.

## WHEN NOT TO FAST

You should avoid fasting if any of the following apply:

- You are pregnant, breastfeeding, or actively trying for a baby (it's okay to fast if you're getting your body ready to conceive, but please don't consider fasting if there's any chance you could already be pregnant).
- You have ever experienced an eating disorder.
- You are underweight

You should seek medical advice first if any of the following apply:

- You have a long-term medical condition such as cancer, diabetes, ulcerative colitis, epilepsy, anemia, liver, kidney or lung disease.
- You have a condition that affects your immune system.
- You are on medication, particularly medicines that control your blood sugar, blood pressure or blood lipids (cholesterol).

## POSSIBLE SIDE-EFFECTS AND HOW TO MANAGE THEM

As we learnt earlier in the book, fasting may make you feel a bit "yucky" at first. Many juice fasters experience headaches through caffeine withdrawal, and feeling hungry is natural when you first try a fast. These effects don't usually last long, and most people find that they're outweighed by the positive effects of fasting.

More serious side-effects may include:

- Dehydration or over-hydration.
- Feeling dizzy or light-headed.
- Extreme fatigue.
- Constipation.
- Nausea or vomiting.
- Insomnia.
- Irregular periods.

Always err on the side of caution and stop the fast if you don't feel well. You can minimize the risk of some side-effects by approaching the fast safely.

# END NOTE

I invite you to think of your goals as a journey. This book as the start, and your goal as the finish. The roads and paths in between will vary, and be full of both victories and losses. Your humble beginning and your eventual triumph mean nothing without the winding roads that link them, and vice versa. Everyone admires those who have "made it". Whether that is in regard to weight loss or some other human want like riches or fame. We are especially motivated by those who appear to have come from nothing or succeeded against all odds, but the road that links these two paradigms is just as important as the factors themselves. The roads are scarcely revered unless the end is reached, otherwise it is simply a road leading nowhere, a lost cause

- failure. Those who have nothing or are underprivileged are seldom celebrated unless they manage to follow a path with a successful ending. Your health and fitness journey are not exempt from such parameters. You have most likely started a hundred times. You have most likely trodden many paths seeking your goal, only to find fleeting success or failure. I hope this book will arm you with enough hope to start once again and lead you on the right path to your ultimate victory, perhaps inspiring those around you to take action and do the same.

# Keto Dessert & Chaffle Cookbook 2021 with Pictures

*Quick and Easy, Sugar-Low Bombs, Chaffle and Cakes Recipes to Shed Weight, Boost Your Mood and Live Ketogenic lifestyle*

**By**

**Dora Gray**

# Table of Contents

## Introduction

The ketogenic diet or Keto is a low-carbohydrate, mild protein, high-fat diet that will help you lose fat more efficiently. It has several advantages for weight reduction, wellbeing, and efficiency, so a rising number of healthcare professionals & practitioners recommend it.

## Fat as a form of nutrition

For nutrition, the body uses three fuel sources: carbohydrates, fats and proteins. Carbohydrates convert into blood sugar or glucose in the bloodstream and are the primary fuel source for the body. If carbohydrates are not accessible, your body then depends on fat as an energy source. Protein is the primary building block of muscles and tissues. Protein could also be processed into glucose in a pinch and utilized for energy.

The keto diet encourages your body to utilize fat as the primary source of nutrition instead of carbohydrates, a ketosis mechanism. You consume too little carbs on the keto diet that the body cannot depend on glucose for nutrition. And your body turns to utilize fat for energy rather than carbs, as keto foods are filled with fat. A major part of the calories, almost 70 to 80% come from fat, consuming 15 to 20% of calories from protein and barely 5% calories from carbohydrates (that makes for about 20 to 30 grams of carbohydrates per day, depending on the weight and height of a person).

## Meal options in regular diets

To conquer the weight reduction fight, it becomes tough to continue the dieting combat for a long period. Many people revert to the previous eating patterns after only a few weeks when confronted with the difficulty and limited food ranges of many diets, especially vegan, low-fat and low-calorie diets. For starters, the ketogenic diet is incredibly beneficial for weight reduction, but following specific food choices can be overwhelming. Only after three weeks can you begin noticing significant effects; however, the complications and inconvenience of transitioning to an effective ketogenic diet may deter you from keeping to the program long enough to reap the benefits.

Thankfully, to render your keto diet ever more efficient, successful and simple to use, you will build an array of foods, preparing strategies, tips and suggestions. One hidden tool can be used from the diet's outset, without much details of the keto diet, which is continued even after achieving the weight loss target.

That hidden preferred weapon is the "Fat Bomb."

## The Fat Bomb

The fat bombs in the keto diet play a major role in motivation for the dieters. Indulging in a high fat dessert gives you a stress-free environment to continue your diet. These fat bombs provide the correct amounts of fat, carbohydrates, and protein resulting in weight reduction while supplying the user with sustained energy. They do this by supplementing your diet with chemicals that hold your body in a fat-burning state, even after you have had a fulfilling meal.

The Keto diet aims to rely on foods that are high in fat and low in carbs. By modifying what the body utilizes as food, it helps facilitate weight reduction. Carbohydrates, like those present in sugars and bread, are usually transformed into energy. If the body cannot have enough nutrients, the body begins to burn fat as a substitute for energy.

Your liver converts the fat into ketones, which are a form of acid. Getting a certain amount of ketones in your body will lead you to a biochemical condition known as ketosis. Your body can burn stored fat for fuel; thus, you will losing weight when you go through ketosis.

To reach a ketosis condition, it takes between one to ten days of consuming a low-carb, high-fat diet; to sustain the fat-burning cycle of ketosis, you have to continue consuming the keto diet. Eating fatty foods will help you more easily get into ketosis and sustain it for longer periods.

Fat bombs are 90% fat, making them the ideal keto addition for beginners and lifetime keto adherents. They hold you in a ketosis state and can provide health advantages unlike many other high protein foods; you can snack on fat bombs or have them as dinners or as have as a side dish too. They are simple to produce and are available in a range of varieties, from sweet to savory.

**Can Fat Bombs Be Healthy?**

Ketogenic fat bombs are fueled by two major ingredients: high-fat dairy and coconut oil. Both of these components have several powerful health advantages. Coconut produces a form of fat known as MCTs (medium-chain triglycerides), which gives the body additional ketones that can be readily consumed and used to sustain ketosis.

There are distinct health advantages of consuming high-fat dairy fat bombs. High-fat dairy products produce fatty acids known as CLA (conjugated linoleic acid), minerals and vitamins. Data indicates that CLA plays a significant role in the body's breakdown of fat and may lower cardiac attack and stroke risk.

Eating high-fat dairy meals prior to bedtime may help burn fat when still sleeping. Fat burned while you sleep the body with an energy that does not need to metabolize stress hormones or depend on sugar.

## Keto Diet and Mood

There are various comments from individuals on a keto diet that probably indicate the association between the keto diet and mood changes. Various hypotheses connect the keto diet to mood regulation, even if only partly.

The explanation of why the keto diet aids in accelerated weight reduction and reversal of multiple chronic weight-related problems lead people to come out of the despair of "I am not healthy." As a consequence of the results themselves, most people report a positive attitude by adopting a keto diet. But is that important? What makes a difference is that it has a positive and long-lasting effect. Some research also shows that a ketogenic diet may help combat depression since it provides anti-inflammatory benefits. Inflammations are associated with, at least certain, forms of depression. A few of the advantages are provided below that create the relationship between the keto diet and mood. A keto diet:

**1. Helps regulate energy highs and lows.**

Ketones offer an immediate energy supply for your brain since they are metabolized quicker than glucose. Ketones give a long-lasting, more accurate and reliable energy supply, and when your body understands it can access your fat reserves for food as well, the brain does not worry.

**2. Neurogenesis improvement**

Dietary consumption is a crucial element in assessing neurogenesis. A reduced degree of neurogenesis is correlated with multiple depressive illnesses. On the other side, a higher rate increases emotional endurance.

**3. Reduces and Brings Down Inflammation**

The Keto Diet provides healthy nutritional options, so you avoid consuming inflammatory and refined products. Consuming anti-inflammatory food can have a direct impact on the attitude. If you eat nutritious food high in protein, healthy fats and low-carb vegetables, it reduces inflammation.

**4. Feeds the brain.**

The good fat you consume on Keto fuels your brain and stabilizes your mood. As your brain is composed of 60% fat, it requires an excess of healthy fats to function properly.

So go ahead and try these easy to make lo carb hi fat desserts and lose weight deliciously!

# Chapter 1- Low Carb Desserts

## 1. 10 Minutes Chocolate Mousse

Prep. Time: 10 minutes

Servings: 4

The serving size is ½ cup

**Nutrition as per serving:**

218 kcal / 23g fat / 5g carbs / 2g fiber / 2g protein = 3g net carbs

**Ingredients**

- Powdered sweetener 1/4 cup
- Cocoa powder, unsweetened, sifted 1/4 cup
- Vanilla extract 1tsp.
- Heavy whipping cream 1 cup
- Kosher salt 1/4tsp.

**Directions**

With an electric beater, beat the cream to form stiff peaks. Put in the sweetener, cocoa powder, salt, vanilla and whisk till all ingredients are well combined.

## 2. The Best Keto Cheesecake

Prep. Time: 20 minutes

Cook Time: 50 minutes

Setting Time: 8 hours

Servings: 12

The serving size is 1 slice

**Nutrition as per serving:**

600kcal / 54g fat / 7g carbs / 2g fiber / 14g protein = 5 g net carbs

**Ingredients**

Layer of crust

- Powdered sweetener 1/4 cup

- Almond flour 1 1/2 cups
- Butter melted 6 tbsp.
- Cinnamon 1tsp.

Filling

- Cream cheese, full fat, room temperature (8 oz.)
- Powdered Sweetener 2 Cups
- Eggs at room temperature 5 Large
- Sour cream at room temperature 8 Oz.
- Vanilla extract 1 Tbsp.

**Directions**

1. Heat the oven to 325F.
2. Arrange the rack in the center of the oven. Mix dry ingredients for the crust in a medium mixing bowl. Mix in the butter. Transfer the crust mixture into a springform pan (10-inch x 4- inch), and using your fingers, press halfway up and around the sides. Then press the mixture with a flat bottom cup into the pan. Chill the crust for about 20 minutes.
3. Beat the cream cheese (at room temperature) in a large mixing container, with an electric beater or a
4. Hand mixer until fluffy and light.
5. If using a stand mixer, attach the paddle accessory.
6. Add in about 1/3rd of sweetener at a time and beat well.
7. Add in one egg at a time beating until well incorporated.
8. Lastly, add in the sour cream, vanilla and mix until just combined.

9. Pour this cheesecake mixture onto the crust and smooth out the top. Place in the heated oven and examine after 50 minutes. The center should not jiggle, and the top should not be glossy anymore.
10. Turn the oven off and open the door slightly, leaving the cheesecake inside for about 30 minutes.
11. Take out the cheesecake and run a knife between the pan and the cheesecake (this is to unstick the cake but don't remove the springform yet). Leave for 1 hour.
12. Chill for at least 8 hrs. loosely covered with plastic wrap.
13. Take off the sides of the springform pan, decorate & serve.

Note: all the ingredients to make the cheesecake should be at room temperature. Anything refrigerated must be left out for at least 4 hrs.

## 3. Butter Pralines

Prep. Time: 5 minutes

Cook Time: 11 minutes

Chilling Time: 1 hour

Servings: 10

The serving size is 2 Butter Pralines

**Nutrition as per serving:**

338kcal / 36g fat / 3g carbs / 2g fiber / 2g protein = 1g net carbs

**Ingredients**

- Salted butter 2 Sticks
- Heavy Cream 2/3 Cup
- Granular Sweetener 2/3 Cup

- Xanthan gum ½ tsp.
- Chopped pecans 2 Cups
- Sea salt

**Directions**

1. Line parchment paper on a cookie sheet with or apply a silicone baking mat on it.
2. In a saucepan, brown the butter on medium-high heat, stirring regularly, for just about 5 minutes.
3. Add in the sweetener, heavy cream and xanthan gum. Stir and take off the heat.
4. Add in the nuts and chill to firm up, occasionally stirring, for about 1 hour. The mixture will become very thick. Shape into ten cookie forms and place on the lined baking sheet, and sprinkle with the sea salt, if preferred. Let chill until hardened.
5. Keep in a sealed container, keep refrigerated until serving.

## 4. Homemade Healthy Twix Bars

Prep. Time: 5 minutes

Cook Time: 20 minutes

Servings: 18 Bars

The serving size is 1 Bar

**Nutrition as per serving:**

111kcal / 7g fat / 8g carbs / 5g fiber / 4g protein = 3g net carbs

**Ingredients**

For the cookie layer

- Coconut flour 3/4 cup
- Almond flour 1 cup
- Keto maple syrup 1/4 cup
- Sweetener, granulated 1/2 cup
- Flourless keto cookies 1/4 cup
- Almond milk 1/2 cup

For the gooey caramel

- Cashew butter (or any seed or nut butter) 1 cup
- Sticky sweetener of choice 1 cup
- Coconut oil 1 cup
- For the chocolate coating
- Chocolate chips 2 cups

**Directions**

1. Line parchment paper in a loaf pan or square pan and set aside.
2. In a big mixing bowl, put in almond flour, coconut flour, and then granulated. Combine very well. Mix in the keto syrup and stir to make it into a thick dough.
3. Add the crushed keto cookies and also add a tbsp. of milk to keep it a thick batter. If the batter stays too thick, keep adding milk by tablespoon. Once desired consistency is achieved, shift the batter to the prepared pan and smooth it out. Chill.
4. Combine the cashew butter, coconut oil and syrup on the stovetop or a microwave-safe dish and heat until mixed. Beat very well to make sure the coconut oil is completely mixed. Drizzle the caramel over the prepared cookie layer and shift to the freezer.

5. When the bars are hard, take out of the pan and slice into 18 bars. Once more, put it back in the freezer.
6. Liquefy the chocolate chips by heat. Using two forks, dip each Twix bar into the melted chocolate till evenly covered. Cover all the bars with chocolate. Chill until firm.

## 5. Best Chocolate Chip cookie

Prep. Time: 5 minutes

Cook Time: 20 minutes

Servings: 15 Cookies

The serving size is 1 Cookie

**Nutrition as per serving:**

98kcal / 6g fat / 12g carbs / 5g fiber / 5g protein = 7g net carbs

**Ingredients**

- Almond flour blanched 2 cups
- Baking powder 1 tsp
- Cornstarch 1/4 cup
- Coconut oil 2 tbsp.
- Sticky sweetener, keto-friendly 6 tbsp.
- Almond extract 1 tsp
- Coconut milk, unsweetened 1/4 cup
- Chocolate chips 1/2 cup

**Directions**

1. Heat oven up to 350F/175C. Line parchment paper on a large cookie tray and put it aside.
2. Place all the dry ingredients in a big mixing bowl, and combine well.
3. Melt the keto-friendly-sticky sweetener, almond extract and coconut oil in a microwave-safe proof or stovetop. Then mix it into the dry mixture, adding milk to combine very well. Stir through your chocolate chips.
4. Form small balls with slightly wet hands from the cookie dough. Set the balls up on the lined cookie tray. Then form them into cookies by pressing them with a fork. Bake for 12 to 15 minutes till they brown.
5. Take out from the oven, allowing to cool on the tray completely.

## 6. White Chocolate Dairy Free Peanut Butter Cups

Prep. Time: 5 minutes

Cook Time: 5 minutes

Servings: 40

The serving size is 1 cup

**Nutrition as per serving:**

117kcal / 6g fat / 14g carbs / 10g fiber / 3g protein = 4g net carbs

**Ingredients**

- White Chocolate Bar, Sugar-free, coarsely chopped 4 cups
- Peanut butter, smooth (or sunflower seed butter) 1 cup
- Coconut flour 2 tbsp.
- Unsweetened coconut milk 2 tbsp.+ more if needed

**Directions**

1. Line muffin liners in a standard muffin tin of 12 cups or mini muffin tin of 20 cups and put aside.
2. Removing ½ a cup of your white chocolate, melt the remaining 3 1/2 cups on the stovetop or in a microwave-safe dish, till silky and smooth. Quickly, pour the melted white chocolate equally amongst the prepared muffin cups, scrape down the sides to remove all. Once done, chill
3. Meanwhile, start making the peanut butter filling. Mix the flour and peanut butter well. Adding a tsp. of milk at a time brings to the desired texture.
4. Take the hardened white chocolate cups, then equally pour the peanut butter filling among all of them. After all, is used up, take white chocolate that was kept aside and melt them. Then pour it on each of the cups to cover fully. Chill until firm.

## 7. Chocolate Crunch Bars

Prep. Time: 5 minutes

Cook Time: 5 minutes

Servings: 20 servings

The serving size is 1 Bar

**Nutrition as per serving:**

155kcal / 12g fat / 4g carbs / 2g fiber / 7g protein = 2g net carbs

**Ingredients**

- Chocolate chips (stevia sweetened), 1 1/2 cups
- Almond butter (or any seed or nut butter) 1 cup

- Sticky sweetener (swerve sweetened or monk fruit syrup) 1/2 cup
- Coconut oil 1/4 cup
- Seeds and nuts (like almonds, pepitas, cashews, etc.) 3 cups

**Directions**

1. Line parchment paper on a baking dish of 8 x 8-inch and put it aside.
2. Combine the keto-friendly chocolate chips, coconut oil, almond butter and sticky sweetener and melt on a stovetop or a microwave-safe dish until combined.
3. Include nuts and seeds and combine until fully mixed. Pour this mixture into the parchment-lined baking dish smoothing it out with a spatula. Chill until firm.

Notes

Keep refrigerated

## 8. Easy Peanut Butter Cups

Prep. Time: 10minutes

Cook Time: 5minutes

Servings: 12

The serving size is 1 piece

**Nutrition as per serving:**

187kcal / 18g fat / 14g carbs / 11g fiber / 3g protein = 3g net carbs

**Ingredients**

Chocolate layers

- Dark chocolate(not bakers chocolate), Sugar-free, 10 oz. Divided
- Coconut oil 5 tbsp. (divided)
- Vanilla extracts 1/2 tsp. (divided) optional

Peanut butter layer

- Creamy Peanut butter 3 1/2 tbsp.

- Coconut oil 2 tsp.
- Powdered Erythritol (or to taste) 4 tsp.
- Peanut flour 1 1/2 tsp.
- Vanilla extracts 1/8 tsp. Optional
- Sea salt 1 pinch (or to taste) optional

**Directions**

1. Line parchment liners in a muffin pan
2. Prepare the chocolate layer on the stove, place a double boiler and heat half of the coconut oil and half of the chocolate, stirring regularly, until melted. (Alternatively use a microwave, heat for 20 seconds, stirring at intervals.). Add in half of the vanilla.
3. Fill each lined muffin cup with about 2 tsp. Of chocolate in each. Chill for around 10 minutes till the tops are firm.
4. Prepare the peanut butter filling: in a microwave or a double boiler, heat the coconut oil and peanut butter (similar to step 2). Mix in the peanut flour, powdered sweetener, sea salt and vanilla until smooth. Adjust salt and sweetener to taste if preferred.
5. Pour a tsp. Of the prepared peanut mixture into each cup with the chocolate layer. You don't want it to reach the edges. Chill for 10 minutes more till the tops are firm.
6. Now, prepare a chocolate layer for the top. Heat the leftover coconut oil and chocolate in a microwave or the double boiler (similar to step 2). Add in the vanilla.
7. Pour about 2 tsp of melted chocolate into each cup. It should cover the empty part and the peanut butter circles completely.

8. Again chill for at least 20 to 30 minutes, until completely solid. Keep in the refrigerator.

## 9. No-Bake Chocolate Coconut Bars

Prep. Time: 1 minute

Cook Time: 5 minutes

Servings: 12 bars

The serving size is 1 bar

**Nutrition as per serving:**

169 kcal / 17g fat / 5g carbs / 4g fiber / 2g protein = 1g net carbs

**Ingredients**

- Keto maple syrup 1/4 cup
- Coconut unsweetened, shredded 3 cups
- Coconut oil, melted 1 cup
- Lily's chocolate chips 1-2 cups

**Directions**

1. Line parchment paper in a large loaf pan or square pan and put aside.
2. Add all the ingredients to a large bowl and combine very well. Shift mixture to the prepared pan. Wet your hands lightly and press them into place. Chill for 30 minutes until firm. Cut into 12 bars.
3. Melt the sugar-free chocolate chips, and using two forks, dip each chilled bar into the melted chocolate and coat evenly. Evenly coat all the bars in the same way. Chill until chocolate solidifies.

4. Keep the Bars in a sealed container at room temperature. If you refrigerated or freeze them, thaw them completely before enjoying them.

## 10. Chocolate Peanut Butter Hearts

Prep. Time: 5 minutes

Cook Time: 5 minutes

Servings: 20 Hearts

The serving size is 1 Heart

**Nutrition as per serving:**

95kcal / 6g fat / 7g carbs / 5g fiber / 5g protein = 2g net carbs

**Ingredients**

- Smooth peanut butter 2 cups
- Sticky sweetener 3/4 cup
- Coconut flour 1 cup
- Chocolate chips of choice 1-2 cups

**Directions**

1. Line parchment paper on a large tray and put it aside.
2. Combine the keto-friendly sticky sweetener and peanut butter and melt on a stovetop or microwave-safe bowl until combined.
3. Include coconut flour and combine well. If the mixture is too thin, include more coconut flour. Leave for around 10 minutes to thicken.
4. Shape the peanut butter mixture into 18 to 20 small balls. Press each ball in. Then, using a heart-molded cookie cutter, shape the balls into hearts removing excess

peanut butter mixture from the sides. Assemble the hearts on the lined tray and chill.

5. Melt the keto-friendly chocolate chips. With two forks, coat the chocolate by dipping each heart into it. Repeat with all hearts. When done, chill until firm.

Notes

Keep in a sealed jar at room temperature for up to 2 weeks, or refrigerate for up to 2 months.

## 11. Magic Cookies

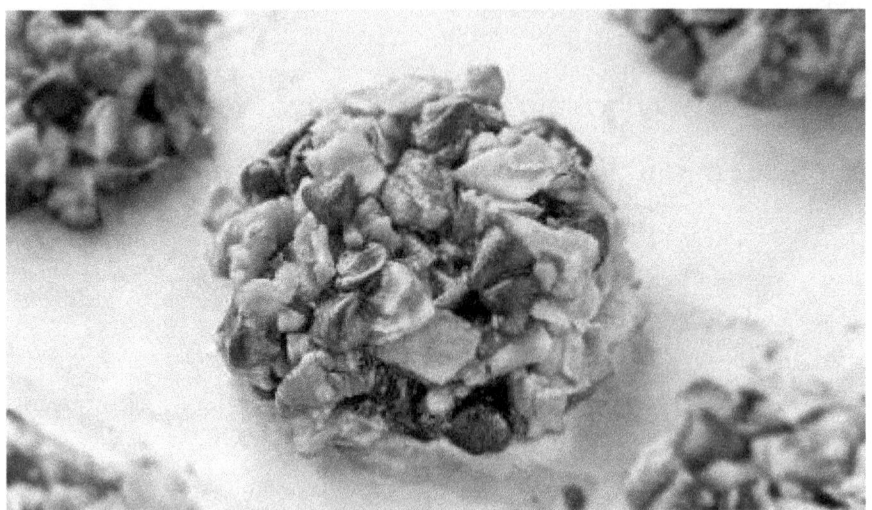

Prep. Time: 10 minutes

Cook Time: 15 minutes

Servings: 15 cookies

The serving size is 1 cookie

**Nutrition as per serving:**

130kcal / 13g fat / 2g carbs / 1g fiber / 2g protein = 1g net carbs

**Ingredients**

- Butter softened 3 tbsp.
- Coconut oil 1/4 cup
- Granulated swerve sweetener 3 tbsp.
- Dark chocolate chips, sugar-free (like lily's) 1 cup
- Egg yolks 4 large
- Coconut flakes 1 cup

- Kosher salt 1/2 tsp.
- Walnuts roughly chopped 3/4 cup.

**Directions**

1. Heat oven up to 350° and line a parchment paper on a baking sheet. In a large mixing bowl, whisk together butter, coconut oil, sweetener, egg yolks and salt; stir in walnuts, coconut, and chocolate chips.
2. Drop spoonfuls of batter onto the prepared baking sheet. Place in the oven and bake for 15 mins until golden,

## 12. No-Bake Coconut Crack Bars

Prep. Time: 2 minutes

Cook Time: 3 minutes

Servings: 20

The serving size is 1 square

**Nutrition as per serving:**

108kcal / 11g fat / 2g carbs / 2g fiber /2g protein = 0g net carbs

**Ingredients**

- Coconut flakes unsweetened & Shredded 3 cups
- Coconut oil, melted 1 cup
- Maple syrup, monk fruit sweetened 1/4 cup (or any liquid sweetener of preference)

**Directions**

1. Line parchment paper on an 8 x 10-inch pan or an 8 x 8-inch pan and put aside. Or use a loaf pan.
2. Combine unsweetened shredded coconut, melted coconut oil, maple syrup (monk fruit sweetened) in a big mixing bowl and mix till you get a thick batter. If you find it crumbling, add a tsp. of water or a bit of extra syrup.
3. Transfer the coconut mixture to the lined pan. Press firmly with slightly wet hands into place. Chill until firmed. Cut into bars & enjoy!

## 13. Candied Pecans

Prep. Time: 5 minutes

Cook Time: 1 minute

Servings: 16 Servings

The serving size is 1 Serving

**Nutrition as per serving:**

139kcal / 15g fat / 3g carbs / 2g fiber / 2g protein = 1g net carbs

**Ingredients**

- Granulated sweetener divided 1 1/2 cups
- Vanilla extract 1 tsp
- Water 1/4 cup
- Cinnamon 1 tbsp.
- Raw pecans 3 cups

**Directions**

1. Over medium flame, heat a skillet or large pan.

2. Add 1 cup of the granulated sweetener, vanilla extract and water, and stir until fully mixed. Let it heat up, stirring in between.
3. Once the sweetener is fully melted, include your pecans. Stir around the pecans ensuring every nut is equally coated in the liquid mixture. Keep occasionally stirring till the sweetener starts to set on the pecans. Take off from the heat. Leave for 2 to 3 minutes.
4. Brea apart the pecans with a wooden spoon before they set together.
5. When cooled, mix with the granulated sweetener that was reserved earlier and cinnamon. Store in a sealed container.

## 14. Sugar-Free Flourless Cookies

Prep. Time: 2 minutes

Cook Time: 10 minutes

Servings: 14 cookies

The serving size is 1 Cookie

**Nutrition as per serving:**

101kcal / 9g fat / 3g carbs / 1g fiber / 5g protein = 3g net carbs

**Ingredients**

For the original style:

- Almond butter 1 cup
- Egg 1 large
- Granulated sweetener, stevia blend monk fruit, 3 /4 cup

For the egg-free style:

- Almond butter smooth 1 cup
- Chia seeds, ground 3-4 tbsp.
- Granulated sweetener, stevia blend monk fruit 3/4 cup

**Directions**

1. Heat the oven up to 350 degrees. Place parchment paper on a cookie sheet or a baking tray.
2. In a big mixing bowl, add all the ingredients and blend until well combined. When using the egg-free recipe, begin with 3 tbsps. of grounded chia seeds. Add an extra tbsp. if the mixture is still too thin.
3. Using your hands or a cookie scoop, shape small balls and place them 3 to 4 inches apart on the baking tray. Make into cookie shape by pressing down with a fork. Bake until cookies are beginning to get a golden brown color but still soft, or for 8 to 10 minutes. Take out from the oven, allowing to cool until firm but soft and chewy.

## 15. Salted Caramel Fudge

Prep. Time: 5 minutes

Cook Time: 5 minutes

Servings: 24 servings

The serving size is 1 fudge cup

**Nutrition as per serving:**

148kcal / 15g fat / 4g carbs / 2g fiber / 4g protein = 2g net carbs

**Ingredients**

- Cashew butter 2 cups
- Keto maple syrup 1/4 cup
- Coconut oil 1/2 cup

**Directions**

1. Line muffin liners in a mini muffin tin of 24-count and put aside.
2. Combine all the ingredients on a stovetop or in a microwave-safe dish and heat till melted.
3. Take off from heat and beat very well till a glossy, smooth texture remains.
4. Split the fudge mixture equally in the lined muffin tin. Chill for about 30 minutes, till firm.

## 16. Healthy Kit Kat Bars

Prep. Time: 5 minutes

Cook Time: 5 minutes

Servings: 20 Bars

The serving size is 1 Bar

**Nutrition as per serving:**

149kcal / 12g fat / 4g carbs / 2g fiber / 7g protein = 2g net carbs

**Ingredients**

- Keto granola 2 cups
- Almond butter (or any seed or nut butter) 1 cup
- Mixed seeds 1/2 cup
- Coconut oil 1/4 cup
- Mixed nuts 1/2 cup
- Dark chocolate chips, 1 1/2 cups
- Sticky sweetener 1/2 cup

**Directions**

1. Mix the mixed nuts, keto granola, and seeds in a big bowl. Put aside.
2. Melt the keto chocolate chips on the stovetop or in a microwave-safe dish. Include almond butter, coconut oil, and sticky sweetener. Heat until well combined.
3. Add the melted chocolate mixture onto the dry and combine until fully unified.
4. Shift the kit kat mixture to a pan of 10 x 10-inch lined with parchment. With a spatula, smooth out to a uniform layer. Chill for about 30 minutes, then slice into bars.

Notes: keep refrigerated

## 17. Healthy No-Bake Keto Cookie Bars

Prep. Time: 5 minutes

Cook Time: 25 minutes

Servings: 12 servings

The serving size is 1 Bar

**Nutrition as per serving:**

149kcal / 5g fat / 10g carbs / 6g fiber / 10g protein = 4g net carbs

**Ingredients**

For the cookie

- Almond flour blanched 1 1/2 cups
- Coconut flour 1/4 cup
- Cinnamon, a pinch
- Protein powder, vanilla flavor (optional) 2 scoops
- Granulated sweetener (like
- Sticky sweetener, keto-friendly, 1/2 cup
- Monk fruit sweetener) 2 tbsp.
- Vanilla extract 1/2 tsp
- Cashew butter (or any nut butter) 1/2 cup
- Sticky sweetener, keto-friendly, 1/2 cup
- Almond milk 1 tbsp.

For the protein icing

- Protein powder,
- Vanilla flavor 3 scoops
- Granulated sweetener, keto-friendly 1-2 tbsp. + for sprinkling 1/2 tsp
- Almond milk, (for batter) 1 tbsp.

For the coconut butter icing

- Coconut butter melted 4-6 tbsp.
- Sticky sweetener, 2 tbsp.
- Almond milk 1 tbsp.

**Directions**

1. Preparing sugar cookie base
2. Place tin foil in a baking pan of 8 x 8 inches and put aside.
3. Mix the protein powder, flours, granulated sweetener and cinnamon in a big mixing bowl, and put aside.
4. Melt the sticky sweetener with cashew butter on a stovetop or a microwave-proof bowl. Stir in the vanilla extract and add to the dry mixture. Beat superbly until fully combined. If the batter formed is too thick, add a tablespoon of almond milk with a tablespoon and mix well until desired consistency.
5. Pour the batter into the lined baking sheet and press tightly in place. Scatter the ½ teaspoon of keto-friendly granulated sweetener and chill for about 15 minutes until they are firm. Then add an icing of choice and chill for 30 minutes more to settle the icing before slicing.
6. Preparing the icing(s)
7. Mix all ingredients of the icings (separately) and, using almond milk, thin down the mixture till a very thick icing is formed.

## 18. Keto Chocolate Bark with Almonds and Bacon

Prep. Time: 30 minutes

Servings: 8 servings

The serving size is 1/8 of the recipe

**Nutrition as per serving:**

157kcal /12.8g fat / 4g protein / 7.5g fiber / 12.7g carbs = 5.2g net carbs

**Ingredients**

- Sugar-free Chocolate Chips 1 bag (9 oz.)
- Chopped Almonds 1/2 cup
- Bacon cooked & crumbled2 slices

**Directions**

1. In a microwave-safe bowl, melt the chocolate chips on high in 30 seconds intervals, stirring every time until all chocolate is melted.
2. Include the chopped almonds into the melted chocolate and mix.
3. Line a baking sheet with parchment and pour the chocolate mixture on it in a thin layer of about 1/2 inch.
4. Immediately top the chocolate with the crumbled bacon and press in with a flat spoon.
5. Chill for around 20 minutes or till the chocolate has solidified. Peel the parchment away from the hardened chocolate and crack it into eight pieces. Keep refrigerated.

# Chapter 2- Chaffles

## 1. Basic chaffle recipe

Prep. Time: 5 minutes

Cook Time: 5 minutes

Servings: 1 chaffle

The serving size is 1 chaffle

**Nutrition as per serving:**

291kcal / 23g fat / 1g carbs / 0g fiber / 20g protein = 1g net carbs

**Ingredients**

- Sharp cheddar cheese shredded 1/2 cup
- Eggs 1

**Directions**

1. Whisk the egg.
2. In the waffle maker, assemble 1/4 cup of shredded cheese.

3. Top the cheese with beaten egg.

4. Top with the remainder 1/4 cup of cheese.

5. Cook till it's golden and crispy. It will get crispier as it cools.

## 2. Keto Oreo Chaffles

Prep. Time: 15 minutes

Cook Time: 8 minutes

Servings: 2 full-size chaffles or 4 mini chaffles

The serving size is 2 chaffles

**Nutrition as per serving:**

381kcal / 14.6g fat / 14g carbs / 5g fiber / 17g protein = 9g net carbs

**Ingredients**

- Sugar-Free Chocolate Chips 1/2 cup
- Butter 1/2 cup
- Eggs 3
- Truvia 1/4 cup
- Vanilla extract 1tsp.
- For Cream Cheese Frosting
- Butter, room temperature 4 oz.
- Cream Cheese, room temperature 4 oz.
- Powdered Swerve 1/2 cup
- Heavy Whipping Cream 1/4 cup
- Vanilla extract 1tsp.

**Directions**

1. Melt the butter and chocolate for around 1 minute in a microwave-proof dish. Stir well. You really ought to use the warmth within the chocolate and butter to melt most of the clumps. You have overheated the chocolate; when you microwave, and all is melted, it means you have overheated the chocolate. So grab yourself a spoon and begin stirring. If required, add 10 seconds, but stir just before you plan to do so.
2. Put the eggs, vanilla and sweetener, in a bowl and whisk until fluffy and light.
3. In a steady stream, add the melted chocolate into the egg mix and whisk again until well-combined.
4. In a Waffle Maker, pour around 1/4 of the mixture and cook for 7 to-8 minutes until it's crispy.
5. Prepare the frosting as they are cooking.
6. Put all the frosting ingredients into a food processor bowl and mix until fluffy and smooth. To achieve the right consistency, include a little extra cream.
7. To create your Oreo Chaffle, spread or pipe the frosting evenly in between the two chaffles.
8. The waffle machine, do not overfill it! It will create a giant mess and ruin the batter and the maker, utilizing no more than 1/4 cup of the batter.
9. Leave the waffles to cool down a bit before frosting. It is going to help them to remain crisp.
10. To make the frosting, use room-temp butter and cream cheese.

## 3. Glazed Donut Chaffle

Prep. Time: 10 mins

Cook Time: 5 mins

Servings: 3 chaffles

The serving size is 1 chaffle

**Nutrition as per serving:**

312kcal / 15g fat / 6g carbs / 1g fiber / 9g protein = 5g net carbs

**Ingredients**

For the chaffles

- Mozzarella cheese shredded ½ cup
- Whey protein isolates Unflavored 2 tbsp.
- Cream Cheese 1 oz.
- Swerve confectioners (Sugar substitute) 2 tbsp.
- Vanilla extract ½tsp.
- Egg 1
- Baking powder ½tsp.

For the glaze topping:

- Heavy whipping cream2 tbsp.
- Swerve confectioners (sugar substitute) 3-4 tbsp.
- Vanilla extract ½tsp.

**Directions**

1. Turn on the waffle maker.

2. In a microwave-proof bowl, combine the cream cheese and mozzarella cheese. Microwave at 30-second breaks until it is all melted and stir to combine completely.
3. Include the whey protein, baking powder, 2 tbsp. Keto sweetener to the melted cheese, and work with your hands to knead until well combined.
4. Put the dough in a mixing bowl, and whisk in the vanilla and egg into it to form a smooth batter.
5. Put 1/3 of the mixture into the waffle machine, and let it cook for 3 to 5 minutes.
6. Repeat the above step 5 to make a total of three chaffles.
7. Whisk the glaze topping ingredients together and drizzle on top of the chaffles generously before serving.

## 4. Keto Pumpkin Chaffles

Prep. Time: 2 mins

Cook Time: 5 mins

Servings: 2 chaffles

The serving size is 2 chaffles

**Nutrition as per serving:** (without toppings)

250kcal / 15g fat / 5g carbs / 1g fiber / 23g protein = 4g net carbs

**Ingredients**

- Mozzarella cheese, shredded ½ cup
- Egg, beaten 1 whole
- Pumpkin purée 1 ½ tbsp.
- Swerve confectioners ½tsp.
- Vanilla extract ½tsp.
- Pumpkin pie spice ¼tsp.
- Pure maple extract ⅛tsp.
- For topping- optional
- roasted pecans, cinnamon, whip cream and sugar-free maple syrup

**Directions**

1. Switch on the Waffle Maker and begin preparing the mixture.

2. Add all the given ingredients to a bowl, except for the mozzarella cheese, and whisk. Include the cheese and combine until well mixed.
3. Grease the waffle plates and put half the mixture into the middle of the plate. Cover the lid for 4- to 6 minutes, based on how crispy Chaffles you like.
4. Take it out and cook the second one. Serve with all or some mix of toppings, like sugar-free maple syrup, butter, roasted pecans, and a dollop of whipping cream or ground cinnamon dust.

## 5. Cream Cheese Chaffle with Lemon Curd

Prep. Time: 5 minutes

Cook Time: 4 minutes

Additional Time: 40 minute

Servings: 2-3 serving

The serving size is 1 chaffle

**Nutrition as per serving:**

302 kcals / 24g fat / 6g carbs / 1g fiber / 15g protein = 5g net carbs

**Ingredients**

- One batch keto lemon curd (recipe here)
- Eggs 3 large
- Cream cheese softened 4 oz.
- Lakanto monkfruit (or any low carb sweetener) 1 tbsp.

- Vanilla extract 1tsp.
- Mozzarella cheese shredded 3/4 cup
- Coconut flour 3 tbsp.
- Baking powder 1tsp.
- Salt 1/3tsp.
- Homemade keto whipped cream (optional) (recipe here)

**Directions**

1. Prepare lemon curd according to Directions and let cool in the refrigerator.
2. Turn on the waffle maker and grease it with oil.
3. Take a small bowl, put coconut flour, salt and baking powder. Combine and put aside.
4. Take a large bowl, put cream cheese, eggs, vanilla and sweetener. With an electric beater, beat until foamy. You may see chunks of cream cheese, and that is okay.
5. Include mozzarella cheese into the egg mixture and keep beating.
6. Pour the dry ingredients into the egg mixture and keep mixing until well blended.
7. Put batter into the preheated waffle machine and cook.
8. Take off from waffle machine; spread cooled lemon curd, top with keto whipped cream and enjoy.

## 6. Strawberries & Cream Keto Chaffles

Prep. Time: 25 minutes

Cook Time: 10 minutes

Servings: 8 chaffles

The serving size is 1 chaffle

**Nutrition as per serving:**

328cals / 12g fat / 8g carbs / 4g fiber /6g protein = 4g net carbs

**Ingredients**

- Cream cheese 3 oz.
- Mozzarella cheese, shredded 2 cups
- Eggs, beaten 2
- Almond flour 1/2 cup
- Swerve confectioner sweetener 3 tbsp. + 1 tbsp.
- Baking powder 2tsps
- Strawberries 8
- Whipped cream 1 cup (canister - 2 tbsp. Per waffle)

**Directions**

1. In a microwavable dish, add the mozzarella and cream cheese, cook for 1 minute, mixing well. If the cheese is all melted, then go to the next step. Else cook for another 30 seconds stirring well.
2. Take another bowl, whisk eggs, including the almond flour, 3 tbsp. of keto sweetener, and baking powder.
3. Include the melted cheese mixture into the egg and almond flour mixture and combine well. Carefully add in 2 strawberries coarsely chopped. Chill for 20 minutes.
4. Meanwhile, slice the unused strawberries and mix with 1 tbsp. of Swerve. Chill.
5. Take out the batter from the refrigerator after 20 minutes. Heat the waffle iron and grease it.

6. Put 1/4 cup of the batter in the mid of the heated waffle iron. Ensuring the waffles are small makes it easier to remove from the waffle maker.
7. Transfer to a plate when cooked and cool before adding whipped cream and topping with strawberries.

This recipe gave me eight small waffles.

## 7. Keto Peanut Butter Cup Chaffle

Prep. Time: 2 minutes

Cook Time: 5 minutes

Servings: 2 Chaffles

The serving size is 1 chaffle + filling

**Nutrition as per serving:**

264kcal / 21.6g fat / 7.2g carbs / 2g fiber / 9.45g protein = 4.2g net carbs

**Ingredients**

For the Chaffle

- Heavy Cream 1 tbsp.
- Vanilla Extract 1/2 tsp
- Egg 1
- Cake Batter Flavor 1/2 tsp
- Unsweetened Cocoa 1 tbsp.
- Coconut Flour 1 tsp
- Lakanto Powdered Sweetener 1 tbsp.
- Baking Powder 1/4 tsp

For Peanut Butter Filling

- Heavy Cream 2 tbsp.
- All-natural Peanut Butter 3 tbsp.
- Lakanto Powdered Sweetener 2 tsp

**Directions**

1. Preheat a waffle maker.
2. Combine all the chaffle ingredients in a small mixing bowl.
3. Put half of the chaffle batter into the middle of the waffle machine and cook for 3 to 5 minutes.
4. Cautiously remove and duplicate for the second chaffle. Leave chaffles for a couple of minutes to let them crisp up.
5. Prepare the peanut butter filling by blending all the ingredients together and layer between chaffles.

## 8. Vanilla Chocolate Chip

Prep. Time: 1 minute

Cook Time: 4 minutes

Servings: 1 serving

The serving size is 1 large or 2 mini chaffle

**Nutrition as per serving:**

297.6 kcal. / 20.1g fat / 5.2g carbs / 1.5g fiber / 22.2g protein = 3.9g net carbs

**Ingredients**

- Mozzarella shredded 1/2 cup

- Eggs 1 medium
- Granulated sweetener keto 1 tbsp.
- Vanilla extract 1 tsp
- Almond meal or flour 2 tbsp.
- Chocolate chips, sugar-free 1 tbsp.

**Directions**

1. Mix all the ingredients in a large bowl.
2. Turn on the waffle maker. When it is heated, grease with olive oil and put half the mixture into the waffle machine. Cook for 2 to 4 minutes, then take out and repeat. It will make 2 small-chaffles per recipe.
3. Enjoy with your favorite toppings.

## 9. Chaffle Churro

Prep. Time: 10 minutes

Cook Time: 6-10 minutes

Servings: 2

The serving size is 4 churros

**Nutrition as per serving:**

189 kcals / 14.3g fat / 5.g carbs / 1g fiber / 10g protein = 4g net carbs

**Ingredients**

- Egg 1
- Almond flour 1 Tbsp.
- Vanilla extract ½ tsp.
- Cinnamon divided 1 tsp.

- Baking powder ¼ tsp.
- Shredded mozzarella ½ cup.
- Swerve confectioners (or any sugar substitute) 1 Tbsp.
- Swerve brown sugar (keto-friendly sugar substitute) 1 Tbsp.
- Butter melted 1 Tbsp.

**Directions**

1. Heat the waffle iron.
2. Combine the almond flour, egg, vanilla extract, baking powder, ½ tsp of cinnamon, swerve confectioners' sugar and shredded mozzarella in a bowl, and stir to combine well.
3. Spread half of the batter equally onto the waffle iron, and let it cook for 3 to 5 minutes. Cooking for more time will give a crispier chaffle.
4. Take out the cooked chaffle and pour the remaining batter onto it. Close the lid and cook for about 3 to 5 minutes.
5. Make both the chaffles into strips.
6. Put the cut strips in a bowl and drizzle on melted butter generously.
7. In another bowl, stir together the keto brown sugar and the leftover ½ tsp of cinnamon until well-combined.
8. Toss the churro chaffle strips in the sugar-cinnamon mixture in the bowl to coat them evenly.

## 10. Keto Cauliflower Chaffles Recipe

Prep. Time: 5 minutes

Cook Time: 4 minutes

Servings: 2 chaffles

The serving size is 2 chaffles

**Nutrition as per serving:**

246kcal / 16g fat / 7g carbs / 2g fiber / 20g protein = 5g net carbs

**Ingredients**

- Riced cauliflower 1 cup
- Garlic powder 1/4tsp.
- Ground black pepper 1/4tsp.
- Italian seasoning 1/2tsp.
- Kosher salt 1/4tsp.
- Mozzarella cheese shredded 1/2 cup
- Eggs 1
- Parmesan cheese shredded 1/2 cup

**Directions**

1. In a blender, add all the ingredients and blend well. Turn the waffle maker on.
2. Put 1/8 cup of parmesan cheese onto the waffle machine. Ensure to cover up the bottom of the waffle machine entirely.
3. Cover the cheese with the cauliflower batter, then sprinkle another layer of parmesan cheese on the cauliflower mixture. Cover and cook.
4. Cook for 4 to 5 minutes, or till crispy.
5. Will make 2 regular-size chaffles or 4 mini chaffles.
6. It freezes well. Prepare a big lot and freeze for the future.

## 11. Zucchini Chaffles

Prep. Time: 10 minutes

Cook Time: 5 minutes

Servings: 2 chaffles

The serving size is 1 chaffle

**Nutrition as per serving:**

194kcal / 13g fat / 4g carbs / 1g fiber / 16g protein = 3g net carbs

**Ingredients**

- Zucchini, grated 1 cup
- Eggs, beaten 1
- Parmesan cheese shredded 1/2 cup

- Mozzarella cheese shredded 1/4 cup
- Dried basil, 1tsp. Or fresh basil, chopped 1/4 cup
- Kosher Salt, divided 3/4tsp.
- Ground Black Pepper 1/2tsp.

**Directions**

1. Put the shredded zucchini in a bowl and Sprinkle salt, about 1/4tsp on it and leave it aside to gather other ingredients. Moments before using put the zucchini in a paper towel, wrap and press to wring out all the extra water.
2. Take a bowl and whisk in the egg. Include the mozzarella, grated zucchini, basil, and pepper 1/2tsp of salt.
3. Cover the waffle maker base with a layer of 1 to 2 tbsp. of the shredded parmesan.
4. Then spread 1/4 of the zucchini batter. Spread another layer of 1 to 2 tbsp. of shredded parmesan and shut the lid.
5. Let it cook for 4 to 8 minutes. It depends on the dimensions of your waffle machine. Normally, once the chaffle is not emitting vapors of steam, it is nearly done. For the greatest results, let it cook until good and browned.
6. Take out and duplicate for the next waffle.

Will make 4 small chaffles or 2 full-size chaffles in a Mini waffle maker.

## 12. Keto Pizza Chaffle

Prep. Time: 10 minutes

Cook Time: 30 minutes

Servings: 2 servings

The serving size is 1 chaffle

**Nutrition as per serving:**

76 kcal / 4.3g fat / 4.1g carbs / 1.2g fiber / 5.5g protein = 3.2g net carbs

**Ingredients**

- Egg 1
- Mozzarella cheese shredded 1/2 cup
- Italian seasoning a pinch
- Pizza sauce No sugar added 1 tbsp.
- Toppings – pepperoni, shredded cheese (or any other toppings)

**Directions**

- Heat the waffle maker.
- Whisk the egg, and Italian seasonings in a small mixing bowl, together.
- Stir in the cheese, leaving a few tsps. for layering.
- Layer a tsp of grated cheese onto the preheated waffle machine and allow it to cook for about 30 seconds.
- It will make a crispier crust.
- Pour half the pizza mixture into the waffle maker and allow to cook for around 4 minutes till it's slightly crispy and golden brown!

- Take out the waffle and make the second chaffle with the remaining mixture.
- Spread the pizza sauce, pepperoni and shredded cheese. Place in Microwave and heat on high for around 20 seconds and done! On the spot Chaffle PIZZA!

## 13. Crispy Taco Chaffle Shells

Prep. Time: 5 minutes

Cook Time: 8 minutes

Servings: 2 chaffles

The serving size is 1 chaffle

**Nutrition as per serving:**

258kcal / 19g fat / 4g carbs / 2g fiber / 18g protein = 2g net carbs

**Ingredients**

- Egg white 1
- Monterey jack cheese shredded 1/4 cup
- Sharp cheddar cheese shredded 1/4 cup
- Water 3/4 tsp
- Coconut flour 1 tsp
- Baking powder 1/4 tsp
- Chili powder 1/8 tsp
- Salt a pinch

**Directions**

1. Turn on the Waffle iron and lightly grease it with oil when it is hot.
2. In a mixing bowl, mix all of the above ingredients and blend to combine.

3. Pour half of the mixture onto the waffle iron and shut the lid. Cook for 4 minutes without lifting the lid. The chaffle will not set in less than 4 minutes.
4. Take out the cooked taco chaffle and put it aside. Do the same process with the remaining chaffle batter.
5. Put a muffin pan upside down and assemble the taco chaffle upon the cups to make into a taco shell. Put aside for a few minutes.
6. When it is firm, fill it with your favorite Taco Meat fillings. Serve.

Enjoy this delicious keto crispy taco chaffle shell with your favorite toppings.

# Chapter 3- Keto Cakes and Cupcakes

## 1. Chocolate Cake with Chocolate Icing

Prep. Time: 10 minutes

Cook Time: 25 minutes

Servings: 9 slices

The serving size is 1 slice

**Nutrition as per serving:**

358kcal / 33g fat / 11g carbs / 6g fiber / 8g protein = 5g net carbs

**Ingredients**

- Coconut flour 3/4 cup
- Granular sweetener 3/4 cup
- Cocoa powder 1/2 cup
- Baking powder 2tsps
- Eggs 6
- Heavy whipping cream 2/3 cup
- Melted butter 1/2 cup
- For chocolate icing
- Heavy whipping cream 1 cup
- Keto granular sweetener 1/4 cup
- Vanilla extracts 1tsp.
- Cocoa powder sifted 1/3 cup

**Directions**

1. Heat the oven up to 350F.
2. Oil a cake pan of 8x8.
3. In a large mixing bowl, put all the cake ingredients to blend well with an electric mixer or a stand mixer.
4. Transfer the batter to the oiled pan and put in the heated oven for 25 minutes or till a toothpick inserted in the center comes out clean.
5. Take out from the oven. Leave to cool fully before icing.
6. Prepare the Icing

7. With an electric mixer, beat the whipping cream until stiff peaks form. Include the cocoa powder, swerve, and vanilla. Keep beating until just combined.
8. Spread the icing evenly all over the cake and serve. Keep any remains in the refrigerator.

## 2. 4 Ingredients Cheesecake Fluff

Prep. Time: 10 minutes

Servings: 6

The serving size is ½ cup

**Nutrition as per serving:**

258kcal / 27g fat / 4g carbs / 0g fiber / 4g protein = 4g net carbs

**Ingredients**

- Heavy Whipping Cream1 Cup
- Cream Cheese, Softened 1 Brick (8 oz.)
- Lemon Zest 1 tsp.
- Keto-friendly Granular Sweetener 1/2 Cup

**Directions**

1. Prepare the Fluff
2. Put the heavy cream in a bowl of a stand mixer and beat until stiff peaks begin to form. An electric beater or a hand beater can also be used.
3. Transfer the whipped cream into a separate bowl and put aside
4. To the same stand mixer bowl, add the cream cheese (softened), sweetener, zest, and whisk until smooth.

5. Now add the whipped cream to the cream cheese into the mixer bowl. Fold with a spatula gently till it is halfway combined. Finish whipping with the stand mixer until smooth.
6. Top with your fave toppings and serve.

## 3. Mug Cake Peanut Butter, Chocolate or Vanilla

Prep. Time: 4 minutes

Cook Time: 1 minute

Servings: 1

The serving size is 1 mug cake

**Nutrition as per serving:**

(For mug cake with almond flour: chocolate flavor and no chocolate chips)

312 kcal / 7 carbs/ 28g fat / 12g protein/4g fiber = 3 net carbs

(Peanut butter flavor and no chocolate chips)

395 kcal / 8 carbs /35g fat / 15g protein/4g fiber = 5 net carb

(Vanilla flavor and no chocolate chips)

303 kcal / 5 carbs/ 28g fat / 11g protein /2g fiber = 3 net carb

**Ingredients**

- Butter melted 1 Tbsp.
- Almond flour 3 Tbsp. or Coconut flour 1 Tbsp.
- Granular Sweetener 2 Tbsp.
- Sugar-free Peanut butter 1 Tbsp. (For Peanut Butter flavor)
- Cocoa powder 1 Tbsp. (For Chocolate flavor)
- Baking powder ½ tsp.
- Egg, beaten 1
- Sugar-free Chocolate Chips 1 Tbsp.
- Vanilla few drops

**Directions**

For Vanilla flavor

1. In a microwave-proof coffee mug, heat the butter for 10 seconds to melt in the microwave.
2. Include the almond flour or coconut flour, baking powder, sweetener, beaten egg and vanilla. Combine well.
3. For 60 seconds, microwave on high, ensuring not to overcook; otherwise, it will come out dry. Sprinkle keto chocolate chips on top if preferred or stir in before cooking.

For Chocolate flavor

In a microwave-proof coffee mug, heat the butter for 10 seconds to melt in the microwave. Include the almond flour or coconut flour, cocoa powder, sweetener, baking powder, beaten egg and vanilla. Combine well. For 60 seconds, microwave on high, ensuring not to overcook; it will come out dry. Sprinkle keto chocolate chips on top if preferred.

For Peanut Butter flavor

1. In a microwave-proof coffee mug, heat the butter for 10 seconds to melt in the microwave.
2. Include the almond flour or coconut flour, baking powder, sweetener, beaten egg and vanilla. Combine well. Stir in peanut butter. For 60 seconds, microwave on high, ensuring not to overcook; otherwise, it will come out dry. Sprinkle keto chocolate chips on top if preferred.

Directions for Baking: Bake in an oven-safe small bowl. Bake in the oven for 15 to 20 minutes at 350.

## 4. Chocolate Coconut Flour Cupcakes

Prep. Time: 10 minutes

Cook Time: 25 minutes

Servings: 12 cupcakes

The serving size is 1 cupcake

**Nutrition as per serving:**

268 kcal / 22g fat / 6g carbs / 3g fiber / 6g protein = 3g net carbs

**Ingredients**

For Cupcakes:

- Butter melted 1/2 cup
- Cocoa powder 7 tbsp.
- Instant coffee granules 1 tsp (optional)
- Eggs at room temperature 7
- Vanilla extracts 1 tsp
- Coconut flour 2/3 cup
- Baking powder 2 tsp
- Swerve sweetener 2/3 cup
- Salt 1/2 tsp
- Hemp milk or unsweetened almond milk 1/2 cup (+more)

For Espresso Buttercream:

- Hot water 2 tbsp.
- Instant coffee or instant espresso powder 2 tsp
- Whipping cream 1/2 cup

- Butter softened 6 tbsp.
- Cream cheese softened 4 oz.
- Swerve powdered sweetener 1/2 cup

**Directions**

For Cupcakes:

1. Heat the oven up to 350F and line silicone liners or parchment on a muffin tin.
2. Mix together the cocoa powder, melted butter, and espresso powder in a large mixing bowl,
3. Include the vanilla and eggs and whisk until well combined. Now add in the coconut flour, baking powder, salt and sweetener, and mix until smooth.
4. Pour the almond milk in and stir. If the batter is very thick, add in 1 tbsp. of almond milk at a time to thin it out. It should not be pourable but of scoopable consistency.
5. Scoop the batter equally among the prepared muffin tins and put in the oven's center rack, baking for 20-25 minutes. Check the cupcakes with a tester inserted into the center comes out clean, then cupcakes are done. Leave to cool in the pan for 5 to 10 minutes, and then cool completely on a wire rack.

For Buttercream:

1. Dissolve the coffee in hot water. Put aside.
2. Whip cream using an electric mixer until stiff peaks are formed. Put aside.
3. Beat cream cheese, butter, and sweetener all together in a medium mixing bowl until creamy. Include coffee mixture and mix until combined. fold in the whipped cream Using a rubber spatula carefully till well combined.
4. Layer frosting on the cooled cupcakes with an offset spatula or a knife.

## 5. Low-carb red velvet cupcakes/ cake

Prep. Time: 15-30 minutes

Cook Time: 20-25 minutes

Servings: 12 slice

The serving size is 1 slice

**Nutrition as per serving:**

193kcals / 12g fat / 6.4g carbs / 1g fiber / 5.9g protein = 5.4g net carbs

**Ingredients**

- Almond flour 1+ 3/4 cups
- Swerve confectioner sweetener (not substitutes) 2/3 cup
- Cocoa powder 2 tbsp.
- Baking powder 2tsp.
- Baking soda 1/2tsp.
- Eggs 2
- Full fat coconut milk 1/2 cup + 2 tbsp.
- Olive oil 3 tbsp.
- Apple cider vinegar 1 tbsp.
- Vanilla extract 1 tbsp.
- Red food coloring 2 tbsp.

For frosting

- Cream cheese at room temperature 1 container (8 oz.)
- Butter softened 2 ½ tbsp.
- Swerve confectioner sweetener 1 cup

- Coconut milk 2 ½ tbsp.
- Vanilla extract 1tsp.
- Salt 1/8tsp.

**Double Frosting for Layer Cake

**Directions**

1. Preheat oven to 350 degrees
2. In a large mixing bowl, add the wet ingredients, eggs, milk, vanilla extract, olive oil, apple cider vinegar and food coloring. Blend until smooth.
3. Now sift together the cocoa powder, Swerve Confectioner, baking powder and baking soda, add to the wet ingredients, and incorporate it into the batter with an electric mixer or a hand whisk.
4. Lastly, sift in the almond flour. Moving the flour back and forth with a whisk will speed up the process significantly. Fold the sifted flour gently into the batter till smooth and all is well incorporated. Use the batter immediately.
5. To make Cupcakes: Scoop batter into the muffin liners, fill only up to 2/3 of liner -do not over-fill. Ensure the oven is heated, put in the oven for 15 minutes at 350 degrees, and then turn the muffin tin in 180 degrees and cook for an extra 10 minutes. (Bear in mind, oven times vary occasionally - humidity and altitude can impact things, so watch closely as they may need a few minutes more or even less).
6. Take out from the oven, do not remove from pan and set aside to cool completely.
7. For Layer Cake: 2 Layer- line parchment paper in two cake pans (8 inches each) and oil the sides. Transfer batter to both pans evenly. Use a wet spatula to spread

the batter smoothly. Apply the same process for three layers, but using thinner pans as dividing the batter three ways-every layers will become thin.

8. Place pans into oven for 20-25 minutes baking at 350 degrees. Cautiously turn the pans 180 degrees halfway through baking and cover lightly with a foil. At 20 to 25 minutes, take out the pans; they will be a bit soft. Set them aside to cool completely. When they are cool, take a knife and run it around the side of the pan and turn them over carefully onto a plate or cooling rack and leave them for an extra 5 to 10 minutes before icing.
9. Meanwhile, prepare. Blend the softened butter and cream cheese together With an electric beater. Include milk and vanilla extract and beat again. Lastly, sift in the Swerve, salt mixing well one last time. If you want a thicker frosting, chill it in the refrigerator. Or adding more Swerve will give a thicker texture or add more milk to make it thinner. * For a layer cake, double the frosting recipe.
10. Spread or pipe frosting onto cupcakes, sprinkle some decoration if desired and enjoy!! To frost layer cake, it is simpler to first chill the layers in the freezer. Then frost and pile each layer to end frost the sides and top.

Keep any leftovers in a sealed box and refrigerate. Enjoy!

## 6. Vanilla Cupcakes

Prep. Time: 5 minutes

Cook Time: 20 minutes

Servings: 10 Cupcakes

The serving size is 1 cupcake

**Nutrition as per serving:**

153kcal / 13g fat / 4g carbs / 2g fiber / 5g protein = 2g net carbs

**Ingredients**

- Butter 1/2 cup
- Keto granulated sweetener 2/3 cup
- Vanilla extract 2 tsp
- Eggs whisked * See notes 6 large

- Milk of choice ** See notes 2 tbsp.
- Coconut flour 1/2 cup
- Baking powder 1 tsp
- Keto vanilla frosting 1 batch

**Directions**

1. Heat the oven up to 350F/180C. Place muffin liners in a 12-cup muffin tin and oil 10 of them.
2. Beat the butter, salt, sugar, eggs and vanilla extract together in a big mixing bowl when combined-well include the milk and mix until blended.
3. In another bowl, sift the baking powder and coconut flour together. Add the wet ingredients to the dry and mix until combined.
4. Pour the batter equally into the ten muffin cups, filling up to ¾ full. Place the cupcakes on the middle rack and bake for 17 to 20 minutes until the muffin top springs back to touch
5. Remove the muffin pan from the oven, set it aside to cool for 10 minutes, and then cool completely on a wire rack. Frost, when cooled.

## 7. Healthy Flourless Fudge Brownies

Prep. Time: 5 minutes

Cook Time: 20 minutes

Servings: 12 servings

The serving size is 1 Brownie

**Nutrition as per serving:**

86kcal / 5g fat / 5g carbs / 3g fiber / 7g protein = 2g net carbs

**Ingredients**

- Pumpkin puree 2 cups
- Almond butter 1 cup
- Cocoa powder 1/2 cup
- Granulated sweetener (or liquid stevia drops) 1/4 cup

For the Chocolate Coconut Frosting

- Chocolate chips 2 cups
- Coconut milk canned 1 cup
- For the chocolate protein frosting
- Protein powder, chocolate flavor 2 scoops
- Granulated sweetener 1-2 tbsp.
- Seed or nut butter of choice 1-2 tbsp.
- Milk or liquid *1 tbsp.

For the Cheese Cream Frosting

- Cream cheese 125 grams

- Cocoa powder 1-2 tbsp.
- Granulated sweetener of choice 1-2 tbsp.

**Directions**

1. For the fudge brownies
2. Heat the oven up to 350 degrees, oil a loaf pan or small cake pan and put aside.
3. Melt the nut butter in a small microwave-proof bowl. In a big mixing bowl, put in the pumpkin puree, dark cocoa powder, nut butter, and combine very well.
4. Transfer the mixture to the oiled pan and put in preheated oven for around 20 to 25 minutes or until fully baked. Remove from the oven, set aside to cool completely. When cooled, apply the frosting and chill for about 30 minutes to settle.

Preparing the cream cheese or protein frosting:

1. In a big mixing bowl, mix together all the ingredients and beat well. With a tablespoon. keep adding dairy-free milk till a frosting consistency is reached.
2. For the coconut chocolate ganache
3. In a microwave-proof bowl, combine all the ingredients and heat gradually until just mixed- whisk till a glossy and thick frosting remains.

## 8. Healthy Keto Chocolate Raspberry Mug Cake

Prep. Time: 1 minute

Cook Time: 1 minute

Servings: 1 serving

The serving size is 1 mug cake

**Nutrition as per serving:**

152kcal / 8g fat / 13g carbs / 8g fiber / 7g protein = 5g net carbs

**Ingredients**

- Coconut flour 1 tbsp.
- Granulated sweetener of choice 1 tbsp.
- Cocoa powder 2 tbsp.
- Baking powder 1/4 tsp
- Sunflower seed butter (or any seed or nut butter) 1 tbsp.
- Pumpkin puree 3 tbsp.
- Frozen or fresh raspberries 1/4 cup
- Coconut milk unsweetened 1-2 tbsp.

**Directions**

1. In a microwave-proof mug, put in the dry ingredients and stir well.
2. Add in the rest of the ingredients, except for milk and raspberries, and combine until a thick batter is formed.
3. Stir in the raspberries and add one tbsp. of milk. Add extra milk if the batter gets too thick. Place in microwave and cook for 1 to 2 minutes. Should come out gooey in the center. If you overcook, it will become dry.

Oven Directions

1. Heat oven up to 180C.
2. Oil an oven-proof ramekin. Add the prepared batter and put in the oven for 10-12 minutes, or until done.

## 9. Keto Avocado Brownies

Prep. Time: 10 minutes

Cook Time: 30 minutes

Servings: 12 squares

**Nutrition as per serving:**

155kcal / 14g fat / 13g carbs / 10g fiber / 4g protein = 2.8g net carbs

**Ingredients**

- Avocado, mashed 1 cup
- Vanilla 1/2 tsp
- Cocoa powder 4 tbsp.
- Refined coconut oil (or ghee, butter, lard, shortening) 3 tbsp.
- Eggs 2
- Lily's chocolate chips melted 1/2 cup (100 g)

Dry Ingredients

- Blanched almond flour 3/4 cup
- Baking soda 1/4 tsp
- Baking powder 1 tsp
- Salt 1/4 tsp
- Erythritol 1/4 cup (see sweetener note *1)
- Stevia powder 1 tsp (see sweetener note *1)

**Directions**

1. Heat the oven up to 350F/ 180C.
2. Sift together the dry ingredients in a small bowl and stir.

3. Place the Peeled avocados in a food processor and process until smooth.
4. One by one, add all the wet ingredients into the food processor, processing every few seconds
5. Now include the dry ingredients into the food processor and blend until combined.
6. Line a parchment paper in a baking dish (of 12"x8") and transfer the batter into it. Spread evenly and put in the heated oven. Cook for 30 minutes or the center springs back to touch. It should be soft to touch.
7. Remove from oven, set aside to cool fully before cutting into 12 slices.

## 10. Low Carb-1 minute Cinnamon Roll Mug Cake

Prep. Time: 1 minute

Cook Time: 1 minute

Servings: 1 serving

The serving size is 1mug

**Nutrition as per serving:**

132kcal / 4g fat / 6g carbs / 2g fiber / 25g protein = 4g net carbs

**Ingredients**

- Protein powder, vanilla flavor 1 scoop
- Baking powder 1/2 tsp
- Coconut flour 1 tbsp.
- Cinnamon 1/2 tsp
- Granulated sweetener 1 tbsp.
- Egg 1 large

- Almond milk, unsweetened 1/4 cup
- Vanilla extract 1/4 tsp
- Granulated sweetener 1 tsp
- Cinnamon 1/2 tsp

For the glaze

- Coconut butter melted 1 tbsp.
- Almond milk 1/2 tsp
- Cinnamon a pinch

**Directions**

1. Oil a microwave-proof mug. In a small bowl, add the protein powder, coconut flour, baking powder, sweetener, cinnamon and mix well.
2. Add in the egg and stir into the flour mixture. Include the vanilla extract and milk. If the batter is too dry, keep adding milk until a thick consistency is reached.
3. Pour this batter into the oiled mug. Sprinkle extra cinnamon and keto granulated sweetener over the top and swirl. Place in microwave and cook for 60 seconds, or till the center is just cooked. Do not overcook, or it will come out dry. Drizzle the glaze on top and enjoy!
4. Prepare glaze by mixing all ingredients and use.

## 11. Double Chocolate Muffins

Prep. Time: 10 minutes

Cook Time: 15 minutes

Servings: 12 muffins

The serving size is 1 muffin

**Nutrition as per serving:**

280 kcal / 27g fat / 7g carbs / 4g fiber / 7g protein = 3g net carbs

**Ingredients**

- Almond flour 2 cup
- Cocoa powder unsweetened 3/4 cup
- Swerve sweetener 1/4 cup
- Baking powder 1 1/2 tsp.
- Kosher salt 1 tsp.
- Butter melted 1 cup (2 sticks)
- Eggs 3 large
- Pure vanilla extract 1 tsp.
- Dark chocolate chips, sugar-free (like lily's) 1 cup

**Directions**

1. Heat oven up to 350° and line cupcake liners in a muffin tin. In a big bowl, stir together almond flour, Swerve, cocoa powder, salt and baking powder. Include eggs, melted butter and vanilla and mix until combined.
2. Stir in the chocolate chips.

**3.** Pour batter equally in muffin cups and bake for 12 minutes or until the muffin top springs back to touch.

# Chapter 4- Keto Fat Bombs

## 1. Cheesecake Fat Bombs

Prep. Time: 5 minutes

Servings: 24Fat Bombs

The serving size is 1 Fat Bomb

**Nutrition as per serving:**

108kcal / 12g fat / 1g carbs / 1g fiber / 1g protein = 0g net carbs

**Ingredients**

- Heavy Cream 4 oz.
- Cream cheese at room temperature 8 oz.
- Erythritol 2-3 tbsp.
- Coconut oil or butter 4 oz.
- Vanilla extracts 2tsp.

• Baking chocolate or coconut for decorating

**Directions**

1. In a big mixing bowl, add all the ingredients and mix for 1-2 minutes with an electric mixer until well combined and creamy.
2. Spoon mixture into an unlined or lined mini cupcake tin. Chill for 1-2 hours in the refrigerator or freezer for about 30 minutes.
3. Take out from the cupcake tins and store them in a sealed container. It can be refrigerated for up to two weeks.

## 2. Brownie Fat Bombs

Prep. Time: 15 minutes

Servings: 16 fat bombs

The serving size is 2 fat bombs

**Nutrition as per serving:**

174 kcal / 16g fat / 4g carbs / 2g fiber / 3g protein = 2g net carbs

**Ingredients**

• Ghee 1/4 cup

• Cocoa butter 1 oz.

• Vanilla extract 1/2 tsp

• Salt 1/4 tsp

• Raw cacao powder 6 tbsp.

• Swerve Sweetener powdered 1/3 cup

• Water 2 tbsp.

- Almond butter 1/3 cup
- Nuts, chopped (optional) 1/4 cup

**Directions**

1. melt the cocoa butter and ghee together In a heat-safe bowl placed over a pot of simmering water,
2. Add in the sweetener, cacao powder, salt and vanilla extract. This mixture will be smooth and thin.
3. Stir in the water and beat the mixture till it thickens to the consistency of a thick frosting.
4. Mix in the nut butter with a rubber spatula. The mixture will look like cookie dough. Mix in the coarsely chopped nuts.
5. Shape into 1 inch sized balls (will make about 16) and chill until firm.

## 3. Coffee Fat Bombs

Prep. Time: 10 minutes

Servings: 8 Fat Bombs

The serving size is 1 Fat Bomb

**Nutrition as per serving:**

140 kcal / 14g fat / 4g carbs / 2g fiber / 1.5g protein = 2g net carbs

**Ingredients**

- Cream Cheese, Full-fat 8 Oz.
- Butter Unsalted, ½ cup (1 Stick )
- Instant Coffee 1 to 2 Tbsps.
- Chocolate Chips, Low Carb, heaped ¼ Cup

- Confectioners Erythritol heaped ⅓ Cup
- Cocoa Powder, Unsweetened 1½ Tbsp.

**Directions**

1. In a large bowl, place the butter and cream cheese (both should be at room temperature)
2. Combine them with an electric mixer until smooth.
3. Then include all the remaining ingredients in the bowl, blending until well-combined
4. Scoop out the batter with a tablespoon or a cookie scoop to make around 12 bombs. Place them on a baking sheet lined with parchment. Chill for about 3 hours.

## 4. Peanut Butter Fat Bombs

Prep. Time: 10 minutes

Servings: 12 fat bombs

The serving size is 1/2 fat bomb

**Nutrition as per serving:**

247 kcal / 24.3g fat / 3.2g carbs / 1.2g fiber / 3.6g protein = 2g net carbs

**Ingredients**

For fat bomb

- Natural peanut butter (no sugar) 3/4 cup
- Coconut oil (melted) 1/2 cup
- Vanilla extract 1 tsp.
- Liquid stevia 3 – 4 drops

• Sea salt 1/4 tsp.

For Ganache

• Coconut oil 6 tbsp.

• Cocoa powder 1 tbsp.

• Liquid stevia 1 - 2 drops

**Directions**

1. Mix the peanut butter, coconut oil, vanilla extract, salt, and liquid stevia together in a small mixing bowl, beat until creamy and smooth.
2. Line muffin paper cups in a six-cup-muffin tray. Fill each cup with about 3 tbsp. of the peanut butter mixture.
3. Refrigerate for about 1 hour to solidify.
4. Meanwhile, beat together the ingredients for Ganache until it's silky.
5. Drizzle about one tbsp. of the chocolate ganache on every fat bomb.
6. Chill for about 30 minutes and enjoy.

## 5. Cream Cheese Pumpkin Spiced Fat Bombs

Prep. Time: 10 minutes

Servings: 12 Fat Bombs

The serving size is 1 Fat Bomb

**Nutrition as per serving:**

80 kcal / 7.5g fat / 2g carbs / 0.25g fiber / 1.5g protein = 1.75g net carbs

**Ingredients**

• Pure pumpkin ⅔ cup

- Pumpkin pie spice ½ tsp
- Cream cheese, full-fat 8 oz.
- Butter melted 3 tbsps.
- Confectioner's erythritol 3 tbsps.

**Directions**

1. Place all the ingredients in a large bowl and mix with an electric mixer until combined.
2. Make 12 equal-sized balls from the dough. Place paper liners in a mini-muffin tin and place the PB cookie dough in the muffin tin.
3. Chill for a minimum of 2 hours

Note:

If the pumpkin pie spice is not available, make some with the following ingredients

¼ tsp cinnamon, a pinch of (each) - nutmeg, cloves, ginger and allspice.

## 6. Brownie Truffles

Prep. Time: 5 minutes

Cook Time: 5 minutes

Servings: 20 Truffles

The serving size is 1 Truffle

**Nutrition as per serving:**

97kcal / 8g fat / 5g carbs / 3g fiber / 4g protein = 2g net carbs

**Ingredients**

- Sticky sweetener, keto-friendly 1/2 cup of choice

- Homemade Nutella 2 cups
- Coconut flour 3/4 cup (or almond flour 1 ½ cup)
- Chocolate chips, sugar-free 2 cups

**Directions**

1. Combine the coconut/almond flour, sticky sweetener and chocolate spread in a big mixing bowl. Add a bit more syrup or liquid; if the mixture is too thick, it should become a creamy dough.
2. Place parchment paper on a large plate. Shape into small balls with your hands, and set on the plate. Chill.
3. Melt the sugar-free chocolate chips. Take the truffles from the refrigerator. Immediately, coat each truffle with the melted chocolate, making sure all are evenly coated.
4. Set back on the lined
5. Plate and chill until firm.

## 7. Coconut Strawberry Fat Bombs

Prep. Time: 10 minutes

Servings: 20 fat bombs

The serving size is 1fat Bomb

**Nutrition as per serving:**

132kcals / 14.3g fat / 0.9g carbs / 0g fiber / 0.4g protein = 0.9g net carbs

**Ingredients**

For Coconut base:

- Coconut cream 1 1/2 cups
- Coconut oil (melted) 1/2 cup
- Stevia liquid 1/2 tsp.
- Lime juice 1 tbsp.

For Strawberry topping:

- Fresh chopped strawberries 2 oz.
- Coconut oil (melted) 1/2 cup
- Liquid stevia 5 – 8 drops

**Directions**

Prepare the coconut base:

1. In a high-speed blender, place all the coconut base ingredients and blend them completely until combined and smooth.
2. Distribute the mixture evenly into an ice cube tray, muffin tray, or a candy mold, leaving room for the topping.
3. Chill in the freezer to set for about 20 minutes.

For the Strawberry topping:

1. In a blender, put all the ingredients for the strawberry topping, then blend until smooth.
2. When the base is set, spoon the strawberry mixture equally over each one.
3. Refrigerate the fat bombs for about 2 hours and enjoy.

## 8. Raspberry & White Chocolate Fat Bombs

Prep. Time: 5 minutes

Servings: 10-12 fat bombs

The serving size is 1 fat Bomb

**Nutrition as per serving:**

153kcal / 16g fat / 1.5g carbs / 0.4g fiber / 0.2g protein = 1.2g net carbs

**Ingredients**

- Cacao butter 2 oz.
- Coconut oil 1/2 cup
- Raspberries freeze-dried 1/2 cup
- Erythritol sweetener, powdered (like swerve) 1/4 cup

**Directions**

1. Place paper liners in a 12-cup muffin pan.
2. In a small pot, heat the cacao butter and coconut oil on low flame until melted completely. Take off the pot from heat.
3. Blend the freeze-dried raspberries in a blender or food processor, or coffee grinder.
4. Include the sweetener and powdered berries into the pot, stirring to dissolve the sweetener.
5. Distribute the mixture evenly between the muffin cups. Don't worry if the raspberry powder sinks to the bottom. Just stir the mixture when pouring them into each mold to distribute the raspberry powder in each mold.
6. Chill until hard. Enjoy.

## 9. Almond Joy Fat Bombs (3 Ingredients)

Prep. Time: 2 minutes

Cook Time: 3 minutes

Servings: 24 cups

The serving size is 1 cup

**Nutrition as per serving:**

72kcal / 8g fat / 6g carbs / 4g fiber / 2g protein = 2g net carbs

**Ingredients**

- Coconut butter softened 1/4 cup
- Chocolate chips, sugar-free, divided 20 oz.
- Almonds 24 whole

**Directions**

1. Place muffin liners in a 24-cup mini muffin tin and put them aside.
2. Melt 3/4 of the sugar-free chocolate chips in a microwave-proof bowl. Distribute the chocolate mixture equally into all the muffin liners. Also, scrape down all the chocolate coated on the sides. Chill until firm.
3. When the chocolate is hard, spoon in the melted coconut butter evenly into every chocolate cup, leaving room for chocolate filling on top. Add in more softened coconut butter if needed.
4. Melt the rest of the chocolate chips and with it, cover each of the chocolate coconut cups. Place an almond on top of each cup and chill until firm.

## 10. Pecan pie fat bombs

Prep. Time: 15 minutes

Servings: 18 balls

The serving size is 2 balls

**Nutrition as per serving**

121 kcal / 12g fat / 3.8g carbs / 2.9g fiber / 2g protein = 0.9g net carbs

**Ingredients**

- Pecans, (or any nut) 1½ cup s
- Coconut butter, ¼ cup
- Coconut shredded ½ cup
- Chia seeds 2 tbsp.
- Pecan butter (or any nut butter) 2 tbsp.
- Flax meal 2 tbsp.
- Coconut oil 1tsp.
- Hemp seeds 2 tbsp.
- Vanilla extract ½tsp.
- Cinnamon 1½tsp.
- Kosher salt ¼tsp.

**Directions**

1. Add the ingredients altogether in a food processor. Process for a minute or two to break down the mixture. First, it will become powdery. Then it will stick together but remain crumbly.
2. Continue to process until the oils begin to expel a bit, and the mixture will begin to stick together easily -be cautious not to process excessively, or you will have nut butter.

3. Using a tablespoon or small cookie scooper, scoop to make equal pieces of the mixture. Roll them into balls with your hands placing them all on a large plate. Chill for about 30 mins.
4. Keep in a sealed container or a zip-lock bag in the freezer or refrigerator.

## 11. PB. Cookie Dough Fat Bomb

Prep. Time: 10 minutes

Servings: 12 Fat Bombs

The serving size is 1 Fat Bomb

**Nutrition as per serving:**

135kcal / 11g fat / 5g carbs / 3.5g fiber / 4g protein = 1.5g net carbs

**Ingredients**

- Lily's chocolate chips ⅓ cup
- Almond flour, superfine 1 cup
- Natural peanut butter 6 tbsps.
- Confectioner's erythritol 2 tbsps.
- Coconut oil (melted) 1 tbsps.
- Vanilla extract 1 tsp
- Salt, a pinch

**Directions**

1. Place all the ingredients in a large bowl and mix with a spoon until crumbly.
2. Form a dough ball with your hands.
3. Line parchment paper on a baking sheet. Scoop out equal-sized 12 cookie dough fat bombs.

4. Chill for about an hour

5. Once they are done setting, keep in a sealed bag in the fridge.

# Conclusion

When going on a ketogenic diet, one retains modest protein consumption but increases their fat intake. The transition to a low-carb diet brings your body into a ketosis state, where fat is used for energy compared to carbohydrates.

It takes some time for fats to decompose through the digestive tract and delay the decomposition of the carbohydrates into sugar, maintain our blood sugar concentrations steady and allow us to feel satiated longer. Based on observational evidence, incorporating a tablespoonful of coconut oil into your diet every day may also result in lower weight.

You may also need to monitor the portion sizes, but as fat is intrinsically pleasing, having one for breakfast will help deter eating during meals.

When consuming high-fat meals, including keto fat bombs, you will further encourage weight reduction by decreasing appetite for the next meal. Be it fat bombs or cheesy waffles or any other hi fat low-carb dessert, they are a dieter's dream come true.

Following the keto diet can positively impact one's brain function.

Advantages of the ketogenic diet and fat bombs.

Keto fat bombs may be seen as a way to reduce sugar habits.

Ketogenic fat bombs are simple to produce, easy to keep, and easy to eat; they often need fewer ingredients than other foods.

Ketogenic fat bombs are tasty and have a broad variety of low-carb recipes.

Ketogenic fat bombs are quick to produce, are easy to store, and are ready to consume at any time.

In this book, you will find the best and easy to prepare keto cakes, chaffles, and yummy high-fat recipes that will fulfill your cravings for desserts after meals or snacks when you don't feel too hungry. Enjoy these recipes by yourself, or even better, share the joy with family and friends!

# Intermittent Fasting for Women

*Look Better, Fell Better and Discover a Modern Approach to Autophagy to Thrive in a Post Pandemic Scenario*

**By**

**Dora Gray**

# Table of Contents

## Introduction

Congratulations on downloading Intermittent Fasting for women: *The Ultimate Beginners Guide for Permanent Weight Loss, Slow the Aging Process, and Heal Your Body with the Self-cleansing Process of Metabolic Autophagy.*

This book is your ultimate guide to intermittent fasting. In this book, you'll explore everything about intermittent fasting; what it is, how it works, and how best you can adapt it to suit your needs as a woman. The intermittent fasting diet is one of the best ways to lose weight since it's not restrictive but instead advocates for a change in lifestyle.

You'll notice that this book covers many facets of intermittent fasting, thus offering as much guidance you need to help you get started. This book also discredits the common belief that breakfast is the most important meal of the days hence can't be skipped. Moreover, nutritionists will tell you to eat multiple small meals during the day to stay healthy, but the intermittent fasting diet overrides this principle. The science behind the intermittent fasting is backed by various research studies that have proved that you can actually skip breakfast.

We all have a tendency to naturally fast that makes it easy to integrate intermittent fasting into our lifestyles. In fact, once you adjust to your new lifestyle of intermittent fasting, you'll be surprised that you actually don't eat as much as you think you do or you need to. Intermittent fasting will help you to not only fulfill your weight loss goals but also meet your dietary needs, fight off diseases, and maintain a healthy lifestyle.

Even then, as you read this book keep in mind that everyone's experience with intermittent fasting is different. This is the key to implementing it in your life because you'll find it easy to stick to the intermittent fasting plan that is convenient for you. It's never too late to make significant changes to your lifestyle with intermittent fasting. You can begin today.

# Chapter 1: Obesity and Its Impact on Women

Obesity has a negative impact on the health of women, yet 2 in 3 women in the United States are obese. What is obesity, and how do you know you are obese? Obesity is a disorder that is characterized by having an excessive amount of body fat. It is diagnosed when your body mass index is (BMI) 30 or higher. This is calculated by dividing your weight in kilograms by your height in meters squared. Wondering what your BMI is? Can you use online BMI calculators to find out your BMI? Even then, BMI is considered less accurate in some people, especially if you're very muscular since muscles weigh more than fat. The other ways to find out if your weight is healthy is by measuring your waist circumference. If your waist circumference is more than 35 inches, then you have a higher risk of experiencing the problems associated with obesity.

Your body needs calories to work properly. However, when your body is storing more calories than its burning over time, you become obese because it means you're gaining weight. However, environmental factors can also influence obesity. When you are extremely obese, you are likely to have a myriad of health problems in addition to having low self-esteem. As a woman, you are also at risk of suffering from diseases like diabetes, heart disease, and even certain types of cancers.

## Obesity Risk Factors

Although women of all ages, ethnicities, and races can be obese, obesity tends to be more common among African American Women and Latina or Hispanic women. Other risk factors for obesity among women include the following:

Genetics and family background. For some people, obesity runs in the family. This is not to say that there's a single fat gene. Rather, many genes work together resulting in your likelihood of gaining excess weight. Additionally, the kind of food you're given as a child by your caregivers and parents can influence your weight gain as an adult.

**Metabolism**. The rate at which your body breaks down calories will often vary from one person to the other due to various reasons affecting your weight loss and gain. When you have more muscle and less fat, your body burns fat quickly. On the contrary, when you have more fat and less muscle, you're more likely to gain weight. Moreover, your metabolism may also be affected by hormonal changes at puberty, during pregnancy, and when you get into menopause.

**Trauma**. You may sometimes go through life issues that you don't have control over or are not your fault that affects how fast you gain weight. Women who experience negative events in their childhood like alcoholic parents or abuse are more likely to be obese as adults.

**Sleep**: Lack of high-quality sleep could also lead to weight gain. This is because not getting quality sleep can affect your hormone levels, which eventually has an effect on your food choices and appetite. Not getting enough sleep may also affect your level or exercise and physical activity throughout the day.

**Medicines**. Some of the medicines that you may be taking such as those used in treating mental health conditions, high blood pressure, and sleep can lead to weight gain. Medicines may also make it difficult to lose weight. If you're taking prescription medicine and you notice you're gaining extra weight, don't hesitate to talk to your doctor to give you alternative medicine or ways of losing weight.

With so many factors contributing to unhealthy weight gain, you always have to be alert to know what is making you gain weight to make sure you keep your weight under control. When you're overweight or obese, it increases your risk of having serious health conditions such as:

**Cancer**. Women who are obese have a high risk of suffering from various types of cancer such as cancer of the thyroid, ovarian, pancreatic, multiple myeloma (blood plasma cells), meningioma (cancer of tissue covering spinal cord and brain, kidney, liver, stomach, esophagus, endometrial, colon, rectal, breast and gall bladder.

**Breathing problems.** When you're overweight, you'll most likely experience sleep apnea. This causes you to stop breathing or take in slow breaths during sleep. Consequently, you'll not get enough oxygen in your body or brain during sleep. This can lead to more serious health issues like heart disease.

**Heart disease**. Your risk of having heart disease increases with excess weight. Therefore, you must strive to keep your weight in check in order to stay healthy and avoid heart disease that is a leading cause of death among women.

**Diabetes**. Having extra weight predisposes you to diabetes. On the contrary, you can prevent diabetes when you lose weight or keep your weight within the recommended range. Weight loss is also important in controlling your blood glucose, especially if you already suffer from diabetes. In fact, you'll less likely need medicine to keep your blood sugar in control.

**Pregnancy problems**. You might find it difficult getting pregnant when you are obese. If you're already pregnant, you're likely to experience complications like preeclampsia (dangerously high blood pressure) and gestational diabetes. Thus, you'll need close monitoring and regular prenatal care to ensure early detection and prevention of such problems.

**High blood pressure**. If you've obesity, you're more likely to have high blood pressure and may be advised by your doctor to lose some weight to reduce your blood pressure. When you have high blood pressure, it can damage your arteries resulting in related health conditions like heart disease and stroke.

**Stroke**. Being obese increases your chances of suffering from a stroke. This is particularly serious when most of your weight is around your waist than thighs and hips.

**High cholesterol**. When your weight is more excess, your body will change the way it processes food. Thus, your bad cholesterol increases while your good cholesterol is reduced. Consequently, the buildup of fatty plaque increases within your arteries. An increase in bad cholesterol can lead to heart disease.

You need to know when to start working towards losing weight. A 3 to 5 % loss is capable of helping lower your risk of health problems while making you healthier. Therefore, take time to discuss with your doctor the amount of weight you must lose.

# Chapter 2: The Skinny on Intermittent Fasting

Losing excessive body weight/fat can be a challenge. In most cases, you'll have to give up something you love and embrace a change of lifestyle by hitting the gym. But did you know that you can lose fat, improve your metabolism, and enjoy all the other health benefits without giving up the foods you love? Intermittent fasting is an incredible solution to shedding off excess fat that comes with other benefits you'll enjoy. So, what is intermittent fasting? Although most people think of it as a diet, it is not. Intermittent fasting is a pattern of eating that cycles between periods of eating and fasting and has been proven to be effective in weight loss while sustaining the results.

Interestingly, intermittent fasting is a practice that has been in existence for a long time. What makes intermittent fasting unique is the way in which you schedule your meals. You don't change what you eat, instead what changes are when you eat. That is, instead of dictating the foods you should eat, it dictates when you should eat. Thus, with intermittent fasting, you get lean and building your muscle mass without cutting down your calories. Even then, most people opt for intermittent fasting for the sole reason of losing fat.

## Who Invented the Intermittent Fasting Diet

Fasting is not a new thing. It has been practiced since human evolution. In fact, the human body is wired to fast. The hunter and gatherer population did have much food to store, and they would sometimes have nothing to eat due to scarcity. As such, they adopted the ability to function without food for long periods that are essentially fasting. There's also a religious angle to fasting for Christians and Muslims alike.

However, the current wave of intermitted fasting diet was popularized by Dr. Michael Mosley. Intermittent fasting has generated a steady positive buzz with more and more people embracing it. Dr. Mosley explains the science behind intermittent fasting. He, however, attributes the success and popularity of intermittent fasting to the fact that it's mostly psychological and teaches you better ways of eating. That is, when you get used to eating vegetables and good protein, you'll eventually crave healthy food whenever you're hungry.

## Why Do You Fast

Intermittent fasting is a simple yet effective strategy for taking shedding off all the bad weight so that you only keep the good weight. This approach requires very little change in behavior. Thus, it's simple yet meaningful enough to make a difference. When you fast, a couple of changes take place in your body both at the molecular and cellular level. To understand why you need to fast to lose weight, you first must understand what happens to your body when it is in the fed and absorptive state. In the fed state, your body is absorbing and digesting food. It actually begins when you start eating and would typically last for five hours as digestion and absorption of the food you ate takes place. When your body is in this state, it can hardly burn fat due to high insulin levels. From the fed state, your body enters the postabsorptive state during which no meal processing is taking place. This stage lasts between 8 and 12 hours after the last meal before you enter the fasted state. It is during the fasted state that your body burns fat because your insulin levels are low. In the fasted state, your body burns fat that is usually inaccessible in the fed state. Fasting helps to put your body in the fat burning state that is rare to achieve when you're on a normal eating schedule.

Intermittent fasting changes the hormones in your body to utilize your fat stores effectively. Your human growth hormone levels go up dramatically, thus speeding up protein synthesis, thereby influencing your body's fat loss and muscle gain by making the fat available for use as a source of energy. What this means is that your body will be burning fat and packing muscle faster. When your insulin levels drop due to heightened insulin sensitivity making the fat stored in your body more accessible to be converted to energy, some changes in gene functions relating to protection and longevity will be amplified, and your cells will initiate repair processes efficiently and quickly. Moreover, fasting promotes autophagy that removes all the damaged cells while contributing to the renewal of cells in addition to supporting the body's regenerative processes.

## What You Should Eat During Intermittent Fasting

One of the reasons why intermittent fasting is appealing is because there are no food rules. The only restrictions are on when you can eat and not what you can eat. However, this is not to say that you should be downing bags of chips and pints upon pints of ice cream. Remember, the idea is to adopt a healthy eating lifestyle. So what should you eat anyway? Well, a well-balanced diet is key to maintaining your energy levels. If your goal is to lose weight, you must focus on including nutrient-dense foods on your menu like veggies, fruits, nuts, whole grains, seeds, beans, lean proteins, and dairy. Think about unprocessed, high fiber, whole foods that offer flavor and variety. Here are some foods you should eat in plenty during intermittent fasting:

**Water**. Although you're not eating, it's important to make sure your stay hydrated to maintain the health of major organs in the body. To tell if you have adequate water, make sure your urine is pale yellow. Dark urine is a sign of dehydration that can cause fatigue, headaches, or even lightheadedness. If you can't stand plain water, you can add mint leaves, a squeeze of lemon juice or cucumber slices.

**Fish**. Dietary guidelines advocate for the consumption of at least eight ounces of fish weekly. Fish is a rich source of protein, ample quantities of Vitamin D and healthy fats. Moreover, limiting your calorie consumption can alter your cognitive ability; hence, fish will come in handy as brain food.

**Avocado**. It's obviously strange to eat high-calorie food when you're actually trying to lose weight. Well, the thing about avocadoes is that they're packed with monounsaturated fat that is satiating. Thus, you can be sure to stay full for longer hours than you would when you eat other foods.

**Cruciferous vegetables**. Foods like Brussels sprouts, broccoli, and cauliflower, are laden with fiber. Eating these foods will keep you regular while preventing constipation. Furthermore, you'll also fee full, which is great when you're fasting for hours.

**Beans and legumes**. Carbs are a great source of energy; hence, you can consider including low-calorie carbs like legumes and beans in your eating plan. Besides, foods like black beans, lentils, and chickpeas have been found to decrease body weight.

**Potatoes**. Potatoes are not necessarily bad. If anything, they offer a satiating effect that could lead to weight loss. However, this doesn't include potato chips and French fries.

**Eggs**. It's important to get as much protein as possible to build muscle and stay full. A large egg will give you six grams of proteins. When you eat hard boiled eggs, you're less likely to feel hungry.

**Berries**. You need immune boosting nutrients like vitamin c, and there's no better way to achieve this than including berries in your meal plan.

**Probiotics**. The bacteria in your gut aren't happy when you go for hours without food. As such, you could experience side effects like constipation. You can counter this unpleasant feeling taking probiotic-rich foods like kefir, kraut, or kombucha.

**Whole grains**. It's ridiculous to be on a diet and eat carbs. Well, with intermittent fasting, you can include whole grains that are rich in protein and fiber to stay full. Moreover, eating whole grains will speed up your metabolism. Think about millet, amaranth, sorghum, kamut, spelled, faro, bulgur, and freekeh, among others.

**Nuts**. Although nuts may contain high calories, they're most certainly important because of the good fat. According to research, polyunsaturated fat found in walnuts has the ability to alter physiological markers for satiety and hunger.

## What to Consider Before Starting Intermittent Fasting

Before you begin intermittent fasting for weight loss, you need to know that this eating pattern is not for everyone. First off, you should not attempt intermittent fasting before consulting a health professional if you're underweight or you have a history of battling eating disorders. Intermittent fasting is also not recommended if you have a medical condition. Some women have also reported various effects like a cessation of a menstrual period. Ultimately, you need to be careful when you go into intermittent fasting because it has been previously found that this eating pattern is not beneficial for women compared to men. If you have fertility issues or are trying to conceive, then consider holding off intermittent fasting. Expectant and lactating mothers are also advised against intermittent fasting.

The main side effect that you'll experience when you go into intermittent fasting is hunger. Additionally, you may experience general body weakness. Your brain may also perform well. However, these are temporary, and your body will adapt to your new eating pattern over time. It's advisable that you consult your doctor before starting intermittent fasting for women if you have any of the following conditions;

- Diabetes/Problems with blood sugar regulations
- Low blood pressure
- You are underweight
- Eating disorders
- Amenorrhea
- Breastfeeding
- Trying to conceive
- Taking medications

Always look at the potential benefits of intermittent fasting before you go for it. If the risks far outweigh the benefits, this could be dangerous hence not worth trying. For instance, if you're pregnant, you definitely have more energy needs; therefore, taking on intermittent fasting would definitely be a bad idea. This also applies when you're having problems sleeping or are under chronic stress. Intermittent fasting is also discouraged if you have a history of eating disorders because it could actually cause further problems that can mess your health. While intermittent fasting has produced results for thousands of people across the globe, you must keep in mind that this is not a gateway to eating a diet comprising of highly processed food or even skipping meals randomly. Generally, intermittent fasting has an outstanding safety profile since it's not dangerous to go without food for a while when you're well-nourished and healthy.

## When Do You Fast

If you're looking to get on the intermittent fasting train, you need to know when you will be fasting in order to achieve the desired outcome. There are three common ways of approaching the fast as follows:

*Eat stop eat.* This involves fasting for 24 hours once or twice in seven days. However, you can take calorie-free beverages during this fasting period. This is one of the best ways to start intermittent fasting because the occasional fasting will equally help you realize the many benefits of fasting.

*Up day, down day.* With this method of fasting, you will keep on reducing your calorie intake daily. That is, when you eat very little one day (down day), you revert to your normal caloric intake the next day (up day). The advantage of this eating pattern is that it allows you to eat every day while you still reap the benefits of fasting.

*Alternate day fasting.* With this schedule, you get to fast for longer periods on alternate days weekly. You fast for 24 hours and only eat one meal every day.

*Lean gains.* With this approach, you'll fast for 16 hours within every 24 hours and only eat during the eight-hour window. Keep in mind that sleep is included so this is not as tough as it may seem. The good thing about this fast is that you can start your 8-hour eating period at a time that works best for you. This means that you could actually skip breakfast and instead have lunch and dinner. Since this is something you'll do every day, it eventually becomes a habit making it remarkably easy to stick to it.

## Chapter 3: Why Intermittent Fasting Is the Best Way for Weight Loss

Most of the weight loss diet fads will often demand that you give up certain things in order for you to see the results. Well, this is not the case with intermittent fasting that almost blends into your normal eating and sleeping pattern. Even then, the truth is that fasting in itself can be intimidating. Not eating for a couple of hours is something many people find difficult. Yet this method comes close to your lifestyle than a diet. So make sure that you identify an intermittent fasting plan that fits into your schedule, and you're able to keep up with comfortably. This will minimize the chance of having to quit because you're not putting any strain on your body.

Think about this; you fast while sleeping and break the fast when you wake up in the morning! Even more interesting, most people often fast for 12 hours and have another 12 hours of eating. As such, you can easily extend the fasting window to 16 hours and eat for eight hours to realize the benefits of intermittent fasting. Here are reasons why you should consider intermittent fasting as your weight loss regime:

**Intermittent fasting is convenient**. One of the reasons many people give up on other kinds of weight loss diets is because they're unable to follow through. When you have a busy lifestyle juggling between a number of things that are vying for your attention and are on a diet, the latter will definitely suffer.

On the contrary, intermittent fasting comes with convenience. For instance, when doing the 16:8 intermittent fast, you don't have to think about preparing breakfast in the morning or even lunch. Yes, you can skip breakfast.

What's more? When it's time to feed, you don't have to worry about what kind of food you should eat. Intermittent fasting is quite flexible with the foods you can include in your diet. In fact, in most instances, nothing will really change. You could even eat at a restaurant yet still enjoy the benefits of fasting.

Moreover, intermittent fasting lets you enjoy special occasions with family and friends without worrying about excess calories. However, this does not mean that you eat highly processed foods. The idea here is to develop a healthy yet convenient to implement eating pattern that can eventually be part of your lifestyle.

**Intermittent fasting makes life simple**. Intermittent fasting is not just convenient but also simple to follow. Whether you're always on the go or are into skipping a meal or two, this eating pattern is convenient and perfect for you. College students will particularly find intermittent fasting appealing because they can hardly find a balance between school work and maintaining a healthy social life. When you take on intermittent fasting, you'll realize there'll be fewer decisions you have to make daily. Instead, you'll have more energy to handle the most important tasks of the day. This is contrary to the effect that most diets will have on your body like feeling overwhelmed and tired in addition to being expensive and complex.

**Intermittent fasting saves you time and money.** If you were to go on a regular diet, no doubt you'll have to go out of your way to spend time and money to conform to a certain menu. Not to mention the amount of time that would go into shopping for the food supplies, prepping and eventually cooking at least six meals in a day. The truth is that this can be draining. However, with intermittent fasting, there's no need to get out of your normal lifestyle. If anything, it will save you money and time since you'll be having fewer meals in a day. Consequently, you don't have to spend time thinking about what you should eat or even spending a lot of time preparing the food.

**Intermittent fasting strengthens your will power while improving your concentration and focus**. Intermittent fasting is all about self-discipline. That is, you must learn to say no. In fact, there'll be numerous times during your fast when you'll crave food, but you must resist this urge to eat. Every time you resist this urge helps you develop your willpower as well as strengthen your ability to steer clear of distractions and temptations even in other areas of life. In addition, it'll also go a long way in improving your ability to focus and concentrate on achieving specific goals that you have yet to accomplish. Generally, you tend to be sharper and alert when you're hungry than when you've got a full tummy. This is attributed to the fact that fasting will free up all the valuable energy hence avoiding distractions while staying focused on an important goal.

**Intermittent fasting lets you eat what you want and still lose weight**. With intermittent fasting, weight loss is more about when you eat as opposed to what you eat. As such, it gives you more freedom to eat what you want to eat. Since you're fasting, you'll typically settle down for a larger meal and consequently more calories than you would normally eat per meal for three to six meals. Therefore, intermittent fasting is more about timing than the composition of your diet. Even then, you should avoid eating processed junk food, particularly those with empty calories since they will undo the benefits of your fast. Since intermittent fasting is more of a lifestyle, you'll do well to cut down on sweeteners and processed sugars and replace processed foods with whole foods. Ultimately, you should focus on having a balanced diet that includes whole grains, vegetables, fruits, and protein. If you're aiming at losing weight, you also must not take in too many calories during your feeding window.

**Intermittent fasting helps you embrace a healthy lifestyle and avoid dangerous eating diets**. Since intermittent fasting is not a diet, it's a lifestyle that can be sustained through the years. Intermittent fasting is more of a wellness revolution because it helps you to adapt to a lifestyle of eating healthy foods and avoiding dangerous diets. If you're on intermittent fasting, you should not overeat junk food; otherwise, you'll end up gaining weight. Remember, intermittent fasting isn't an excuse for indulging in your favorite chocolate cookie or ice cream without giving a care. Rather, intermittent fasting reprograms your brain so that you're accustomed to taking reduced calories than you would normally consume. This helps you to avoid the trap of overeating. In fact, you'll be surprised that over time you'll be able to say no to your favorite cookies not because you deny yourself a treat, but you simply don't want. When you're consuming fewer calories than you're taking, you'll definitely begin to burn fat and lose weight over time.

**Intermittent fasting lets you have bigger meals that are more satisfying**. When you have to eat every 2-3 hours, you tend to think about food for the better part of the day. Consequently, you'll hardly have big meals, particularly if you are physically inactive. Having infrequent meals in a large volume will often provide you with more calories and is much more satisfying hence a great way to feel fuller for longer periods. When you eat large meals infrequently, you'll have increased adherence to the diet over time.

**Intermitted fasting helps to establish a more structured way of eating.** When you are on the regular eating plan, you will, in most instances, find yourself snacking in between meals mindlessly. From a couple of cookies to a slice of cake and ice cream, there's always something you can chew on. This will definitely contribute to you gaining excess weight. Intermittent fasting helps you to structure your eating pattern without necessarily getting rid of your favorites. Instead, you eliminate the habit of eating every so often by taking better control of your diet.

**Intermittent fasting improves your hunger awareness.** Hunger and thirst are processed in the same part of the brain. Thus, it is common to find that you're eating throughout the day not because you're hungry but for other reasons. This can be anything from stress, boredom, happiness, or even sadness, among others. Sometimes, the mere smell of food can make you assume you're actually hungry. Thus, when you're on a fast, you'll have a heightened sense of hunger awareness that will make you realize that real hunger feels like and how to differentiate it from the hunger that is triggered by other factors.

**You can still eat out and enjoy social gatherings during intermittent fasting**. Unlike many weight loss diets, intermittent fasting is not restrictive in terms of the foods you need to include on your menu. So you don't have to worry about missing out on social gatherings or even eating out! In fact, this pattern of eating accommodates the social nature of human beings as we tend to build social events around food. Since most of the occasions take place in the evening, you can always stick to your fasting routine and join the rest of the gathering at the table. Intermittent fasting gives you the freedom to eat food that is served at social gatherings as well as restaurants while staying within your calorie range for the day. This makes it simple and easy to maintain. So you don't have to write off the idea of eating out.

**You can still travel the world while fasting**. If you love traveling, you might be hesitant about attempting intermittent fasting. However, the interesting thing is that you can still travel the world and not worry about missing new experiences because of breaking your fast outside your feeding window. You can easily integrate intermittent fasting into your diet so that you are enjoying new experiences while losing weight. This way, you don't have to eat unhealthy food or even abandon your intermittent fasting plan for weight loss. Intermittent fasting can work for you whenever and wherever you are.

**Intermittent fasting helps to improve the quality of your sleep**. Although most people embrace intermittent fasting solely to lose weight, it comes with other added benefits among them quality sleep. This is attributed to the fact that when you're fasting, your body digests food before you sleep. This eventually helps you to sleep better because your insulin and fat levels are better controlled. Getting quality sleep can also contribute to weight loss.

**Intermittent fasting makes you feel happy**. This is another added advantage of fasting for weight loss. When you lose excess weight, you will not only feel lighter but also happier because you'll be more confident in your body. Moreover, you'll also have more energy because generally, digestion often takes much of your body's energy. This is in addition to feeling more healthier and in control.

**Intermittent fasting is easy to follow.** In most cases, starting a diet is easy. However, many people tend to give up after several weeks of watching what you're eating and counting calories. On the contrary, intermittent fasting gives you much freedom making it a lot easier to stick with it in the long term.

**Intermittent fasting helps in muscle growth.** Although many people have reported that intermittent fasting resulted in the loss of muscle when done properly, intermittent fasting can contribute to muscle building. However, this will require you to tailor your intermittent fasting approach in a manner that limits your fasting period to between 10 and 12 hours so that you're not inhibiting the body's ability to build muscle. You may also have to extend your feeding window to 10 hours so that you get all the nutrients you need.

Well, intermittent fasting does more than just helping you achieve your goal of losing weight. It actually presents many other benefits that will generally improve your lifestyle. This means that you must stay committed to the intermittent fasting plan that works for you to make sure that you get the results you desire. Eventually, intermittent fasting will become part of your lifestyle.

## Chapter 4: Impact of Intermittent Fasting on Your Body

A number of studies have backed up the fact that intermittent fasting presents powerful benefits to your brain and body. Some of the top benefits you'll experience when you embark on intermittent fasting for weight loss include the following:

**Speeds up fat burning and weight loss**. Intermittent fasting is one of the top strategies for burning fat effortlessly. Fat burning during intermittent fasting is actually a result of being in a calorie deficient state that promotes loss of fat. A study done on animals found that intermittent fasting for a period of up to 16 weeks helps in the preventions of obesity with the results being seen in just six weeks. According to researchers, intermittent fasting activates metabolism while also helping to burn more fat through the generation of body heat. When you're fasting, your insulin levels will be low. The body will break down carbohydrates into glucose that the cells will draw energy from or convert it into fat hence store it for later use. Insulin levels are low when you're not consuming food. Thus, during fasting, your insulin levels are likely to be low, prompting the cells to get their glucose from fat stores as energy. When this process is done repeatedly, it results in weight loss. Most research suggests that intermittent fasting may be an effective weight management strategy. The fact that you'll most likely be eating fewer calories than you're burning means that your body will mostly be relying on the fat stores for energy which will translate to significant weight loss.

**Boosts growth hormone production**. The physiology of fasting is interesting. As such, the power of fasting is not in the reduction of calories, but hormonal changes that take place. Fasting triggers increased the production of the human growth hormone (HGH) that is produced in the pituitary gland. This hormone is instrumental in the normal development in adolescents, children, and adults. In adults, a deficiency of the growth hormone results in an increase in body fat, a decrease in bone mass, and lower lean body mass. Upon release by the pituitary gland, the growth hormone lasts for just a few minutes in the bloodstream. This hormone goes to the liver for metabolism before conversion into various growth factors with the most important one being the Insulin-Like Growth Factor 1 (IGF1).

This Insulin-Like Growth Factor 1 is linked to high insulin levels as well as most poor health outcomes. Even then, the brief pulse of IGF1 from the human growth hormone only lasts for a few minutes. All hormones are secreted in brief bursts naturally ostensibly preventing the development of resistance that requires high levels as well as the persistence of those levels. This explains how insulin resistance develops. The human growth hormone is usually secreted during sleep as a counter-regulatory hormone. Together with adrenaline and cortisol, this the growth hormone increases your blood glucose by breaking down glycogen to counter insulin. These hormones are secreted in a pulse just before you wake up during a counter-regulatory surge. This is normal as it helps the ready prepare for the upcoming day.

It's, therefore, wrong to say that you derive the energy for the day from breakfast because usually, your body has already given a big shot for great stuff and fuel for the day. Therefore, you absolutely don't need to rely on all your sugary cereals for energy. This is also the reason why you least feel hungry in the morning even when you haven't eaten for 12 hours. The growth hormone tends to go down with age while abnormally low levels can result in low bone and muscle mass. Fasting stimulates the secretion of the human growth hormone. That is, when you fast, there's a spike in the morning and regular secretion throughout the day. This is critical to the maintenance of lean bone and muscle mass while the stored fats burn. When the growth hormone is elevated by fasting, your muscle mass increases.

**Prevents insulin resistance.** When you eat, the body breaks down the food into glucose that goes in the bloodstream for transportation to the cells. Your cells rely on this glucose as fuel to function properly. Insulin is a hormone that allows the cells to absorb glucose. Thus, whenever you eat insulin is produced, signaling the cells to absorb glucose. When the cells receive this glucose, they effectively receive energy. Even then, this is not always the case. In some instances, the communication between insulin and the cells can go off so that the glucose is not received in the cells but is instead stored as fat. This is referred to as insulin resistance. That is, as more and more insulin is produced, the cells do not respond by receiving glucose. Insulin resistance can be caused by various reasons, yet your pancreas can only produce so much insulin before it is fatigued, leading to insulin deficiency and subsequently, diabetes. When this happens, you'll constantly feel tired, cold, and lousy. This resistance is dependent on not only the levels of insulin but also the persistence level. Intermittent fasting is a great and easiest way of increasing your insulin sensitivity. When you burn the available glucose and glycogen that is the stored glucose, your body goes into ketosis where you draw energy from ketones.

**Reduces the risk of heart disease.** Heart disease is a leading killer across the world. CDC puts the number of people who die from heart disease in the United States at 610,000 annually. According to research, intermittent fasting can improve certain aspects of cardiovascular health. You can reduce the risk of heart disease by making changes to your lifestyle. This includes exercising, eating right, limiting your intake of alcohol, and not smoking. Intermittent fasting restricts the calories you consume on a given day it will improve your glycemic control, cardiovascular risk as well as insulin resistance. In one study, individuals who followed an alternate day fasting plan for successfully lost weight had a notable reduction in their blood sugar levels, inflammatory markers, blood pressure, triglycerides, LDL cholesterol, and the total cholesterol. Triglycerides are a type of fat that is found in the blood and is linked to heart disease.

**Increases metabolic rate.** Intermittent fasting helps in improving insulin sensitivity that is key in the prevention of diabetes, increasing metabolic rate, and weight management. It's a common belief that skipping meals will result in the body adapting to the calorie deficit by lowering the metabolic rate to save energy. It has been established that extended periods of fasting can lead to a drop in metabolism. However, some studies have also shown that when you fast for short periods, you can increase your metabolism. In fact, one study conducted among 11 healthy men found that after a three day fast, their metabolism actually increased by 14%. This increase is attributed to the rise in norepinephrine hormone that, together with insulin, promotes fat burning. Based on these findings, intermittent fasting is far much significant with great weight loss advantages when compared to the other diets that are aimed to focus on calorie restriction for losing weight. Even then, the effects of intermittent fasting on metabolism are still under study because several other studies have found that your muscle mass doesn't decrease much during intermittent fasting.

**Intermittent fasting changes how cells, genes, and hormones function**. There's a raft of activities that go on in your body when you fast for extended periods. One of the things that happens is that your body will initiate important cellular repair processes as well as a change in the levels of hormones to make stored fat more accessible. More specifically, there'll be a significant drop in the insulin levels resulting in fat burning as the stored fats become a primary source of energy. The growth hormone in the blood may increase up to five times that also facilitates fat burning and muscle gain. Fasting also results in beneficial changes, molecules, and genes that are related to protection against disease and longevity. Cellular repair processes are also initiated when you're fasting promoting the removal of waste material from the cells.

**Reduces inflammation and oxidative stress in the body.** Oxidative stress is a step in most of the chronic diseases and aging. It involves unstable molecules known as free radicals that react with other molecules like DNA and protein and damage them. A number of studies show that intermittent fasting enhances your body's resistance to oxidative stress. In addition, intermittent fasting also helps in fighting inflammation that is a common cause of diseases, especially when your body is able to go into autophagy.

**Induces a number of cellular repair processes**. When you fast for extended periods, the cells in your body begin to initiate a waste removal process that is known as autophagy. This process not only involves breaking down but also metabolizing dysfunctional and broken proteins that accumulate in within the cells over time. Increased autophagy is able to offer protection against a number of diseases such as Alzheimer's disease.

**Helps in the prevention of cancer**. Cancer is a disease that is characterized by the growth of cells that is uncontrolled. Studies have found that fasting has a number of benefits on metabolism that could actually lead to a reduced risk of cancer. There's also evidence on cancer patients showing that fasting reduced some of the side effects of chemotherapy. It's important to note that these studies have mostly been done in animals; hence, there's a need for further studies in humans.

**Fasting has anti-aging effects**. Various forms of fasting have been found to improve healthspan and lifespan significantly. This has been demonstrated with caloric restriction in animals that reduces the number of calories by between 20 and 30%. Intermittent fasting also slows down the aging process and increases your lifespan by manipulating mitochondrial networks. Mitochondria are power generators found in the cells. They produce most of the energy the cells need for survival. Studies have shown that intermittent fasting helps to keep the mitochondrial networks fused hence keeping the mitochondria strong with the ability to process energy. This is crucial for vibrant aging and longevity. Fasting also delays the aging process and prevent diseases by triggering adaptive cellular stress responses that result in a better ability to cope with more stress while counteracting the disease. Thus, when your mitochondria work better, so will your body.

**Intermittent fasting is therapeutic.** When practiced well, intermittent fasting offers therapeutic benefits that are psychological, spiritual, and physical. For physical benefits, intermittent fasting can help cure diabetes. In addition, it has been proven to be extremely useful in the reduction of seizure-related brain damage as well as seizures themselves as well as improve symptoms of arthritis. Fasting also offers spiritual benefits, as is widely practiced by different religions around the world. It contributes towards purifying your soul and body when practiced within the religious context. The psychological angle of fasting is in the fact that it takes your will and self-control, which is a powerful psychological benefit. You learn how to ignore hunger and practice restraint from eating for a certain duration. This is a great practice because it's about training your mind. A successful intermittent fasting plan will have powerful effects on your psychological perspective. In fact, intermittent fasting has been proven to have positive results in women, especially in relation to improving the sense of control, pride, achievement, and reward. Moreover, it is handy for improving your self-esteem.

You need to understand how intermittent fasting will affect you before you get into it because this signals a change of lifestyle. While it may seem difficult to execute because your body is used to a certain way of eating, it's doable, and the results are incredible. The only thing you should never do is wake up one morning and jump into it. Rather, take time to prepare psychologically and begin slowly to increase your success rate, especially if you're looking to embrace healthy living by making a lifestyle change.

## Chapter 5: Benefits of Intermittent Fasting

You've probably been told to make sure that you eat a balanced diet. Thus, it's odd to think that depriving yourself a meal or more can actually be a necessity. Interestingly, evidence points to the benefits of intermittent fasting on your wellbeing. Different forms of intermittent fasting will yield different benefits that go beyond weight loss. Some of the benefits of intermittent fasting include:

**Weight and body fat loss.** The majority of people who try intermittent fasting do it because they want to lose weight. Unlike other weight loss plan, intermittent fasting makes you adapt to an eating pattern that defines when you should eat and when you should fast. The whole idea behind intermittent fasting it offers you flexibility while making you eat fewer meals. This is not equivalent to counting calories as is usually the norm with most of the weight loss regimens. When you alter your eating pattern, then you're likely to eat much less hence taking fewer calories. In addition, intermittent fasting will enhance the hormonal function that facilitates weight loss. That is, a dip in the levels of insulin, along with a higher presence of the growth hormone and an increase in the amount of norepinephrine increases the rate at which fat is broken down into energy. As such, fasting on a short-term basis will increase your metabolic rate, thus helping you to burn more fats. Thus, intermittent fasting works to lose weight by reducing the amount of food you eat as well as boost your metabolic rate. It's estimated that you can experience up to 8% weight loss over a period of 3-24 weeks with intermittent fasting. When you have significant weight loss, your waist circumference will also reduce indicating loss of belly fat that is actually harmful.

**Stable glucose level**. Studies conducted in both people and mice show that various kinds of intermittent fasting can improve the way your body responds to sugar. In mice, researchers were able to reboot the pancreas that produces insulin, thereby reversing diabetes. Various forms of fasting that involve extended hours of unrestricted eating, followed by five days of eating a restricted fasting diet has been found to cause big improvements in individuals with high blood sugar. Losing weight, eating healthy, and moving more can help in fighting off the development of type 2 diabetes. Losing weight makes you more insulin sensitive hence driving your blood sugar down. When you eat, your body releases insulin in your bloodstream to supply cells energy. However, if you're pre-diabetic, your insulin resistant meaning your blood sugar levels are constantly elevated. Thus intermittent fasting can help to stabilize your glucose levels since it requires your body to produce insulin less often hence restoring your insulin secretion and promoting the generation of new insulin-producing pancreatic beta cells according to research.

**Improves digestive health.** The cells with the gastrointestinal tract are constantly working. In some instances, these cells work to the extent of being passed out a part of excreta. You can repair these digestive cells with intermittent fasting by making sure your body gets to autophagy. This gets rid of the old cells and activates your immune system accordingly. This also applies to a chronic gut immune response that is capable of inflaming bowels. Getting them to rest allows them a chance to restore and repair. An extended night fast and autophagy will give your gut a chance not only to relax but also recharge.

**Improved brain health.** Studies conducted in mice show that intermittent fasting could actually improve brain health by boosting your brainpower. As you grow older, the amount of blood flowing to your brain decreases while the neurons shrink, and the brain volume declines. Intermittent fasting halts the aging process keeping you mentally healthy and sharp. By boosting your brain health, intermittent fasting can lower your risk of neurodegenerative diseases like Parkinson's and Alzheimer's.

Furthermore, fasting reduces obesity and is able to protect you from diabetes, both of which can increase your risk of developing Alzheimer's disease. Intermittent fasting also helps in improving your brain by hindering the degeneration of nerve cells. According to one study, intermittent fasting plays an important role in guarding neurons in the brain from excitotoxic stress. In addition, it also speeds up autophagy in the neurons helping your body to eliminate all the damaged cells while generating new ones. This is important in helping the body defend itself from diseases. Your memory and learning ability also improve with intermittent fasting. Studies have shown that memory and mood are boosted after periods of caloric restriction.

**Decreased risk of cancer**. Cancer has become prevalent over the past few years, affecting people of all ages and race. The good news is that autophagy promises to reduce the likelihood of having cancer. Autophagy has received attention from medical professionals for its role in the prevention of cancer. This is because cancer occurs when there's a cellular disorder thus by promoting cell inflammation as well as regulation of damage response to the DNA by foreign bodies and regulating genome instability it helps to keep cancer at bay.

**Promotes longevity**. Intermittent fasting can help promote the overall length of life. This concept dates back to the 1950s when scientists discovered autophagy as well as the great potential it holds in determining the quality of life. That is, you don't necessarily need to take in too many nutrients to ensure your wellbeing rather, work toward promoting the internal process that recycles the damaged cell parts and eliminates the toxic body cells.

**Improve immune system.** Autophagy is powerful and highly effective when it comes to keeping your immune system in top shape. It achieves this by promoting inflammation in cells as well as actively fighting diseases through non-selective autophagy. When cellular inflammation happens, it boosts the cells of the immune system whenever it is attacked by diseases. Autophagy induces inflammation by depriving cell proteins of nutrition, thereby causing them to work more actively. This initiates the required immune response that keeps diseases and infections away. It also eliminates harmful elements that include tuberculosis, micro bacterium, as well as other viral elements from the cell.

**Regulates inflammation**. You can either reduce or boost the immune response with autophagy depending on what is required. This, in turn, prevents and promotes inflammation. When there's a dangerous invasion, autophagy will boost inflammation by signaling the immune system to attack. On the other hand, it can also decrease the inflammation within the immune system by getting rid of the signals that cause it.

**Improved quality of life.** The internet is awash with tons of methods and techniques that guarantee quality health and quality life in general. The truth is that none of these methods that include diets, anti-aging creams, and other products can lead closer to autophagy during intermittent fasting. The cellular degeneration and regeneration processes during autophagy are guaranteed to make you appear youthful in contrast to your actual age. This is especially important to your skin that is exposed to harsh elements of pollution as well as other substance that cause wrinkles leading to a decline in your skin quality with layers of toxic substances forming over your skin cells.

**Decreased risk of neurodegenerative diseases**. When your body achieves autophagy, you'll have a decreased risk of developing neurodegenerative diseases like Alzheimer's and Parkinson's. Here's how. Neurodegenerative diseases will work well on the basis of the accumulated toxic and old neurons that pile up in certain areas of the brain spreading to the surrounding areas. Therefore, autophagy replaces the neuron parts that are useless and, in their place, regenerate new ones effectively keeping these diseases in check.

**Enhanced mental performance.** Intermittent fasting enhances the cognitive function in addition to being useful in boosting brain power. Intermittent fasting will boost the brain-derived neurotrophic factor (BDNF) levels. This is a protein within the brain that is able to interact with the other parts of your brain that are responsible for controlling the learning, memory, and cognitive functions. The brain-derived neurotrophic factor is also capable of protecting and stimulating the growth of new brain cells. When you are on intermittent fasting, your body will go into the ketogenic state, thereby using ketones to burn body fat to energy. Ketones are also capable of feeding your brain, thus improving your mental productivity, energy, and acuity.

**Prevention of diseases.** Intermittent fasting has been associated with the prevention of diseases. According to research, intermittent fasting plays an important role in improving the number of risk markers for chronic disease that include lowered cholesterol, lowered blood pressure, and reduced insulin resistance. A study in the World Journal of Diabetes reveals that patients who have type 2 diabetes and are on short term daily intermittent fasting are likely to experience a drop in their lower body weight and have better variability of post-meal glucose. Intermittent fasting will also enhance stress markers resistance, reduce inflammation and blood pressure and promote better glucose circulation and lipid levels hence reducing the risk of cardiovascular diseases such as cancer, Alzheimer's, and Parkinson's. Intermittent fasting can also slow down the progression of certain cancers like skin and breast cancer by increasing the levels of tumor-infiltrating lymphocytes. These are the cells that are sent by the immune system to attack the tumor.

**Improved physical fitness**. Intermittent fasting influences your digestive system; hence, your level of physical fitness. Having a small feasting window and an extended fasting window encourages proper digestion of food. As a result, you have a healthy and proportional daily intake of food as well as calories. As you get used to this process, it is unlikely that you will experience hunger. You don't have to worry about slowing down your metabolism because, in reality, intermittent fasting will enhance your metabolism making it more flexible as your body has the capability to run on fats and glucose along for energy effectively. The use of oxygen is important in the success of your training. In fact, in order to perform well, you must adjust your breathing habits during workouts. Generally, the maximum amount of oxygen that your body uses per kilogram of your body weight or per minute is referred to as VO2. This is also known as wind. The amount of wind you have influences your performance. More wind means better performance.

Consequently, top athletes will have twice as much VO2 level compared to those without training. A study carried out on a fasted group that skipped breakfast and a non-fasted group that had breakfast an hour before found that the VO2 levels of both groups were 3.5L/min at the beginning. There was a notable increase in the wind in the fasting group at 9.7% compared to an increase of 2.5% in those who took breakfast.

**Enhances bodybuilding**. When you have a short feasting window, it automatically translates to fewer meals meaning you can concentrate your daily intake of calories in 1-2 meals. Bodybuilders find this approach to be great compared to splitting your calories in 5-6 meals spread throughout the day. You need a certain amount of protein in maintaining your muscle mass. You can still maintain your muscle mass with intermittent fasting even though this eating pattern doesn't focus on your protein intake. Since your growth hormone reaches unbelievable levels after 48 hours of fasting, you're able to maintain muscles even without having to eat proteins or even having protein shakes and bars.

**Increased insulin sensitivity.** Insulin sensitivity refers to your body cell's level of sensitivity in response to insulin. High levels of insulin sensitivity are good as it allows the cells to use blood glucose effectively, thereby reducing the amount of blood sugar in your system. When your insulin levels are low, you will experience insulin resistance. When this happens, you will experience abnormal levels of blood sugar, which, when not managed, will result in type 2 diabetes. Insulin sensitivity will vary between different people and will change according to various dietary factors and lifestyle. Therefore, improving it could be beneficial to those people who are living with or are at risk of developing type 2 diabetes. According to a 2014 review investigating the effect of intermittent fasting in obese and overweight adults, intermittent fasting has the ability to reduce insulin resistance. Even then, there was no significant effect on glucose levels.

Intermittent fasting will provide amazing results when done right. From the loss of excessive weight to a reversal of type 2 diabetes, many benefits are linked to intermittent fasting. Even then, you need to stay committed and be consistent with your intermittent fasting protocol in order to achieve results. Most importantly, make sure you have a goal you'd like to achieve at the beginning of your fasting period. While at it remember that unlike many weight loss diets, fasting doesn't have a standard duration because it's just about depriving your body food for a given time.

Intermittent fasting is nothing curious or queer rather; it's part of normal everyday life. It's the most powerful and oldest intervention you can think of, yet so many people are not aware of its power to rejuvenate the body as well as its therapeutic potential. You don't have to put pressure on yourself to produce results in the beginning, especially if your goal is to lose weight. Take time to transition, allowing your body to adjust accordingly. This may mean starting with a plan that is close to your current eating plan, slowly advancing to intermittent eating plans that require you to fast for longer durations.

## Chapter 6: Intermittent Fasting: The Best Anti-Aging Diet

Countless celebrities and entrepreneurs use intermittent fasting to reverses the effects of aging. However, not everyone understands the scientific aspect of intermittent fasting and its link with anti-aging. This chapter looks into the scientific aspect of intermittent fasting while introducing concepts related to aging healthily. To understand the relationship between fasting and anti-aging, you first need to understand the difference between the various fasting methods. For starters, the short-term fasting plans with a fasting window of between 16 and 20 hours offer multiple independent benefits. These fasts that are also known as micro-fasts support metabolic healthy by controlling body weight, lowering your insulin levels, and improving glycemic control. As such, short term fasting is an incredible choice to embrace when your goal is solely weight loss. During short fasts, your fat mass may reduce while physical strength remains the same.

The other benefits of fasting include an increase in brain-derived neurotrophic factor (BDNF) signaling within your brain, cardiovascular support, and reduced risk of cancer recurrence. On the other hand, fasting for extended periods will stimulate physiological changes that offer unique benefits of fasting that fall within functional areas like longevity, immune strength, and healthy aging.

The physiological effects of extended fasting are more pronounced than the effects of short-term fasts lasting less than 24 hours because of the body's ability to switch to fat and ketone catabolism upon the depletion of glycogen reserves during extended fasting. Extended fasting also increased the white blood cells that are a biomarker for immune health and is useful for adjunct therapy alongside chemotherapy for killing cancer cells. The rationale behind this is that cancer cells grow and thrive on glucose; thus, when you go on extended fasts; you starve the cancer cells and support the anti-cancer immune efforts.

## Anti-Aging Benefits of Intermitted Fasting

Out of all interventions that are aimed at countering aging, calorie restriction is that most efficient. Generally, fasting for extended periods results in calorie restriction that reduces calories by between 20 and 40%. This is not recommended for performance and is unpopular among biohackers owing to mental distraction. Calorie restriction promotes five mechanisms that are essential for healthy aging. The following are mechanisms of extended fasting that promote healthy aging.

These processes are:

*Cell proliferation (IGF-1 and TOR; specifically mTOR):* Cell proliferation promotes balanced cell growth. It is the ability of the human system to be in the anabolic state with the presence of calories. That is, whenever calories are abundant, cells are in an anabolic state. When you're intermittent fasting results in caloric restriction that tends to shift the balance in the system through stimulation of catabolic pathways. The two pathways that are important in this process are the mammalian target of rapamycin (mTOR) and insulin-like growth factor-1 (IGF-1). Both IGF-1 and mTOR are nutrient sensors that regulate the cellular resources depending on the availability of calories. When you fast, fewer calories are leading to the down-regulation of mTOR and IGF-1, thus signaling repurposing and recycling of organelles and cells. A decline in mTOR signaling has been found to lead to lifespan extension.

Moreover, its inhibition is known to be a longevity assurance mechanism with the availability of rapamycin as well as other mTOR inhibitors making this pathway a valuable target for interventions that extend lifespan. Dr. Jason Fung, a proponent of intermittent fasting, agrees that mTOR is a protein sensor. He further says that eating fats alone and no protein can theoretically modulate MTOR positively. Thus, you can include fat-based drinks in your micro-fast.

*Decreased Inflammation (NF-kB)*: The human body is bound to experience cumulative damage as you age. The damage is often identified by the immune receptors, thereby stimulating the production of multiple proinflammatory molecules. In the worst-case scenario, the accumulated damage is so extensive that the inflammation becomes continuous that either accompanies numerous age-related diseases or contributes to them. Inflammation on its own is not necessarily bad since its part of healing. However, evidence suggests that chronic inflammation and specifically age-associated inflammation, also referred to inflaming, heavily correlates with poor health biomarkers. Calorie restriction during intermittent fasting will inhibit nuclear factor kB (NF-kB) that exerts the anti-inflammatory effect. NF-kB is believed to the master regulator of inflammation, thus minimizing its activity will downregulate various parts of the proinflammatory signaling. Animal models suggest that this anti-inflammatory effect may have cognitive enhancing properties. One study focused on fasting as eustress; a form of stress that is beneficial versus distress; the negative stressors of life that speed up aging. The conclusion was that intermittent fasting led to a reduction of the plasma inflammatory factors. Thus, intermittent fasting can improve cognitive function and preserve the brain from distress through regulation of inflammatory response pathway. By engaging in intermittent fasting, you're able to attain the beneficial levels of stress that is necessary for your physiology and psychology.

*Improved mitochondrial physiology (AMPK/SIRT)*: Mitochondria are the organelles that make up a cell. They're crucial in the production of cellular energy that enables the cells to do more work. This work is equivalent to physical labor, as is the case with the muscle cells or cognitive tasks in the case of brain cells. Aging tends to weaken the general quality of your body's mitochondrial network, thereby decreasing the destruction of already damaged or dysfunctional mitochondria as well as the generation of new mitochondria. However, when you fast and experience calorie restriction, these processes will be supported, giving rise to a high quality of your mitochondrial network. The two pathways that are mostly associated with mitochondrial support are sirtuins (SIRT genes) and AMP-dependent kinase (AMPK). Both pathways are sensitive to the shifts in the NADH/NAD+ ratio. Calorie restriction triggers an increase in NAD+ accumulation that activates sirtuins and AMPK. Studies have concluded that the fact that sirtuins need NAD for their enzymatic activity links metabolism to diseases associated with aging and aging. Both sirtuins and AMPK are central to mitochondrial biogenesis as well as processes of mitophagy (mitochondrial removing and recycling of the organelles that are dysfunctional that are associated with age) are important in maintaining a younger mitochondrial network. When cells are deprived of glucose during an extended fast, the production of ATP initially drops. When AMPK senses the decrease in ATP, it limits the utilization of energy as it upregulates numerous other processes that replenish ATP. As a result, mitochondria and cells are able to better make ATP in the future. Calorie restriction activates the AMPK pathway in a number of tissues in animal models. However, this has not been studied in humans. Sirtuins also play an important role in aging as a biological stress sensor. Increasing and manipulating the expression of sirtuins in yeast promotes longevity.

*Enhanced autophagy (FoxO):* Autophagy can loosely be translated to self-eating. That is a cleaning mechanism that involves removal of organelles, old cell membranes as well as other cellular junk that has accumulated with time and is an impediment to optimal cellular performance. When the old and broken parts of your cells are removed, the growth hormone that is usually amplified during fasting will signal the body to start the production of new replacements. The result of autophagy is the renovation and recycling process of cells. mTOR will induce the activation of the forkhead box proteins. Both mitophagy and autophagy are FoxO-dependent suggesting that the transcriptional molecule is an integral component of the processes.

*Increased antioxidant defenses (Nrf2)*: As humans age, there's an increase in the reactive oxygen species (ROS) while the natural antioxidant defenses decrease. Over time, this imbalance becomes greater even as the damage accumulates while the mitochondrial dysfunction becomes more prevalent. The normal production of oxidants in specific types of cells is important in the regulation of pathways (ROS are involved in some of the signaling processes). Therefore, it is valuable to strike the right balance as we age. This balance is may be critical for the optimization of mitochondrial performance and is referred to as mitohormesis with the idea being the need for the right amount of ROS with too little resulting in subpar performance while high amounts of ROS cause damage. This is important for those tissues that rely on the production of large amounts of ATP for metabolism such as heart, brain, and muscle. Among the understandings from mitorhormesis is that a certain amount of ROS is required to trigger adaptive responses that upregulate the antioxidant defenses as well as make mitochondria and cells better in dealing with toxins and stress. Thus, intermittent fasting can help in promoting anti-oxidant defenses. Calorie restriction will activate the nuclear factor (erythroid-derived 2) like 2 (Nfr2) that is a regulator of the cellular resistance to the oxidants. This protein plays a role in supporting antioxidant defenses through:

- Catabolism of peroxides and superoxide; eliminating all the bad stuff.
- Regeneration of oxidized proteins and cofactors (regrowing more of the good old stuff)
- Increase of redox transport (increasing efficiency of existing machinery)
- Synthesis of reducing factors (Creation of new good stuff)

Overall, Nrf2 is not the only mechanisms that promote antioxidant support and defenses. All the five mechanisms that are interrelated owing to the complex nature of human systems contribute to healthspan longevity. Like it is with all these other mechanisms, they support each other. For instance, mTOR is not only categorized under cell proliferation and autophagy.

## Intermittent Fasting for Lifespan and Healthspan

Lifespan refers to the duration of time that you've lived. On the other hand, the duration within which you've been functional and healthy, and not just being alive is referred to as the healthspan. Calorie restriction that is initiated by any form of intermittent fasting is important in affecting both your lifespan and healthspan. It's not unusual to focus on the lifespan within the longevity and aging space at the expense of the quality of life you're living.

On the contrary, the duration of time you're functional and healthy is correlated with a higher quality of life. Your healthspan can be mediated by many things among them; dietary interventions, social interactions, exercise, family, and community. Social interaction is positively related to life satisfaction and longevity. Thus, healthspan it may be more valuable to emphasize lifespan alone.

## Damage Accumulation vs. Programmed Aging

The debate between the importance of damage accumulation and programmed aging is unending. Humans are complex systems that involve a combination of both. Damage accumulation is characterized by mitochondrial and cellular damage, both of which happen at the cellular level with each amplifying the effects of the other. That is the changes in gene expression speed up damage accumulation, which in turn affects the ability of the cell to have healthy gene expression. On the other hand, programmed aging refers to changes in the manner in which our genes are expressed as we age. Some of the genes are underexpressed, while others are overexpressed.

## Aging Benefits of Intermittent Fasting

The scientific aspect of the mechanisms that are involved in promoting longevity and aging go beyond the context of fasting. These mechanisms determine nootropics as well as the other techniques that we can use in supporting healthy aging. Although there are many benefits that arise when a certain degree of temporary starvation is induced, it's important to note that there are more ways to trigger these responses. Most importantly, you need to keep in mind that while some of the benefits will occur while you're in the fasted state, others will happen when you start eating normally. Thus, starvation primes the systems for rejuvenation even though it is refeeding that is credited for rebuilding new organelles and cells, thus increasing health.

## Intermittent Fasting and Anti-aging Compounds

Excessive levels of pyrimidine and purine are signs that your body might be experiencing an increase in the levels of certain antioxidants. Specifically, researchers have found significant increases in carnosine and ergothioneine. A study on the individual variability in human blood metabolites found that the number of metabolites decreases as you age. These metabolites include ophthalmic acid, isoleucine, and leucine. This study also found that fasting significantly boosted the three metabolites and concluded that this explains how fasting extends the lifespan in rats. It is believed that the hike in antioxidants may be a survival response because when in the fasted state, the body experiences extreme levels of oxidative stress. Thus, the production of antioxidants can help in avoiding the potential damage that is a result of free radicals.

## Intermittent Fasting and the Anti-Aging Molecule

Research has found that being in the fasted state is instrumental in triggering a molecule that can cause a delay in the aging of arteries. This is important in the prevention of chronic diseases that are age-related like cardiovascular disease, cancer, and Alzheimer's and is evidence that aging can be reversed. Vascular aging is the most important aspect of aging. Thus, when people grow older, they vessels supplying blood to various organs become more sensitive and more likely to experience aging damage; thus studying is vascular aging is important. According to the research done on starving mice generated a molecule known as beta-hydroxybutyrate that prevented vascular aging. This molecule is also a ketone that is produced by the liver and is handy as an energy source; then the glucose level is low. Ketones are mostly produced during starvation or fasting or when you're on a diet comprising low carbs and after a prolonged exercise. This molecule also promotes the multiplication and division of cells lining the blood vessels. This is a market of cellular youth.

Additionally, this compound is also able to delay vascular aging through endothelial cells that line lymphatic vessels and blood vessels. This can prevent the kind of cell aging that is referred to as cellular aging or senescence. Cellular senescence is defined as the irreversible cell cycle while at the same time preserving the cellular viability. Cellular senescence is suggested to work as a tumor suppressor mechanism as well as tissue remodeling promoter after wounding. These cells show marked changes in morphology that includes irregular shape size, enlarged size, multiple and prominent nuclei, increased granularity, accumulation of lysosomal, and mitochondrial mass.

# Chapter 7: The Golden Key: Autophagy

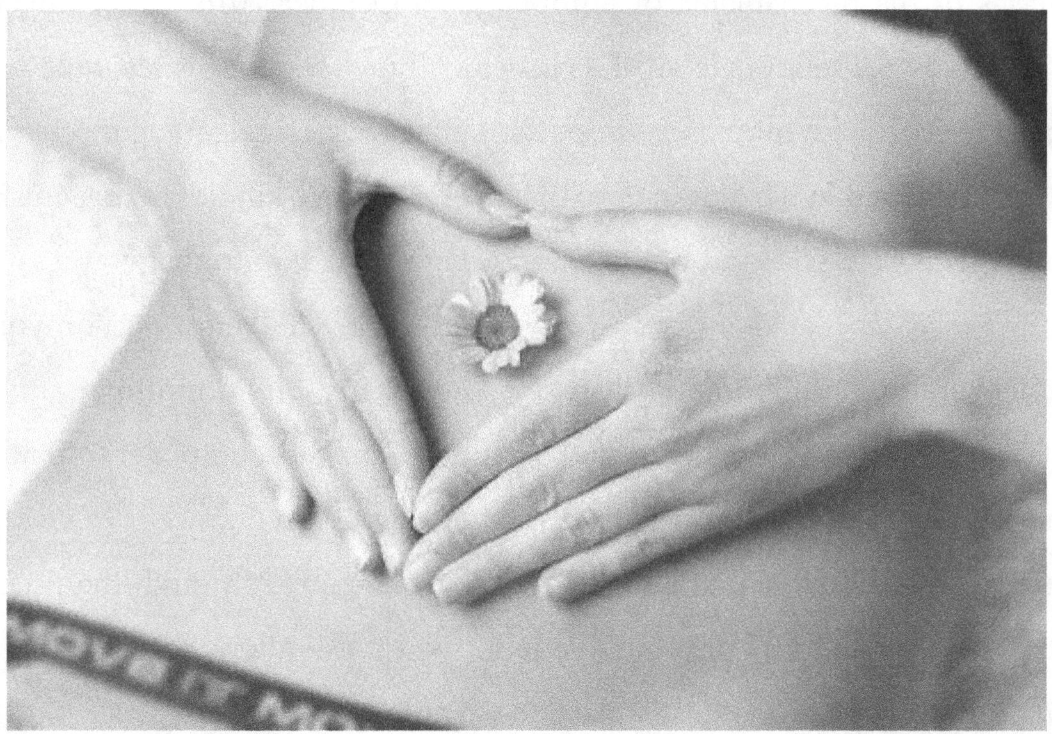

The cells in the human body are constantly being damaged as metabolic processes take place hence the need for autophagy to clear these damaged cells. The word autophagy comes from two Greek words; 'auto' which means self and 'phagy' meaning eating. Thus, autophagy is the process where the body consumes its own tissue in the wake of metabolic processes that occur due to certain diseases and starvation. Researchers consider autophagy to be a survival mechanism or the body's clever way of responding to stress to protect itself.

When you think of it as a form of self-eating, it's definitely scary. So is autophagy good for your health? Definitely! This is the body's normal way of initiating the process of cellular renewal. Autophagy may seem like a relatively new concept, yet our bodies have been using it for millions of years. The first autophagy studies were conducted on yeast with the progress of this study leading to a Nobel Prize in

Physiology or Medicine for Dr. Yoshinori Ohsumi, a Japanese scientist for his discoveries of the mechanisms of autophagy in October 2016. According to the study, the body can eliminate all the clutter within whenever it feels the need to conserve the energy for other most important purposes. The cleaning mechanism of autophagy is critical in the elimination of just about every kind of toxins, misfolded proteins, germs, bacteria, and pathogens. So beneficial is autophagy that is key in preventing diseases like liver disease, cancer, infections, diabetes, cardiomyopathy, neurodegeneration, autoimmune diseases. Autophagy offers multiple anti-aging benefits by helping in destroying and reusing damaged components that occur within cells. Thus, this process uses the waste generated within cells to create new building materials that facilitate regeneration and repair. Although the process of autophagy doesn't require any outside help, you'll definitely begin feeling more relaxed and energetic once it takes place.

While recent studies have revealed the role of autophagy in cleaning and defending the body from the negative effects of stress, the exact way autophagy processes work is just beginning to be understood. Several processes are involved. For instance, lysosomes form part of the cells that are capable of destroying large damages cells such as mitochondria as well as help in transporting the damaged parts, so they are used to generate fuel. To sum it up, the damaged material must be transported by a lysosome, before it's deconstructed and spit back out for repurposing.

## Essential Autophagy Steps

The process of autophagy involves the following steps as follows:

1. Creation of phagophore by a protein kinase complex as well as a lipid kinase complex. These two work together in sourcing a membrane that will eventually become the phagophore.
2. Once the phagophore is formed, the next step is its expansion. In this stage, a protein that is known as LC3 is bonded with the just formed phogophore through multiple autophagy-related proteins that are referred to as the ATG. When the bonding of the two is complete, the LC3 protein then becomes LC3-II. This formation occurs around cytoplasm material, which is then due to be degraded. This material may be random or selected specifically if it includes misfolded proteins and damaged organelles. When the process of replacement begins, ATG-9, a transmembrane protein acting as a protector of the site of phagophore formation is formed. This protein is assumed to help in expansion by increasing the number of phagophore membrane by supplying them from adjacent membrane locations.
3. The phagophore undergoes changes in its shape becoming elongated and closing, thereby becoming an autophagosome. The autophagosome serves as a holder of materials that are then degraded.
4. Both lysosome and autophagosome membranes fuse together. The lysosomal lumen (space within a lysosome) have hydrolases. Hydrolases break down molecules into smaller pieces using water to demolish the chemical bonds. When the lysosome and autophagosome fuse together, an exposure of the material that is inside the autophagosome to chemical wrecking balls occurs. The fusion converts the lysosome into an autolysosome.

5. The hydrolases degrade all material found within the autophagosome together with the inner membrane. The macromolecules that are the result of this process are waddled around by permeases that are on the autolysosome membrane until they get back to their original cytoplasm. At this point, the cell may reuse the macromolecules.

Well, this is how autophagy works. It's a complex yet important process that is still being studied to ensure further understanding.

There are different kinds of autophagy that include micro and macroautophagy as well as chaperone-mediated autophagy. Macroautophagy is the most popular of the three. It is an evolutionarily conserved anabolic process that involves the formation of autophagosomes (vesicles) that surround cellular organelles and macromolecules. Apart from humans' mold, yeast, flies, worms, and mammals also benefit from autophagy.

Macroautophagy is the process where catalyzation of non-functional cellular constituents to lysosome of cells takes place. What this process does is a separation of the cytoplasm of cells that includes different cell organs, degrading them to amino acids.

## Inducing Autophagy With Intermittent Fasting

One of the common questions about autophagy is when does it occur? Generally, autophagy is usually active in all the cells. However, there's increased response to acute energy shortage, nutrient deprivation, and stress. This means that you can cause your body to go into autophagy using good stressors such as temporary calorie restriction and exercise. These have been linked with longevity, weight control as well as inhibiting a number of age-related diseases.

You can induce autophagy through intermittent fasting. When you restrain yourself from eating food for a while, it will eventually trigger autophagy. When you fast for long, your body will start feeling deprived of supply hence can begin catabolic processes at the macromolecular level. This means identifying those processes that are misusing the available energy like parasites, pathogens, mold, fungi, and bacteria within that don't give back anything for elimination. Once your body goes into autophagy, it begins the elimination by identifying all misfolded proteins and recycling them to produce energy and new cells. Not only does this process clean your body but also promote restrengthening. The body also identifies chronic inflammations, disorders, and diseases that make us ill and use the energy of the body and eliminates them. When the elimination begins, even chronic inflammations that have troubled you for years will go away, making autophagy a powerful mechanism of treatment. This also has a powerful anti-aging effect because it stops those processes that hasten the signs of aging. Autophagy also has a great impact on the cognitive function in addition to stopping neurodegenerative disorders and reversing their effects. This means that disorders like Parkinson's and Alzheimer's can be brought under control. Autophagy also promotes cardiovascular health, lowers immunity problems, hypertension, and chronic inflammation. This process is guaranteed to give you a boon for a rejuvenated life.

Studies suggest that the autophagy process starts anywhere between 24 and 48 hours after your last meal. This is perhaps one of the best ways of inducing autophagy. Therefore, if you would like to trigger autophagy, then you must fast for longer. Alternate day fasting and water fasting are the most ideal. If you opt for alternate day fasting, make sure that you don't eat anything during the 36-hour fasting window. Don't consume any calories from soft drinks or juices either. On the other hand, if you go for the water fast, you must do it for 2 to 3 days as your recommended fasting window of between 24 to 48 hours.

Ultimately, the best intermittent fasting you can employ to induce autophagy is alternate day fast without consuming any calories in the fasting window. If you feel you're up to it, you can take it a notch higher with a 2- t0 3-day water fast once in three months. Looking at the benefits, it's definitely worth restraining yourself from eating to get your body into autophagy.

Exercise is another source of good stress that has been found to induce autophagy. According to recent research, exercise induces autophagy in a number of organs that take part in metabolic regulation like liver, muscle, adipose tissue, and pancreas. Although exercise has many benefits to the body, it's a form of stress since it breaks down tissues and causes them to be repaired so that they grow back stronger. Although the extent of exercise required to boost autophagy is not clear, research suggests that going into intense exercise is most beneficial. If you want to combine fasting and exercise, then you must approach it with caution. You just might be surprised that you actually feel energetic once you get the hang of fasting.

Apart from fasting and exercise, there are certain foods which, when eaten, will contribute towards inducing autophagy. Generally speaking, you need to focus on low carb foods, some of which include the following:

Herbs and spices such as cayenne pepper, black pepper, ginseng, ginger, cinnamon, turmeric, cumin, cardamom, parsley, thyme, cilantro, coriander, rosemary, and basil.

Berries and other fruits; strawberries, raspberries, blueberries, elderberries, cherries and cranberries.

Drinks; tea and coffee. Your coffee and tea should have no cream, milk, or sugar. As such, it's better to go for herbal, green, or black tea. Avoid fruit tea since it's too sweet. You may also have distilled vinegar or apple cider.

Alcoholic drinks; vodka, vermouth, gin, whiter, and red wine.

You could also try foods that are healthy for your body that include the following:

Fruits such as; olive, avocado, coconut, watermelon, cantaloupe, and honeydew.

Veggies; squash, tomato, peas, spinach, bell pepper, pickles, beetroot, green beans, carrots, and turnip.

Seeds and nuts; brazil nuts, almonds, cashews, chia seeds, chestnuts, flax seeds, macadamia, hazelnuts, pecans, peanuts, pistachios, pine nuts, pumpkin seeds, sunflower, sesame seeds, walnuts, peanut butter, almond butter, cashew butter, and macadamia nut butter.

Dairy and milk; blue cheese, buttermilk, brie cheese, Colby cheese, cheddar cheese, cottage cheese, cream cheese, Monterey jack cheese, mozzarella, feta cheese, swiss cheese, parmesan, mascarpone, sour cream, heavy cream, skimmed milk, and whole milk.

Fats; coconut milk, coconut cream, red palm oil, olive oil, MCT oil, macadamia oil, flaxseed oil, coconut oil, cocoa butter, avocado oil, beef tallow, lard, lard, ghee and butter.

Protein shakes with water; whey protein shake, hemp protein shake, rice protein shake, pea protein shake, and microgreens blend.

Drinks; almond water, almond milk, coconut water, kombucha, and coconut milk.

Alcoholic drinks; cognac, tequila, champagne, beer, mint liquor and chocolate liquor.

There's more to learn about autophagy and the best way of inducing it. Combing fasting and regular exercise as part of your daily routine is a great place to start. If you're taking certain medications for any health condition, you must consult your doctor before you go into fasting.

## Uses of Autophagy

The main function of autophagy is degrading and breaking down organelles in cells. This process contributes to the repair of cells. Autophagy also acts as part of the body's repair mechanism. Autophagy also plays an important role in a number of cellular functions like yeast the high levels of autophagy are activated by nutrient starvation. In addition to degrading unnecessary proteins, autophagy is also helpful in recycling amino acids that in turn, are important in synthesizing proteins that are crucial for survival. In the case of animals, they experience nutrient depletion after birth due to severing transplacental food supply. It is at this point that autophagy is activates helping to mediate the nutrient depletion. Another function of autophagy is xenophagy, which is the breaking down of the infectious particles.

## Benefits of Autophagy

Although autophagy presents multiple benefits, there are two major benefits of this process:

**Autophagy eliminates waste cells, misfolded proteins, and pathogens from your body**. Autophagy is instrumental in ridding the body of all waste that is making you sick and contributing to inefficient functioning. It removes the pathogens that live inside your body, thriving on your energy and making you experience good health. The presence of wasted cells and misfolded proteins often clutter your body. Autophagy comes in to recycle and clean them up, giving your body new cells while also releasing energy that your body can use when there's an extreme shortage.

**Autophagy helps to improve muscle performance**. When you exercise, the stress on your cells causes energy to go up, making parts get worn out faster. Autophagy, therefore, helps in removing the damage and keeping the energy needs in check.

**Autophagy helps in the prevention of neurodegenerative disorders**. Most of the neurodegenerative disorders are a result of damaged proteins forming around neurons. Thus, autophagy offers protection by eliminating these proteins. In particular, autophagy will help clear proteins associated with Alzheimer's, Parkinson's, and Huntington's diseases.

**Autophagy enhances metabolic efficiency.** Autophagy can be activated to help in improving the work of mitochondria the smallest part of the cell. This makes the cells work efficiently hence becoming more efficient.

**Autophagy slows down the progression of certain diseases.** Diseases too need energy for them to spread in the body. Thus, by starving them of energy, they're unable to function. For instance, cancer cells usually function like the normal body cells thriving on glucose obtained through food. When you go on a fast and deprive the body of this energy, the progression of cancer stops dramatically since they can't rely on fat energy to spread. In the same way, when you live on a fat diet, your body will begin burning fat hence literally starving cancer. This also applies to other chronic inflammations that flourish in your body silently because of the availability of energy that will begin to go when you're on extended fasts.

**Autophagy helps fight against infectious diseases.** Autophagy removes toxins that cause infections in addition to helping your body improve the way your body responds to infections. Most importantly, viruses and intracellular bacteria can be removed by autophagy.

## Common Misconceptions About Autophagy

Intermittent fasting has become popular over the years, effectively shifting the spotlight on autophagy. As a result, many people have come up with speculations and assumptions about autophagy that are untrue. Here are some of the false beliefs about people hold autophagy:

**You can trigger autophagy with a 24-hour fast**. Neither will a 16-hour or 24-hour fast trigger autophagy. This is because this is such a short time frame. Instead, if you want to trigger autophagy within a short time, then high-intensity exercise is recommended. The reason autophagy can't happen after a 24-hour fast is simple. Fasting doesn't happen soon after your last meal because then your body has to digest the food and draw energy from it. Thus, after your last fast, the body will be in a postabsorptive state of metabolism for a couple of hours. Remember, it takes more time to digest certain foods. Foods like fibers, vegetables, fat, and protein don't digest that easy. Because of this, the body will not be getting into the fasted state until after a period of 5 to 6 hours of going without food. The reason is simple. Before that, you're still in a fed state as your body thrives on the calories you've consumed. For example, if you had your last meal at 7pm, it will not be until midnight when you actually begin the actual physiological fast. Therefore, while you'll claim to be going on a 16- to 20-hour fast, in reality, you've spent about 12 hours fasting. This is such a short time to trigger autophagy. Even then, your fast is not in vain because you'll still experience the other benefits of intermittent fasting that include; low inflammation levels, reduced insulin levels, and fat burning.

**More is better**. You need a minimum of three days fasting to experience autophagy. That is by the time you're getting to your third day of fasting; you'll enjoy benefits of autophagy and fasting as this will energize your body to fight off tumors, cancer cells as well as boost the production of stem cells. Even then, prolonged autophagy is not the best. If anything, it can have side effects that include providing ample ground for the production of bacteria and Brucella. Extended autophagy may also see the resilience of tumor cells because they're strengthened, thus becoming more resistant to treatment. The essential autophagy gene ATG6/BECN1 that encodes Beclin 1 protein and is vital in reducing cancer cells may instead feed the cancer cells, thus giving them the strength they need to survive. Finally, there's a risk of muscle wasting and sarcopenia that affects longevity. Although you can't dispute the fact that autophagy is incredible, you need to be aware that it's not good to always be in this state. Otherwise, you'll end up with unwanted repercussions as well as health hazards. Thus, it's best to induce autophagy intermittently; don't make it a constant process.

**Autophagy means starvation**. Some people believe that autophagy will make you starve. This is untrue. Although you have to avoid eating for an extended period to achieve autophagy, this is totally different from starvation. Staying away from food for a couple of days will not make you starve because people who are starving don't even have the energy to go about their lives and daily activities like someone who is practicing intermittent fasting will. Intermittent fasting doesn't deprive your body of energy since the body stores unused energy as fats that it resorts to whenever there's scarcity. This is not only in overweight and obese people but also those with a lean mass.

Additionally, autophagy breaks down misfolded proteins and old cells that serve as additional sources of energy when you are not feasting. Thus, your body turns to other body components for energy. After a couple of days of fasting, you get to experience ketosis where your normal metabolism is suspended due to the absence of new food consumption. Thus, the body begins to use ketones and stored fats to draw energy for the muscle and brain. You eventually get to improve your lifespan through basal autophagy.

**Autophagy makes you build muscle**. This is an outright lie because you need calories to build muscles. Therefore, building muscles during autophagy will be close to impossible since there's no additional source of energy when you're staying away from food. Moreover, proteins are essential to muscle building are it requires a vital process that is referred to as protein synthesis. Intermittent fasting limits your protein intake is limited; thus, your body easily switches to a catabolic state where it breaks down as opposed to an anabolic state where it grows. Remember, autophagy can still breakdown old protein floating around your body cells that are central to muscle protein synthesis. However, experts point to the fact that with proper meal choice, you can maintain your muscle mass during intermittent fasting.

**Coffee hinders autophagy.** Taking coffee doesn't have any impact on your body's ability to achieve autophagy. In fact, taking coffee is good for inducing autophagy and ketosis because coffee contains polyphenols, that is a compound that promotes autophagy. Thus, coffee supports the process of autophagy. Caffeine also contributes to the body enjoying lipolysis that burns fat while reducing insulin, thus improving ketones and boosting AMPK. Although it doesn't hinder autophagy, you shouldn't take your coffee with sugar, sweeteners or even cream as these can increase the insulin level, thus stopping any benefit, you'd get from fasting.

**When you exercise, you stop autophagy**. Exercising is among the proven ways of inducing autophagy. Simply put, activity triggers autophagy. Resistance training is an excellent way of increasing mTOR signaling. While exercising will not activate mTOR in the same manner that eating does, exercise will translocate mTOR complex near the cellular membrane, preparing it for action as soon as you begin eating. By working out, you become more sensitive to activating mTOR; this will trigger more growth after working out. In addition, you also get to activate autophagy with in-depth resistance training that can help in reducing the breakdown and destruction of muscles by regulating the IGF-1 as well as its receptors. Apart from fasting, the other best approach to increasing autophagy is working out. Ultimately, you can combine both in order to attain the best results.

**Eating fruits will not stop autophagy**. Most of the fruits are laden with fructose that is digested by the liver before being stored as liver glycogen. When you have excess levels of fructose, it's converted to triglycerides. Thus, eating fruits will definitely work against ketosis and autophagy as it promotes liver glycogen storage. The content of glycogen in the liver makes sure that there's a balance between the mTOR and AMPK. When you consume fruits with a regulated amount of fats and protein may help in remaining in a catabolic state of breaking down molecules. Even then, the chance of experiencing autophagy is quite slim.

Most of the autophagy research has been done on yeast and rats. Genetic screening studies have found at least 32 different autophagy-related genes. Research continues to show the importance of autophagic processes as a response to stress and starvation. As you may know, insulin is the hormone that is responsible for letting glucose in the blood to enter the cells, thus energizing them for proper functioning. Thus, the more glucose you ingest, the more likely it will be stored in the blood effectively raising your insulin levels and blood sugar. Even then, the insulin will only get active and begins working if magic when its level decreases, thereby regulating your blood level. It's important to understand that fasting for extended periods is not easy; hence, you'll do well to start with intermittent fasting, which, when done on a regular basis produces the benefits of autophagy.

# Chapter 8: The Seven Types of Intermittent Fasting Diets

Intermittent fasting is about changing your pattern of eating. You can choose to abstain from eating partially or entirely for a specified period before you can begin eating again. As such, there are many different methods of fasting. These methods vary in terms of the number of days, hours, and calorie allowances. With intermittent fasting, every person's lifestyle and experience is unique; hence, different styles will suit different people. Here are 7 common types of intermittent fasting diets:

## The 12:12 Diet

With this diet, you need to adhere to a 12-hour fasting window and a subsequent 12-hour feeding window every day. This means that if you eat dinner at 9 p.m., you won't have breakfast until 9 a.m. the following morning. This intermittent fasting protocol is perhaps the easiest to follow. This plan is particularly good for beginners because of the relatively small fasting window. You can also opt to incorporate sleep in the fasting window, which means you'll be asleep for most of the fasting window. Apart from helping you lose fat and weight, this plan offers numerous benefits. First, it helps you break from the habit of binge eating or snacking at midnight mindlessly. Secondly, it helps in clearing inflammation as well as getting rid of damaged cells, thereby preventing cancer while also promoting healthy gut microbes. Fasting at night stimulates cell regeneration that has a positive effect on cancer, dementia, heart attacks, and dementia.

When you go for the 12:12 fasting plan, caution must be taken when choosing food so that you only take low-fat food with high protein and low carbohydrates. Most importantly, stay away from processed food. When followed to the latter, the 12:12 plan yields incredible results that include improved brain health, reduced inflammation, enhanced detoxification, and weight loss. To incorporate the 12:12 plan in your day, make sure that you leave 12 hours between your evening and morning meal. You can, however, take water and unsweetened tea.

## 16:8 Intermittent Fasting Plan

The 16:8 intermittent fasting plan limits your consumption of foods and beverages containing calories to 8 hours a day while abstaining from eating for the remainder of the 16 hours. You can repeat this cycle frequently from once to twice a day or even make it your daily routine depending on what you prefer. This plan is common among those looking to burn fat and lose weight. There are no strict regulations and rules, making it easy to follow and see the result with so little effort. It's also flexible and less restrictive hence can fit into just about any lifestyle. Apart from weight loss, the 16:8 will also help to improve blood sugar control, enhanced longevity, and boost brain function.

## Getting Started With 16:8

The 16:8 plan is safe, simple, and sustainable. To begin, you need to pick an appropriate eating window within which you limit your food intake. Most people prefer eating between noon and 8 p.m. so that they skip breakfast. You may also have your eating window between 9 a.m. and 5 p.m. allowing you plenty of time for healthy breakfast, a normal lunch and a light dinner or snack. Since everyone is different, you can experiment with different timings and see what works for your lifestyle and schedule. Regardless of what you choose to eat, make sure you space out to have several small meals and snacks throughout the day. This is important in stabilizing your blood sugar levels and keeping hunger under control. To maximize the potential of health benefits, make sure you're only consuming nutritious whole beverages and foods during your eating.

Having nutrient-rich foods helps in rounding out your diet so that you reap the rewards of this eating plan. While at it, make sure you're drinking calorie-free beverages such as water and unsweetened coffee and tea to keep your appetite in check. The 16:8 plan is easy to follow since it cuts down the time you spend preparing food and cooking every week. Some of the benefits associated with this plan include improved blood sugar control, increased weight loss, and enhanced longevity. On the flipside, this plan also has drawbacks. Restricting your food consumption to eight hours can cause you to eat more during the eating window in a bid to make up for the time spent fasting. This can lead to weight gain, development of unhealthy eating habits, and digestive weight gain. You may also experience some short-term negative side effects like weakness, fatigue, and hunger when starting out. Some research findings suggest that intermittent fasting affects women differently and could interfere with reproduction and fertility. Therefore, make sure you consult your doctor before you start.

## 5:2 Intermittent Fasting Plan

The 5:2 intermittent fasting plan is also referred to as The Fast Diet. This plan, which was popularized by British journalist Michael Mosley, lets you have five days of normal eating and two days of restricted calories to a quarter of your daily needs, usually 500-600 per day. The plan doesn't spell out the specific days you should eat or fast. You're at liberty to make this decision. For instance, you can decide to fast on Mondays and Thursdays where you eat two to three small meals and eat normally for the rest of the days. Even then, you need to know that eating normally doesn't imply eating anything, including junk or even binge eating because then you won't lose weight but instead gain.

A study on the 5:2 diet found that this diet has the potential of causing weight loss that is similar to regular restriction of calories. This plan was also effective in the reduction of insulin levels as well as improving insulin sensitivity.

The 5:2 plan can be effective when done in the right manner because it lets you consume fewer calories. Thus, you shouldn't compensate for the fasting days by eating more than you'd normally eat when you're not fasting. There's no rule on when and what you should eat on the days when you're fasting. One of the side effects you'll experience at that beginning of this program is extreme episodes of hunger accompanied by feelings of weakness and sluggish. However, this tends to fade with time, especially when you're busy with other things. Eventually, they find it easier to fast. Should you notice that you're repeatedly feeling unwell or faint, be sure to talk to your doctor. The 5:2 plan, just like any other plan is not suitable for everyone. Some of the people who should avoid this plan include people who experience drops in blood sugar levels, people with an eating disorder, and people who are malnourished and underweight with known nutrient deficiencies.

## Alternate Day Intermittent Fasting

With this plan, you fast on one day and eat the next day. This means that you're restricting what you'll be eating half the time. When you're fasting, you can drink calorie-free beverages like unsweetened tea, coffee, and water. Studies on alternate day fasting reveal that you can lose 3-8% of your body weight between 2 and 12 weeks. You can also consider modified alternate fasting that lets you have 500 calories on fasting days and is more tolerable because of the decreased amounts of hunger hormones and an increase in the satiety hormones. Alternate day fasting will not only help you to lose weight but also help in lowering insulin levels in type 2 diabetes patients. Type 2 diabetes makes up 90-95% of diabetes cases in the US.

Moreover, more than two-thirds of Americans are considered to be pre-diabetic, which means they've higher blood sugar levels that can't be categorized as diabetes. Restricting calories and losing weight is an effective means of improving or reversing the symptoms of type 2 diabetes. Alternate day fasting also contributes to mild reductions in risk factors for type 2 diabetes in obese and overweight individuals.

Most importantly, alternate day fasting is especially effective in reducing insulin resistance and lowering insulin levels with a minor effect on blood sugar control. Excessive insulin levels have been linked to obesity, cancer, heart disease, and other chronic diseases. Thus, insulin resistance and a dip in insulin levels can lead to a significant decline in type 2 diabetes. Evidence suggests that alternate day fasting is a great option for weight loss and reducing risk factors for heart disease. Other common health benefits of alternate day fasting are:

- Decreased blood triglycerides
- Lower LDL cholesterol concentration
- Decreased blood pressure
- Reduced waist circumference
- Increased number of large LDL particles and reduction in dangerous small, dense LDL particles.

One of the common effects of alternate day fasting is its ability to stimulate autophagy. This gives you the added advantage of having parts of old cells degraded and recycled. This process is crucial in preventing diseases like cancer, neurodegeneration, cancer, and infections. In addition, it also contributes to delaying aging as well as reducing the risk of tumors.

## Warrior Fasting Diet

The warrior diet was created by Ori Hofmekler, who was a former member of the Israeli Special Forces. This intermittent fasting plan is based on the eating patterns of ancient warriors that feasted at night and ate little during the day. This plan is designed to improve the way we feel, eat, look, and perform by stressing the body through reduced consumption of food hence triggering survival instincts. According to Ori Hofmekler, this diet is not based on science but on personal observations and beliefs. When you follow this diet, you're required to under eat for at least 20 hours a day, that is considered to be the fasting period but eat as much food at night. You should aim at eating small amounts of foods such as hard-boiled eggs, dairy products, vegetables and fruits, and non-caloric fluids. You then have a four-hour feeding window. It is recommended that you stick to healthy, organic, and unprocessed food choices. Like other intermittent fasting plans, warrior fasting helps you burn fat, boost your energy levels, improve concentration/brain health, decrease inflammation, control blood sugar, and stimulate cellular repair.

Despite all these health benefits that the warrior diet promises, it also has some potential downfalls that include the following:

*It's inappropriate for most people.* This diet is inappropriate for most people, including expectant women, children, extreme athletes, people with diseases such as type 1 diabetes, and underweight people.

*It can be difficult to stick to for some people.* This is an obvious limitation of this diet because it restricts the time that you can eat substantial meals to just four hours. This can be difficult to maintain, especially if you desire to go out for lunch or breakfast.

*Warrior fasting can cause disordered eating.* This plan emphasizes on overeating that can be problematic for most people. However, Ori argues that you should know when you're satisfied and stop eating.

*It can result in negative side effects.* Some of the negative side effects that the warrior diet can potentially cause some of which can be severe include dizziness, fatigue, anxiety, low energy, insomnia, lightheadedness, constipation, fainting, hormonal imbalance, irritability and weight gain among others. Additionally, health professionals hold the opinion that this fasting plan can result in nutrients deficiency. However, you can take care of this by making sure you're eating nutrient-dense food.

Unlike other intermittent fasting plans, the warrior fasting plan has three phases:

Phase 1 - Detox. Start by under eating for 20 hours daily. You can eat anything from the clear broth, vegetable juices, hard boiled eggs, raw fruits, and vegetables. In your four-hour eating window, include whole grains, plant proteins, cooked vegetables, salads, and cheese. You can also take water, small amounts of milk, tea, and coffee throughout the day. The whole idea is to detox.

Phase 2. This week, your focus should be on high fat. Therefore, you shouldn't consume any starches or grains but instead focus on eating foods like vegetable juices, dairy, clear broth, raw fruits, hard boiled eggs lean animal protein as well as cooked vegetables.

Phase 3. This is the phase where you conclude your fat loss. Thus, it cycles between periods of high protein and high carb intake. This would mean 1-2 days of high carbs, followed by 1-2 days of high protein and low cards.

## Eat Stop Eat Intermittent Fasting

The Eat stop eat intermittent fasting regimen involves fasting for 24 hours once or twice weekly. This method was made popular by Brad Pilon, a fitness expert and has been quite popular over the past few years. You fast from dinner one day to dinner the next day amounting to 24 hours of being in the fasted state. This means that if you finish dinner at 8 p.m., you don't eat anything until 8 p.m. the next day to make a full 24-hour fast. This fasting plan is not restricted to dinner alone; you can also fast from breakfast to breakfast or better still lunch to lunch and get the same end result. Like other intermittent fasting plans, you can take coffee, water, and other beverages with zero calories during the fast. However, no solid food is allowed. If your goal of doing the 24-hour weekly fast is to lose weight, make sure you're eating normally during your eating period. That is, just consume the same amount of food you'd be normally consuming without keeping the fast in mind. The challenge with this 24-hour fast is that it's fairly difficult for many people because of the length of the fasting window. Thus, you don't have to go all the way at the beginning. You can begin with 14-16 hours of fasting, increasing the duration with time. Generally, the first few hours of the fast will be easy before you become ravenously hungry. However, with discipline and taking enough fluid during the fasting duration, you can be sure to pull through. Soon, you'll get used to doing these fasts.

## Spontaneous Meal Skipping

You don't have to stick to a specific intermittent fasting plan to reap the benefits. You could actually consider meal skipping. You can opt to skip meals from time to time when you're too busy to cook, or you don't feel hungry. Skipping one or two meals whenever you feel inclined basically means you're doing a spontaneous intermittent fast. It is simple; you can skip your lunch and have an early dinner. Alternatively, if you eat a large dinner, you can skip breakfast instead. Skipping meals can boost your metabolism Skipping meals is a good place to start your intermittent fasting experience, especially if the idea of going for long periods without food intimidates you. This intermittent fasting plan bursts the myth that you need to eat after every few hours; otherwise, your body will get into starvation mode or even lose muscle. The truth is that the human body is equipped very well to handle extended periods of famine, let alone having to do without a meal or two from time to time. Therefore, if there's a day you're really not hungry, you can skip breakfast so that you have healthy lunch and dinner. This fast is also convenient if you're traveling somewhere but just can't find something you can eat. You just must sure that you eat healthy foods.

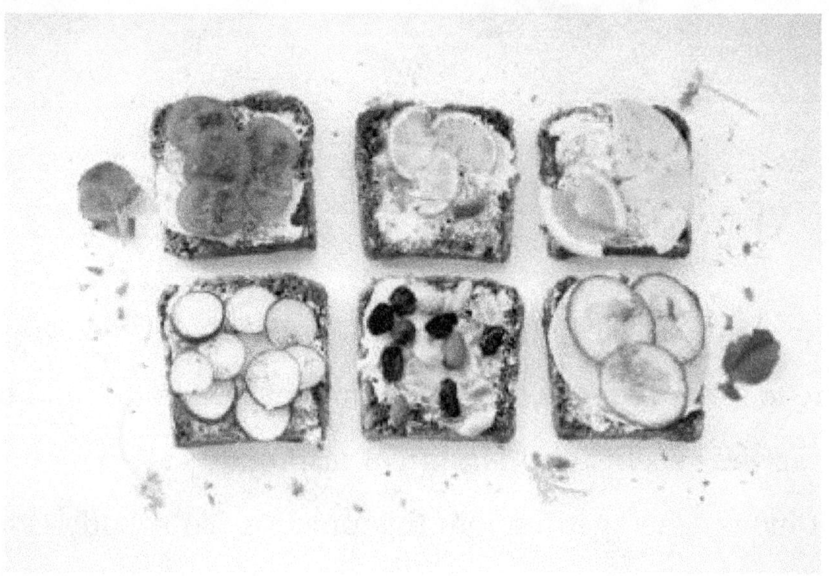

# Chapter 9: Cautions While Making the Transition to Intermittent Fasting

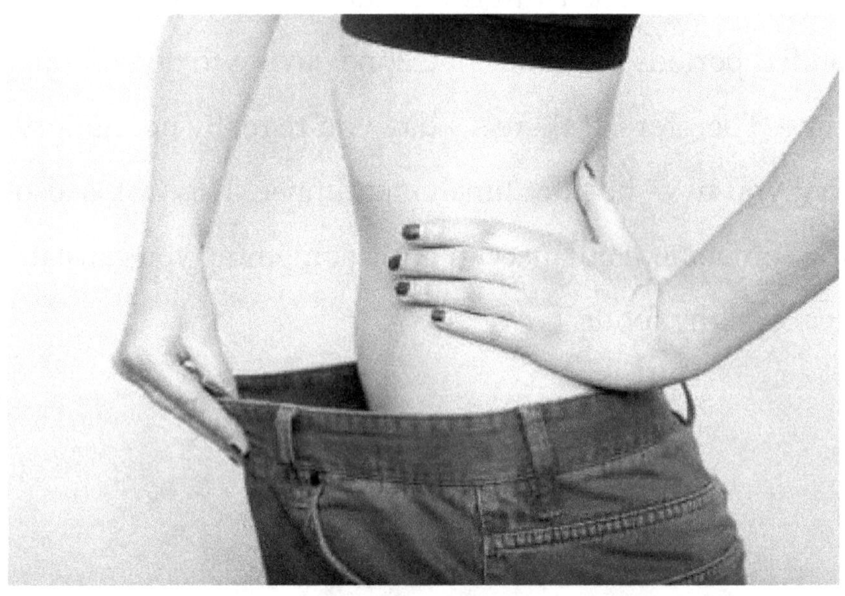

Preparation is the key to succeeding in intermittent fasting. When you prepare well, you can be sure to stay in control so that you're not feeling lost and out of place. If you want to reap the benefits of intermittent fasting quickly, you must be keen to make the right move when getting into this practice. Your body is accustomed to eating after 2-3 hours; therefore, you need to immerse yourself into fasting systematically. Although this sounds simple in principle, it's actually not easy when you start out. However, when you take caution and come up with a good plan, you'll have a smooth transition that will contribute to the success of your intermittent fasting quest. Here are some cautions you can consider while making the transition to intermittent fasting:

**Transition slowly**. It's okay to be ambitious about going without food for several hours. However, as you're starting out, you need to be careful not to be too ambitious by immersing yourself into intermittent fasting that requires you to fast for extended periods. It's advisable to consider starting with the simpler intermittent fasting protocols and advance to the extended protocols over time. If anything, you gained the weight you're trying to shed off after a long time, so don't expect to lose weight overnight. For instance, you can start with the 12:12 intermittent fasting protocol where you have a fasting window of 12 hours to advancing on to 16:8 that lets you fast for 16 hours and eat for 8 hours. You can even take a break after a couple of days or weeks before attempting again. The trick is to make sure that you're adding on another day every week until you're able to stick to your intermittent fasting plan. Only then can you consider trying intermittent fasting protocols that require you to fast for extended periods of between 18 and 24 hours like 5:2 or warrior depending on how comfortable you're. Don't hesitate to tailor the fasting protocol to your preference, even if it means not doing it every day.

**Take your schedule into account**. It's very important to keep your schedule in mind while planning for the intermittent fasting protocol that's right for you. Your choice of an intermittent fasting protocol should not be influenced by peer pressure rather, by what is suitable for you in relation to your schedule. Don't go for an extreme plan in the beginning just because your friends are doing it. If there's no way you can have your meals within an 8-hour window because your schedule is erratic, then the LeanGains 16:8 protocol is not appropriate for you. However, if you are sure you can't go for 24 hours without food, then this intermittent plan might be the most suitable for you. Ultimately, you must think about your schedule, your preferences, and if the plan will affect the other people that you live with before deciding what is best for you. This will make your transition to intermittent fasting smooth.

**Don't start intermittent fasting alongside a new diet**. If your goal is to lose weight and you're also interested in taking on a new diet like low-calorie diet or keto, make sure you're not starting it alongside intermittent fasting. This is because it takes time for your body to adjust to the new meals and foods included in your diet. Moreover, whether you're cutting down on meat on your vegetarian diet or you're simply reducing your carbs dramatically, it will have a huge effect on your body when combined with intermittent fasting. Therefore, to succeed with intermittent fasting, make sure that you stick to your diet for up to two weeks before adding intermittent fasting. This way, you will have a great understanding of your body, hence a smooth transition.

**Eliminate snacks.** Snacks refer to anything that will add empty calories to your system and cause cravings. Before beginning intermittent fasting, make sure you prepare your body to stay without food for longer periods than usual. The first step towards this is eliminating snacks. Although not evident, snacks are your biggest enemies because they're not nutritious; rather, they're only full of salt, sugar, flours, and refined oil. Thus, you must learn to avoid them in order to stay in shape. Snacks often cause your blood sugar levels to spike while loading your system with empty calories and provide very little to your gut. Make sure you eliminate snacks from your routine. You also need to avoid carbonated beverages that add empty calories and are full of sugar.

Most importantly, keep in mind that intermittent fasting is not based on restricting your calorie intake so you can consume calories within a limit that is reasonable. Rather, your calorie intake will automatically reduce since your eating windows are short. Remember, intermittent fasting is based on when you eat and not what you eat. One of the best ways to avoid processed foods is staying away from foods that are served at fast food chains, including salads that have various dressings. Instead, make it a habit to cook your own food. This will ensure you're only eating healthy food.

**Stay true to your purpose.** There's definitely a reason why you're getting into intermittent fasting. Staying true to this reason is the only way you'll stay grounded to the cause. Therefore, make sure you have defined the reason why you're going into fasting. This may be losing weight; fasting will reduce the level of hormones like insulin while increasing the human growth hormone and norepinephrine that make the stored body fat more accessible hence making it possible for you to burn fat and effectively lose weight. Fasting also helps in the prevention of heart disease, diabetes, as well as reduce inflammation. Most importantly, fasting will also offer protection against cancer, Alzheimer's while increasing longevity.

**Face your fears**. It's normal to feel nervous and even harbor doubts before beginning intermittent fasting, especially because we have been cultured to believe that breakfast is the most important meal of the day. However, you need to know that when unaddressed these worries can cause you to stop. Therefore, face them. It's important to know that breakfast is a neutral meal hence can be skipped. In fact, the reality is that skipping breakfast will not make you gain weight while eating breakfast will not rave up your metabolism. You also need to keep in mind that fasting will increase your metabolic rate and help you lose weight while retaining more muscle.

**Begin with 3 meals.** Intermittent fasting is all about a total lifestyle change. Therefore, you need to start by taking three meals. This may be surprising, and you may be wondering whether the fact that you're already skipping a meal means you are doing intermittent fasting. Well, the answer is no. Here's why; while you don't have time to consume three meals on any given day, you somewhat take improper meals in the course of the day. This kind of munching counts for intermittent fasting. Thus, we must consider starting off with a balanced breakfast, eat moderate lunch, and finish with a light dinner. When you get to a point where you're able to sustain without difficulty with the three meals you'll be ready to move on to intermittent fasting.

**Be consistent with your intermittent fasting protocol.** It's likely that you will be excited to make a change and transition to the next intermittent fasting protocol after some time. This is especially the case when you begin seeing results. Even then, you must remember that intermittent fasting mustn't be rushed. Make sure you stay on a single fasting protocol for at least two weeks before moving on to the next. Keep in mind that each of the intermittent fasting protocols presents its own unique results and advantages. Only when you get comfortable should you consider moving on to the next one.

**No fasting protocol is superior**. It's a common misconception that you can only get better results when you go for the tougher regimen. While there's some degree of truth in this belief, it's important to focus on individual capacity. Everyone has their unique capabilities, thus imitating someone else is utterly meaningless. Some people may post impressive results with a 12-hour fasting protocol while for others, it will take another protocol to experience similar results. So don't go for the toughest protocol but instead find a protocol that suits you.

**Focus on eating healthy eating**. One of the things that you're likely to ignore when starting intermittent fasting is the quality of food you're eating. Although your fast will generally involve cutting down on the number of calories you're consuming, it's equally important to be deliberate about your food choices. More specifically, focus on healthy eating, especially if you're aiming to make this a lifestyle. While you can eat unhealthy food while doing intermittent fasting, eating healthy foods contribute towards living a long and healthy life. Therefore, be sure to include fruits, nuts, vegetables, healthy fats, and lean proteins in your diet.

**Know when to quit**. It is important that you're flexible and adapts to your changing needs. For instance, if your plan is to fast for 16 hours, but you begin feeling tired, you might as well shorten your day. You may also be working out, but you generally feel you don't have enough energy, this is also a reason to break your fast early. You shouldn't aim to be perfect at the expense of your wellbeing. If you begin feeling sick during your fasting window, it's also a good reason to cut short your fasting and pay attention to you your health. It's better to be consistent than to be perfect.

**Keep it simple**. Unlike many other diets that are designed to help in losing weight, intermittent fasting doesn't require you to deviate from your usual meals to some sophisticated menus. Therefore, aim at eating your usual meals during your eating window. However, you can also consider combining your intermittent fasting regimen with a low carb-high fat diet comprising real whole foods.

Get enough rest. Fasting, by itself, is not enough if you want to embrace a healthy lifestyle. Make sure you're also getting enough sleep. Your body requires sleep to be able to carry out some of the important functions. Therefore, don't work at night unless it's important. We aren't wired as other nocturnal beings; thus, we need to follow through our circadian rhythm. When you get sound sleep at night, no doubt your body will be able to fight off the weight in a better way even as your stress and cholesterol levels improve. If anything, intermittent fasting puts emphasis on giving the body adequate sleep. Make sure you plan your day so that you free up some time for good sleep. Most importantly, make sure you rest more when you fast for extended periods.

**Practice perseverance.** It's unfortunate that most people that have a problem with their weight are also impatient. This is probably because they're already under pressure to lose weight, yet it's just not happening. Moreover, most people trying to lose weight have already tried other ways of shedding off excess fat unsuccessfully and are looking for quick results. Unfortunately, intermittent fasting is not an overnight success. It takes time and consistency before you can see the results. You must be ready to see the change happen after a while since you're correcting problems/weight that has accumulated over the years. Don't lose hope in the process because by quitting, you can't tell whether you had made any progress. You can stall hunger by laughing, running, or talking to friends or engage in activities that stall hunger.

**Hydrate during fasting.** It's extremely important always to make sure you're drinking up enough during intermittent fasting. Yet it's common to find beginners thinking that they should not actually consume anything during the fasting window. This is wrong because intermittent fasting allows you to take water, tea, or coffee as long as you don't use any cream, milk, or sugar. Staying hydrated is important in extending your feeling of satiety; thus drinking water will help you to get rid of that feeling of hunger.

**Manage your fasting time properly.** It's a common thing for people to mismanage time during the fasting window just as is with our normal schedules. You need to know that not managing your fasting time well is likely to be a cause of distress. This can make your journey of losing weight painful and difficult. Stop thinking about food the entire time you're in the fasted state. This will create problems since your gut will be confused. You can manage your fasting time by staying busy while making sure that you're engaged until the last leg of your fasting window. When you're idle, it's likely that you'll only be thinking about food. Think about ways of putting off hunger. After all, our bodies have ample energy reserves that can run without food for a long time.

**Don't rush the process**. We all want quick results, but with intermittent fasting, you have to follow through the process. Don't attempt to make quick jumps because the body doesn't work this way. The transition process of your body is quite slow. Thus, you need to allow more time to adjust to change that comes with intermittent fasting. To succeed with each of these processes, make sure you stay at every stage for some time. This gives your body time to adjust to the changes. Remember, you're trying to change habits that are decades old, so you need to be patient to make your body adjust to the process. The other thing you must remember is that fasting is different in men and women. While a man's system is rugged and doesn't get to be affected by periods of extended fasting, fasting can affect a woman's health adversely; hence, it takes time to normalize. Hence, the need to start small and advance with time.

**Have realistic expectations.** It's okay to have a goal and dreams about your weight loss goals. Even then, make sure that you're grounded in reality. This is a good place to start as you're able to accept facts and avoid lots of disappointments. Having unrealistic expectations often contributes to the failure to recognize the benefits you derive from the process. For instance, if your goal is losing weight, then you must really think about the amount of time, you'll put into fasting and your overall commitment. Not taking all the relevant factors into consideration will leave you feeling frustrated and difficult to achieve the results you desire.

**Determine how long you want to fast/create a routine**. Since intermittent fasting is more of a pattern of eating than a diet fad, you can only get the best results when you follow it in routine. This means that you will not get the results if you're only practicing fasting in a way that is unstructured. If anything, doing intermittent fasting in an irregular manner will not yield any results; rather, it'll leave you feeling hungry. Your gut releases the hunger hormone with so much accuracy. As such, the gut is able to sense the time when you eat so that you feel gurgling in your stomach around exactly the same time the next day. This means that if you're keeping a 14-hour fast regularly, you'll notice you feel hungry hunger just about the time you need to break your fast. This means that if you don't keep a regular routine, then this will not happen. Making intermittent fasting a usual routine will help you get over the hassle of being too conscious. After a while, this would be part of your lifestyle hence easy to follow.

**Don't be greedy when it's time to breaking your fast.** Food is the most alluring thing you can come across when you've been deprived of it for long hours. It's actually tempting. You need to make sure that you don't get greedy when breaking your fast, rather get off the fast in a proper manner. The biggest mistake you can make is eating a lot as it can lead to various problems among them poor digestion. Your gut can be dry after long periods of fasting. Thus, stuffing it with heavy food can result in problems. When breaking your fast start with liquid food, slowly transitioning to semi-solid and finally solid foods. You also need to check the quantity of food that you eat because the brain takes time to decode the leptin signals that you're full. When the brain finally signals you're full, you'll have overeaten. This means that you need to eat slowly so that your brain has enough time to determine your satiety levels. Alternatively, stop eating when you're at 80% full after which you're unlikely to feel hungry again.

You only require a few calories during intermittent fasting because your body is running on just a few calories or no food at all for a longer period than usual. This can result in having a hangover initially. You can train your body to come with the stress that is linked to food deprivation in order to get used to staying for long without food. If you realize that you can't cope with your intermittent fasting plan, then you can consider switching to another plan. You might have chosen a plan that is not suitable for your needs or lifestyle. Don't be discouraged if one plan doesn't work. Rather, make sure you work towards finding the right fasting protocol that you'll be comfortable with while getting the results you need.

By transitioning into intermittent slowly, you're giving your body a chance to self-regulate and gradually adapt to your eating pattern that is changing. It also helps in diminishing or avoiding symptoms of early transition that include dry mouth, insomnia, and digestive changes.

## Chapter 10: Common Myths About Intermittent Fasting

Before joining the intermittent fasting bandwagon, it is important to have a clear picture of what it is you're getting into and the kind of results you should expect. Like with any other programs, there are several misconceptions and myths associated with the intermittent fasting lifestyle that is as popular as the benefits. Let's debunk some of the myths about this eating pattern so that you feel more confident embarking on this weight loss and wellness strategy:

**You'll definitely lose weight.** While one of the primary reasons why most people take on intermittent fasting is to lose weight, the results are not guaranteed. Several factors come into play. Thus, intermittent fasting will not always lead to weight loss. This is especially true if you're fasting faithfully while at the same time throwing down pizza, candy, and burgers. Intermittent fasting works well when you're on a healthy diet. Don't treat your eating window like a cheat day and expect to see positive results.

**Intermittent fasting will slow down your metabolism**. There's a general fear that when you go into intermittent fasting, your metabolism slows down. This is not actually true because intermittent fasting doesn't restrict the number of calories you take. Rather, it makes you wait for a few hours before you can have your first meal. This doesn't make a difference in your metabolic rate. Instead, changes in your metabolic rate will only come about when you're not eating enough, which is not the case with intermittent fasting.

**You can eat as much food during your feeding window**. It's not exactly true that you can eat as much as you want during your feeding window. Here's the thing.

When you start intermittent fasting, your aim should be entering a healthier lifestyle. Unfortunately, most people only go into it to lose weight before going back to their reckless eating at the end of the fast. Experts warn that this is counterproductive to the results you've attained during your fasting window. The key to success with intermittent fasting is eating normally when you end your fast so that you don't negate the time spent fasting.

**It's better to fast than snack for weight loss.** Most conventional diet regimens recommend snacking in between meals. Those who opt for intermittent fasting think it should be a substitute for snacking. Ultimately, weight loss is occasioned by a constant deficit in calories. Whether those calories are consumed within a four to eight-hour window or spread throughout the day is not an issue. Instead, you should aim to do what is beneficial to your body.

**Intermittent fasting for weight loss is far much better compared to other weight loss strategies**. If you believe that intermittent fasting is the best strategy for your weight loss, you need to think again. It is important to keep in mind that intermittent fasting is simply about exercising caloric restriction in terms of when you take your food. If anything, there's no evidence to prove that intermittent fasting works better than the other methods and means of losing weight. It all boils down to your approach and discipline.

**You can't skip breakfast.** You must have heard this one even with other diets that are designed to help in weight loss. It's largely believed that breakfast if is the most important meal of the day hence must be taken even during intermittent fasting. In fact, this is part of the American tradition. Although you'll be told you need to consume a good breakfast to get fuel for the day, this is not necessarily true. If anything, it's likely that you don't have an appetite when they wake up. However, you can always listen to your body and have a small breakfast. Depending on the intermittent fasting protocol you choose, you can always have your meals at a time of day when its convenient.

**Skipping breakfast makes you fat**. It's believed that when you skip breakfast, you'll experience excessive hunger and cravings that lead to weight gain. While a number of studies have linked skipping breakfast to obesity, this is not the case with intermittent fasting. However, another 2014 study conducted between obese adults who skipped breakfast and those who didn't find any difference in weight. That is, there's no difference in weight loss whether you eat breakfast or not. Eating breakfast can have benefits, but it's not essential.

**You can't work out when you're fasting.** Contrary to popular belief that you can't work out when you're fasting, you can carry on with your work out routine when fasting. In fact, working out when fasting is a positive thing. It is believed that working out on an empty stomach, especially when it is the first thing you do in the morning is more rewarding. This is because you'll be burning stored fat instead of using up the calories from the food you just consumed. You can then eat your breakfast after working out to replenish your body.

**All fasting is the same, and everyone gets the same results**. There are many forms of intermittent fasting that you can follow. There's no official fasting protocol leaving the flexibility of choosing what works for you. Therefore, you can opt to fast daily while someone else fasts for on alternate days. Consequently, you can be sure that everyone will get results that are unique to them depending on the fasting protocol they're following and their goal.

**Fasting makes you extremely fit and healthy.** Intermittent fasting in itself is not a magic bullet to achieving health and fitness. You'll do well to combine your eating pattern with proper care and exercise. You must work to maintain health and fitness in your entire life. They should not be taken for granted. Fasting alone will not give you an ideal body overnight. Moreover, when you lose excess weight, you'll have to make sure you continue maintaining it with healthy eating habits that include regular exercise and a nutritious diet.

**Intermittent fasting is productive because the body doesn't process food at night.** Although it's a common misconception that your body doesn't process food at night, it's actually the reason you lose weight during intermittent fasting. Your body is wired to digest food no matter the time. However, when you allow the body a certain time, usually between 12 and 18 hours, the focus shifts to other metabolic processes like cellular repair and autophagy taking the attention from digestion. Your body will digest food even if you eat at 3a.m.

**Intermittent fasting will decrease your training performance.** One of the fears most people have when contemplating intermittent fasting is a decrease in training performance. This because of the possibility of having to skip or having a light pre-workout meal. The truth is that a closer look at athletes who train while in the fasted state have not experienced any hindrance to their performance due to nutrient deprivation. Moreover, it's important to keep in mind that intermittent fasting doesn't deprive the body of fluids and water.

**Intermittent fasting will lead to loss of muscle mass.** The fact that you've reduced the frequency of eating especially proteins doesn't mean your body is in the catabolic state as it is largely assumed. The idea that fasting reduces muscle mass is based on the idea that your body relies on a constant supply of amino acids to maintain, build, or repair muscle tissue. It is important to keep in mind that when you have a large meal of protein at your last meal prior to your 16-20 hour fast, your body is likely to be releasing the amino acids they need by the time you break the fast. It's common to have a complete meal that digests proteins slowly to the time you have your next meal. The thing is that fasting for extended periods will cause muscle loss only when you are not eating a large balanced diet during your feeding window.

**Eating big meals with a lot of carbohydrates in the evening causes weight gain**. Most fitness and nutrition experts will link carbs to insulin. While this is correct, there's a tendency to overgeneralize the psychological effects of insulin. The fear is that an increase in insulin, especially in the evening, will result in the conversion of nutrients to fats because insulin sensitivity is highest in the morning and lowest at night.

**Fasting leads to glorified, binge eating, and bulimia disorders**. This is another ridiculous claim that has been continually advanced about intermittent fasting by classifying it as disordered eating. The truth is that with intermittent fasting, the time you eat is not as important as meeting your daily macronutrient and calorie goals. What this means is that you're able to stick to your diet. Moreover, fasting presents a number of health benefits that disqualify the idea of promoting binge eating and bulimia. Besides, it's unrealistic to expect someone who is on an intermittent fasting protocol not to eat a large meal. Eating a large meal does not necessarily equal to binge eating, especially if you're staying within your nutrient needs.

**Intermittent fasting has limited uses in limited populations**. This myth in itself suggests that intermittent fasting is less applicable to the majority. This is not true because most of the people that have found success with intermittent fasting will attest to the fact that it's such a huge relief from having to constantly obsess about following the clock all day just to make sure that you're eating after every 3 hours. Intermittent fasting is most likely to work well with most people's routines, especially if you're working. Not many people like to have a large meal in the morning or at midday owing to the nature of their schedules.

**Eating frequently will help reduce hunger**. Some people, especially those that are keen on following conventional weight loss diets, believe that when you snack in between meals, you'll prevent excessive hunger and cravings. Well, knowing when to eat is far much better because you get to eat one large meal that is packed with nutrients; hence, you'll experience satiety for longer periods. If anything, there's no evidence to show that snacking will reduce hunger.

**Fasting puts your body in starvation mode**. A common argument against intermittent fasting is that it can activate the starvation mode. That is, failure to eat will make your body assume it's starving hence shut down metabolism and the ability to burn fat. Long term weight loss reduces the calories you burn, which can aptly be described as starvation mode. Even then, this tends to happen whenever you're trying to lose weight regardless of the method you're using. There's no evidence that this is more with intermittent fasting. Evidence points to the fact that fasting for short term can increase metabolic rate.

**Intermittent fasting is not for people with diabetes.** Findings of a recent study point to the fact that intermittent fasting will result in improved weight loss, fasting blood sugar, and stabilize blood sugar after dinner in group 2 diabetics. In some instances, prolonged fasting will restore your insulin sensitivity, especially in type 2 diabetes. When your insulin sensitivity is improved, your body will produce less insulin and experience less inflammation. This shows intermittent fasting is important for individuals with diabetes by reducing the risk of kidney and heart disease.

There are many myths about intermittent fasting. While some have merit, others are outrightly wrong. For most people, intermittent fasting presents real benefits. It's one of the best tools to lose weight.

# Chapter 11: Common mistakes people make While Intermittent Fasting

Although it is billed as the most effective method of losing weight, you can easily have difficulty with intermittent fasting. Research has found intermittent fasting to have a 31% drop out rate. There are many mistakes people make when making a switch from your regular eating plan to intermittent fasting. This can jeopardize your expectations by influencing the results because you might not see the results everyone is raving about, resulting in giving up. Having a workable and realistic approach to intermittent fasting can be the difference between your success and failure. Here are some of the common pitfalls you're likely to be making in your intermittent fasting:

***Having a wrong plan for your lifestyle.*** Intermittent fasting is flexible; hence, you have the liberty of selecting a plan that suits your lifestyle. You need to understand the dynamics of the different forms of intermittent fasting to make sure you choose what will work well with your lifestyle, needs, and schedule. By signing up for a plan that you can't keep up with, you're definitely setting yourself up for failure. For instance, if you're working in a full-time job, have an intense workout routine and an active family, the 5:2 plan will not be realistic instead of the 16:8 plan will be more sensible and easier to maintain because you'll have a reasonable feeding window. Therefore, take time to do your research and pick a plan that will work well for you, and you're able to stick with comfortably.

***Getting into intermittent fasting too soon.*** One of the reasons most people give up on diets is because it presents a departure from the natural and normal way of eating. As such, you'll find it impossible to keep up with. This is often the case when you jump into intermittent fasting too fast. For instance, if you're accustomed to eating after every 2-3 hours, it's unrealistic to switch to a 24-hour fast suddenly. As a beginner, you can begin by fasting for 12 hours and have a 12-hour eating window. This comes close to your regular pattern. You can then extend your fasting window gradually until you reach your goal. It takes time to stop feeling hungry when you take on intermittent fasting. This way, you'll find better success. The secret is to be patient and see a lifestyle change

***Eating too much during the eating window***. Although you don't have to count calories as is typical with most diets, intermittent fasting requires discipline in terms of determining how much you should eat. While it's true that you may be too hungry from too many hours of fasting, caution must be taken so that you don't overeat during your eating window. In fact, you try not to be preoccupied with your next meal because this can lead to binge eating. Instead, consider sitting down to a larger meal that is more satisfying so that you're not completely famished when you enter your feeding window. When you do this correctly, you won't feel too hungry during the fasting window to want to eat everything.

***Failure to hydrate adequately***. Although your intermitted fasting plan alternates patterns of eating and fasting, you must make sure that you're taking in enough water. You actually need to have a bottle of water by your side because you're missing out on the water from veggies and fruits. Failure to stay dehydrated can results in headaches and cramps while worsening hunger pangs. You can also have tea or coffee but without sugar. You don't want to take any sweetened drink that can have an effect on your insulin levels and stimulate your appetite giving you the desire to eat. Avoid fluids that are filled with proteins since they can halt autophagy that you need to promote during fasting. If you find drinking up difficult, you can consider using an app to ensure you're sipping up in between your fasting and feasting windows.

***Overlooking what you're while focusing on when you're eating.*** While it's true that intermittent fasting is more of time centered eating regimen with no specific rules on what you should eat, your goal should be to eat healthy, nutrient dense foods. Therefore, you should not dwell on milkshakes, French fries, and the likes in your diet as these can easily undo the gains of fasting. Shift your focus from treating yourself after hours of fasting to getting nutrient-dense foods that are nourishing. Generally, your meals should have a protein, complex carbs, fiber, and good fats. These will keep you feeling satiated and carry you through the fasting window while helping you to build muscle, feel energetic, and maintain a healthy brain.

***Eating too little.*** While it is wrong to overeat during your feeding window, you should also not eat too little. Fasting affects the hormones that control your appetite leaving you feeling less hungry. Consequently, when you get to eat, you'll only eat a small portion of food and feel full. Even then, you need to be careful so that you don't consume too little because failure to eat enough will leave you feeling extremely hungry the next day so that you can end up feeling lethargic and unable to perform any work. Failure to eat adequate food will cannibalize your muscle mass, resulting in slowed down metabolism. Lack of metabolic muscle mass will sabotage your ability to maintain fat. Eventually, you may end up feeling the need to skip fasting or even give up on intermittent fasting altogether.

***Leading a sedentary lifestyle.*** You may likely want to skip your workout session because you're used to having a pre-workout snack. Exercising when fasting will definitely seem foreign. Although it is advisable that you check with your doctor before exercising while intermittent fasting, it's safe to carry on with your exercise routine, albeit with some alterations. This is because your body has lots of stored energy in the form of stored fat that is used up when there's no food. Aim to keep up with your routine or consider low impact exercises like walking. For instance, if you're fasting overnight, you can exercise in the morning after which you can eat a protein-rich meal for better muscle build.

***Obsessing over intermittent fasting.*** When your fasting, you might be inclined to decline invitations to parties or even opt out for dinner with friends. When this is the case, your intermittent fasting goal may not be sustainable. You can fix this by shifting your fasting schedule either backward or forward by a couple of hours on the days when you have a date with friends so that you can still enjoy your social life without being guilty or the fear of being left out. Remember, intermittent fasting as a lifestyle is flexible; hence, it has to fit in your special occasions.

# Keto diet Cookbook

## Best and easy diet to follow and maintain

**Dora Gray**

# Table of Contents

# Introduction

We as human are all different, the effect of these eating systems can vary from one person to another but with several modifications to them so that they can suit you, there will only be benefits. Unfortunately, there are some individuals who should not attempt these fat loss regiments. If you have any severe health issues, it is mandatory to seek medical advice prior to beginning the new lifestyle, even if you are generally healthy, it is still advisable to consult a professional.

To clarify things even before diving right into the pool of data contained in this book, it is best to understand the difference between IF and the keto diet. IF is not a diet, but a meal planner that is designed to enhance weight loss and other health advantages, the keto diet is a diet that highly restricts carbohydrates and increases the amount of fat that you take so that you can be fuller for longer and be able to make fat your main energy source in the midst of other advantages that will be discussed later on.

The main reason why many doctors and nutritional experts give the "calories in-calories out" advice is that on paper it is simple and direct. They think that excessive calorie intake is the main cause of obesity; thus, the direct way of reversing this is consuming fewer calories. The 'eat less and move more' approach has been done for a very long time, and it simply does not work. The reason is that obesity and excessive weight gain is more of a hormonal imbalance than a calories imbalance. You will learn more about this and how the IF and the ketogenic diet can assist you in correcting this.

By reading this book, you will find a vast amount of information about IF and the ketogenic diet. You will know why and how they work so well and how they can work together to enhance your weight loss experience. You will also know about their benefits and downsides and how to be safe as you practice them.

During intermittent fasting, your body utilizes stubborn fat as it encourages metabolism that results in heat manufacture. This helps preserve muscle mass during weight loss and increases energy levels for keto dieters who want to lose weight and improve their athletic prowess. Combining the scheme of intermittent fasting and the ketogenic diet can lead to more body fat melting than individuals who follows IF but still consume junk food.

It can also increase your body structure as intermittent fasting improves human growth hormone output but at very large proportion. This hormone performs an enormous part in constructing muscles. The human growth hormone helps an individual reducing body fat concentrations and boost lean body and bone mass, according to studies conducted. Working out in a fasted state can result in metabolic adjustments in your muscle cells arising in energy fat burning. The human growth hormone also enables you to recover from injury or even difficult exercise at a quicker pace. It also decreases skin swelling.

The mixture of the two can even affect the aging process in a beneficial way. They cause the process of stem cells to rise. These are like construction blocks for the body as they can be transformed into any cell the body requires, as well as replacing ancient or harmed cells that keep you younger internally for longer. These stem cells can do wonders to old wounds, chronic pain, and much more. This can enhance your life expectaction as your general health is enhanced by balancing blood glucose, reducing swelling, and improving the free radical defense.

It can boost autophagy. This is simply cell cleaning measures. When it starts, your cells migrate through your inner components and remove any harmed or old cells and replace them with fresh ones. It's like an organ upgrade. It decreases inflammation and improves organ life.

There are no cravings, tiredness, and mood changes when exercising the ketogenic diet and intermittent fasting. This is accomplished through constantly small concentrations of blood sugar. This is because your blood sugar concentrations are not increased by fat. You will be prepared to keep small concentrations of blood sugar that can significantly assist individuals with Type 2 diabetes, even get off their drugs.

The liver transforms fat into packets of energy called ketones that are taken into the blood to offer your cells energy. These ketones destroy the ghrelin, the primary hunger hormone. High concentrations of ghrelin leave you famished while ketones decrease hormone concentrations even if your digestive tract does not contain any meals. This means you can stay without eating for a longer period of time and you won't get hungry. Undoubtedly, the ketogenic diet makes fasting much easier for you to do.

Some individuals follow the ketogenic diet integrated with intermittent fasting. This is by observing the ketogenic nutritional laws while also pursuing the trend of intermittent fasting eating. This can have many advantages, including high-fat burning levels, as both are important in using fats for energy over carbohydrates, providing you energy, reducing cholesterol in your body, controlling your blood sugar that can assist manage type 2 diabetes, helping to cope with hunger, and reducing skin inflammation.

For most individuals, combining the two is comfortable and can significantly speed up the fat burning process, making you accomplish your objectives quicker. However, one or the other can be done alone as they have many comparable advantages. Choosing an intermittent fasting unit that fits you is also essential and always makes sure you consume enough of the macro ingredients. Depending on what was in the meals, the functions can be comparatively fine for both. The job performed will be ideal when you mix both of them and will make weight loss much easier for you to do as both operate in distinct aspects but complement each other superbly.

## Successful stories

1. Actor.

John Cusack, the actor, is on a completely Keto diet and the majority of his life revolves around his Keto commitment. He is always seen doing physical activities with his wife, and their children. John admits to never ever getting sick. He follows a diet plan that has proven effective as seen from his movies. He is a big believer in the keto diet and the keto lifestyle.

You look good, where did you lose weight? Shusaku, the man in the center, did a diet that was popular in 2015. The year was 2015, and it was one of the worst years that American History would witness. John -John, the football player, hated tofu and chicken. He is a huge meat eater. That was why he implemented a Keto diet. It is a long-term diet, and it is relatively simple to follow. The kind of food you are going to eat will depend on your daily activity and the activity level on the day. The diet also depends on the activity and physical condition. There are those that enter the diet when they are sick. They do it because we feel good and we are looking good.

2. President Donald Trump.

Donald Trump wanted to lose weight. He was so overweight that he needed to take surgical precautions of his heart as he had developed heart problems. He is exploring various ways to take advantage of the positive effects of the Keto diet he is on. Trump was happy with the results that he was getting from the Keto diet. His heart surgeon had no choice but to say, "it is looking good. We are seeing the pounds melting off that boy." Trump said, "I am a believer in the Keto diet."

3. Kathryn Dennis.

Kathy says she has lost 60 pounds and that she hopes to do another 26-pound weight loss in the next year. She wants to get from 240 pounds to 119 pounds.

The girlfriend of professional football player Nate Washington says she went from a size 26 to a size 4, without taking shots of insulin. She decided to do the Keto diet in order to lose weight. She wanted to do the keto diet because of the weight loss, and the other benefits that the diet has to offer.

4. George W. Bush.

George Bush is a very avid Keto supporter. He has recently joined the Keto diet program and has gotten a lot of compliments and also a lot of medical advice. He started the Keto diet after he was diagnosed with coronary artery disease. His doctor told him to do away with food that has a high-fat content like meat and eggs, He was advised to fish, fruits, and vegetables and to do away with the high carb and fat drinks. He was advised to do away with all that has a high carbohydrate content. These include sugar, sugary drinks, potatoes, rice, pasta, and bread. As a result, he began to lose weight rapidly. He does not drink any high carb or fat meal. He does not like drinking any alcohol as he only drinks small quantities of beer once in a while. He can happily say he is enjoying his life on the Keto diet.

5. Shakira

Shakira is a singer. She is from Columbia, and she has Spanish ancestry. At a certain point in her life, she gave birth to her son, Milan. She gained a lot of weight because she wanted to nurse him. She could not give up on her baby. One day, she looked into the mirror, and she did not recognize herself. She realized that she was not happy. She researched on the Internet, and she came across the Keto diet. She went through it, and she did not move from step one to step two. She was determined to do everything properly. She followed what she was told to do, and she fully embraced the Keto lifestyle. She went on a diet with high fat, protein, and low carb content. She lost weight successfully.

6. Serena Williams.

Serena Williams is a tennis player. She is very successful. She is one of the best tennis players in the world, and she is primarily using the keto diet plan. She has been using the Keto diet because of her desire to lose weight. She does not eat any good that is high in carbs; she only eats vegetables, healthy food, fish, and meat. She consumes coconut oil, coconut milk, and salad dressings. She consumes something that has a high-fat content. She only eats one serving of carbs. This is a very good development for people that are trying to lose weight, and people that are trying to improve theirs constantly. Kick-off your new year by losing weight. You do not need a better reason to do it other than your desire to look good.

Eating is good for your health, and it keeps you healthy, but when you eat high-fat foods, and high carb foods, you could develop health problems, and you could get sick. What you want is to be healthy. When you are healthy, you are happy, and you can get new opportunities to be something you have always wanted to be.

# Recipes

## Almond Pancakes

Preparation:4 min
cooking:6 min
servings:

Ingredients:

- ½ cup almond flower
- ½ cup cream cheese
- 4 eggs
- Cinnamon to taste
- Truvia to taste/vanilla extract
- Sides:
- 3 eggs

- Sea salt and pepper to taste
- 1 tablespoon grass-fed butter
- ¼ cup sugar free syrup

Directions:

1. Mix all ingredients in a blender until smooth
2. Spray nonstick cooking spray in a medium pan, fry remaining 3 eggs, season with salt and pepper, cook to desire doneness
3. Enjoy your pancakes (2 pancakes are enough for a meal) with butter, syrup and eggs on the side.

*TIPS:* if you like, add some crunchy bacon

## Keto bread

Preparation: 6 min
cooking:50 min
servings: 6

Ingredients:

- 5 tablespoons of psyllium husk powder
- 1 ¼ cups almond flour
- 2 teaspoon baking powder
- 1 teaspoon sea salt
- 1 cup water
- 2 teaspoon cider vinegar
- 3 egg whites

- 2 tablespoon sesame seed if desired

Directions:

1. Preheat oven to 350 F
2. In a bowl mix all the dry ingredients
3. Bring the water to boil
4. Add vinegar and egg whites to the dry ingredients and combine well, add boiling water and mix for 30 seconds until you have the consistency of play-doh
5. Shape 6 rolls and put on the oven tray, top with sesame seeds if desired
6. Bake on lower rack for about 50-60 minutes.Serve with butter or toppings of your choice

## Jarlsberg Omelet

Preparation: 6 min
cooking:10 min
servings:1

Ingredients:

- 4 medium sliced mushrooms
- 2 oz. 1 green onion
- 1 tablesppon of butter sliced
- 2 eggs
- 1 oz Jarlsberg or Swiss cheese
- 2 slices of ham

Directions:

1. Cook the mushrooms the diced ham and the green onion in half of the butter in a big non-stick pan until the mushrooms are ready. Season with salt lightly, remove and set aside.
2. Melt over medium heat the remaining butter.
3. Add the beaten eggs
4. Now put the mushroom, ham and the grated cheese, on one side of the omelet.
5. Fold the plain side of the omelet over the filling once the eggs are almost ready.
6. Turn off the heat and leave until the cheese melts.
7. Enjoy it!

## Crockpot Southwestern Pork Stew

Preparation:10 min
cooking:  8 min
servings:4

Ingredients:

- 1 teaspoon of paprika
- 1 teaspoon of oregano
- 1/4 teaspoon of cinnamon
- 2 Bay leaf
- 6 oz. button mushrooms
- 1/2 Jalapeno
- 1 lb. sliced cooked pork shoulder
- 2 teaspoons Chili Powder
- 2 teaspoons cumin
- 1 teaspoon minced garlic

- 1/2 teaspoon Salt
- 1/2 teaspoon Pepper
- 1/2 Onion
- 1/2 Green Bell Pepper, chopped
- 1/2 Red Bell Pepper, chopped
- Juice from 1/2 Lime
- 2 cups bone broth
- 2 cups Chicken Broth
- 1/2 cup Strong Coffee
- 1/4 cup Tomato Paste

Directions:

1. Cut vegetables and stir fry on high heat in a pan. Once done, remove from heat.
2. Put sliced pork into the crockpot, add the mushrooms, bone broth, chicken broth, and coffee.
3. Add all the seasoning with the sauteed vegetables and stir well.
4. Cover the crockpot and cook for 4-10 hours at low temperature.
5. This recipe can be done with a cast iron boiler, the cooking time will be around 1 hour 20 minutes

## Pan-Roasted Rib Eye Steak with Pan Jus

Preparation:45 min
cooking:20 min
servings: 3

Ingredients:

- 1 (1 pound) rib-eye steak
- 4 spoons of olive oil
- 1⁄2 cup Chicken Broth
- 3 spoons of room temperature butter
- sea salt and pepper to taste

Directions:

1. Before cooking, remove steak from the fridge for about 45 minutes, pat it dry, and salt it completely. Flip it through for about 20 minutes, remembering when flipping to pat it dry, and then again before cooking.
2. If you want to cook your steak medium or medium-well, preheat your oven to 200 ° F. Heat on the stovetop a cast-iron skillet or another pan over elevated heat.
3. Add the oil to the casserole.
4. Place the meat in the pan just before it starts smoking, then listen to the searing sound.
5. Leave it to cook for 3 to 5 minutes without shifting it.
6. Once the bottom has a pleasant brown color (you can check by lifting one edge of the steak to look at the bottom) flip over the steak and do the same on the other.
7. This will offer you a steak that is medium-rare. If you want to continue cooking, place medium-well in the oven at 200 ° F for 5 to 6 minutes and medium-well for 7 to 8 minutes.
8. Once done, put it on a cutting board for 5 minutes to rest.
9. Slice it and serve it.
10. Make the pan jus while the meat rests.
11. Transfer the pan to the stovetop, add the broth and water over medium heat, reduce the sauce by half, add the butter and stir from 2 to 4 minutes.
12. Pour the Jus over the meat and enjoy.

## Conclusion

Thank you for making it through to the end of *Intermittent Fasting for Women,* let's hope it was informative and able to provide you with all of the tools you need to achieve your goals whatever they may be.

The next step is to take action that will usher you into a new level of wellness. If you still need help getting started, you are likely to get better results by evaluating your current schedule before you can select an appropriate intermittent fasting plan that is realistic, to begin with. Remember, you'll not be doing this to please anyone but for your own benefit.

Intermittent fasting is a great concept of scheduling your meal times, not just for weight loss but also living holistically because it gives you access to numerous health benefits. What's more? Unlike many weight loss diets that are restrictive, expensive, and offer minimal results, intermittent fasting is free and easy to follow through. You simply need to change your eating pattern so that you have periods of fasting followed by periods of feasting.

This book is especially a great resource that will help you through your journey in carving a new lifestyle. Remember, you don't have to change your way of living but instead embrace the new way of feeding to suit your way of living. In fact, you can still carry on with your exercise routine even though you may have to tailor it to your current situation in terms of when you eat and how intense your workout is.

What are you waiting for? Go ahead and start preparing for your intermittent fasting experience to tap into its benefits. Use the information you have acquired in this book as a springboard to prepare and transform your life.

CPSIA information can be obtained
at www.ICGtesting.com
Printed in the USA
BVHW011358030821
613533BV00003B/585

9 781802 951899